THE COMPLETE IDIOT'S GUIDE® TO

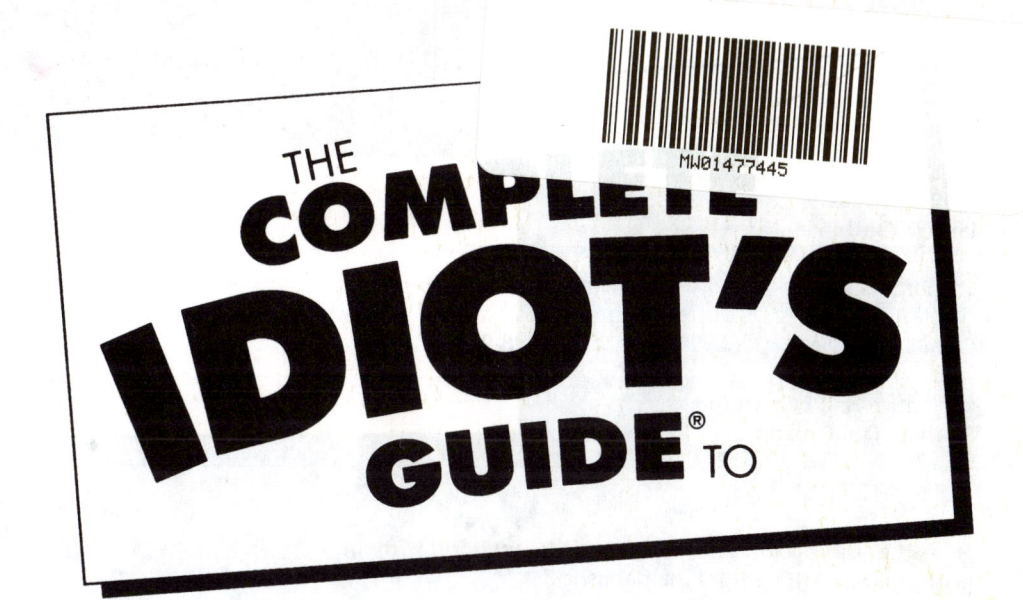

Canadian Sports History and Trivia

by Malcolm G. Kelly

alpha
books

Prentice Hall Canada Inc., Scarborough, Ontario

Canadian Cataloguing in Publication Data

Kelly, Malcolm (Malcolm G.)
  The complete idiot's guide to Canadian sports history and trivia

Includes index.
ISBN 0-13-014658-7

1. Sports – Canada – History. I. Title

GV585.K44 1999   796'.0971   C99-93179

© Prentice-Hall Canada Inc.
Scarborough, Ontario

ALL RIGHTS RESERVED

No part of this book may be reproduced in any form without permission in writing from the publisher.

Prentice-Hall, Inc., Upper Saddle River, New Jersey
Prentice-Hall International (UK) Limited, London
Prentice-Hall of Australia, Pty. Limited, Sydney
Prentice-Hall Hispanoamericana, S.A., Mexico City
Prentice-Hall of India Private Limited, New Delhi
Prentice-Hall of Japan, Inc., Tokyo
Simon & Schuster Southeast Asia Private Limited, Singapore
Editora Prentice-Hall do Brasil, Ltda., Rio de Janeiro

ISBN 0-13-014658-7

Editorial Director, Trade Group: Andrea Crozier
Acquisitions Editor: Paul Woods
Copy Editors: Greg Ioannou & Wendy Yano/Colborne Communications
Production Editor: Jodi Lewchuk
Art Direction: Mary Opper
Cover Image: The Image Bank
Production Coordinator: Barbara Ollerenshaw
Page Layout: Arlene Edgar

1 2 3 4 5   RRD   03 02 01 00 99

Printed and bound in the United States of America.

ALPHA BOOKS and THE COMPLETE IDIOT'S GUIDE TO are trademarks of Macmillan General Reference, a division of Simon & Schuster. All rights reserved. Used under license from Macmillan General Reference.

Visit the Prentice Hall Canada Web site! Send us your comments, browse our catalogues, and more. **www.phcanada.com.**

Contents at a Glance

Part 1: Roots — 1

1 No Autopsy, No Foul? — 3
Sports the natives played.

2 Roughing It in the Bush, or, Rounders with Susanna Moodie — 9
Sports of the early settlers.

3 Towards the New Century — 15
From hockey's roots to the beginnings of baseball and football.

4 My Canadian Can Beat Your (Fill in the Blank) Anytime! — 23
Our first international heroes, including Ned Hanlan and a procession of giant men.

Part 2: Hockey: Our Game — 31

5 We'll Take Your Puck and Start Our Own League — 33
Hockey in this century up to the founding of the National Hockey League.

6 Blood Sport — 43
Canadian teams appear and disappear in an era of violence.

7 An Original Six — 53
Six men who changed the face of the game from 1940–1967.

8 Expansions, Explosions, and a Kid Named Bobby Orr — 63
The NHL expands, violence rages, and one of the two best players ever takes the ice.

9 The Great One, The Magnificent One, and the International Pastime — 75
Wayne Gretzky, Mario Lemieux, and the expansion of hockey internationally.

10 The Dispossessed — 85
Blacks and women in hockey.

Part 3: The Olympic Spirit: A New Kind of Drug   95

11   Faster, Higher, Stronger   97
Canada's early Olympic appearances and successes.

12   Pure Amateurism   107
Canada struggles during the Olympic golden era.

13   State-Sponsored T & S   115
Montreal hosts the Olympics at a time when terrorism and steroids become prevalent.

14   Back from the Depths of Despair   125
From Ben Johnson to Sylvie Frechette to Donovan Bailey and more.

15   The Winter Olympics: In the Arena   137
Canada's hockey and figure skating history at the Games.

16   The Winter Olympics: The Great Out (and In) Doors   149
Skiing, bobsleighing, speed skating, and more.

Part 4: Canadian Football: The Heroes of the Game   159

17   The Family of Football   161
The game in the first 40 years of this century.

18   Heroes from Coast to Coast   171
The glory days of Canadian football.

19   From the Penthouse to the Outhouse   181
Politics, anti-Canadian feeling, and self-inflicted wounds in the Canadian Football League.

20   E Pluribus Unum, Eh!   191
Canadian football heads south and comes back with its tail between its legs.

Part 5: Baseball: Diamonds of the Great White North   201

21   A Tip O' the Cap, and Other Stories   203
From Tip O'Neill to the Babe's teacher and struggles in the Depression.

22	**Minor only in Name**	**211**
	Heroes from the Great White North hit the Major Leagues while Canadian women make their mark.	
23	**Developing Some Reputations**	**221**
	Fergie Jenkins, Dr. Ron, talent from Saskatchewan, and Larry Walker.	
24	**Triumphs and Tragedies: The Montreal Expos**	**229**
	Up and down the roller coaster with Canada's first Major League team.	
25	**Climbing the Tallest Mountain: The Toronto Blue Jays**	**239**
	The history of Canada's second big league club from birth to the World Series.	

Part 6: All The Sports You Can Eat — 249

26	**Curling: Hogging the Spotlight**	**251**
	A short history of the other game on ice.	
27	**Basketball: Just a Humble Peach Basket**	**257**
	Basketball, the Canadian invention.	
28	**Racing: The Asphalt Jungle**	**265**
	The Villeneuves and other speed sport heroes.	
29	**Horse Racing: A Star in the Barn and Other Stories**	**271**
	A quick look at Canada's quickest athletes, including Northern Dancer, the best sire in modern history.	

Appendices

I	**Special Events**	**279**
	The Miracle Mile, Marilyn Bell, Cindy Nicholas, Rick Hansen, and the great Terry Fox.	
II	**Other Things You Should Know**	**283**
	A run through the plethora of Canadian heroes.	

Bibliography — 289
Index — 293

Contents

Part 1: Roots — 1

1 No Autopsy, No Foul? — 3
  Lacrosse, or A Guide to Pre-Invasion First Aid 4
  The Mother of Invention 5
    Shinny Night with the Ottawa 6
    Bob, Bob, Bobbin' Along 7
  Twenty-Five Men in a Dugout Canoe 7
  Deerfoot 8

2 Roughing It in the Bush, or, Rounders with Susanna Moodie — 9
  The Buzz About Bees 10
  Bob's Yer Uncle, and He Can Curl, Too! 10
  I'll Box Your Ears Off, My Boy! 11
  Uptown Boys 11
  Imports and Exports 12

3 Towards the New Century — 15
  From Windsor, by Way of the Mi'kmaq 16
    A Young Game Goes West 17
  Three Yards and a Kick in the Head 17
  Buy Me Some Peanuts and Back Bacon, Eh! 18
    Around the Canadian Bases 20
  Anybody Seen the Canadians? 21

4 My Canadian Can Beat Your (Fill in the Blank) Anytime! — 23
  On the Waterfront 24
  The Talent Coming up Behind 25
  The Boy in Blue 25
    A Match Race Made in Blue Heaven 26
    Ned's Legend 27
  One Big, Fair-Haired Boy 27
  A Procession of Giants 28
  You Want Ice? We've Got Ice! 29
  A Couple of All-Arounders 29

Contents

Part 2: Hockey: Our Game — 31

5 We'll Take Your Puck and Start Our Own League (1890–1919) — 33
A Fifty Dollar Investment in the Future 34
A Scalper's Dream 34
Give That Man a Pacifier 35
After the Gold Rush 36
Les Canadiens sont là (Here Come the Canadiens) 37
Three Patricks on the Left Coast 38
Up the Vimy Ridge, Boys! 39
It Was All Because of Eddie 40
Influenza 41
Other Stars of the Era 41

6 Blood Sport (1920–1939) — 43
The Disappearing-Reappearing Canadian
   Franchise Boogie 44
Quit Yer Cryin' Howie, You're About to Be a Star 45
   Killed by a Broken Heart 46
The Maple Leafs: Conn's Emblem Dear 47
   Spinning Gold Out of Straw 48
Ace Bailey is Crowned in Boston 48
Hello Canada… 49
Other Stars of the Era 50

7 An Original Six (1940–1967) — 53
An Unstoppable, Unforgiving Rocket 54
   That Richard, He's Such a Riot 55
There, But for the Grace of the Hockey Gods 56
If You Won't Sign with Us, Big Jean, We'll Buy
   Your Whole League 57
The Troubles of Terry 58
The Golden Jet? How Did They Know? 59
A Man Not Named Maholovich 60
Other Stars of the Era 61

8 Expansions, Explosions, and a Kid Named Bobby Orr (1967–1980) — 63
The Wrong Left Coast 64
The Greatest, Part One 64
Coming In on Left Wing and a Prayer 65

      What Do You Mean, You Can't See the Puck? 66
   God Bless You, Paul 67
   The Gruesome, Violent Seventies 69
      Giving In to the Bullies 69
      All Hell Breaks Loose 70
   Les Habitants sont là, Again 71
   And So... 71
   Other Stars of the Era 72

9 The Great One, The Magnificent One, and the International Pastime (1981–Present)   75

   The Great One 76
      He Did What? 77
   Magnificent Mario 78
   Bring Us Your Tired, Your Hungry... 79
   The Truly Unthinkable 80
   Bite Him, Blue! Bite That Bad Man! 81
   Goodbye to The Greatest One 82
   Other Stars of the Era 82

10 The Dispossessed   85

   Casting a Shadow on the Game 85
   Ignoring Jackie Robinson 86
   O'Willie! 86
   If They Don't Want Him... 87
   Filled with Sound and Fuhry 88
   We Got Puck! 88
   Look Dad, There's a Girl in Goal 90
   Gail, Justine, and the Big Question 91
   A Touch of National Angst 92

Part 3: The Olympic Spirit: A New Kind of Drug   95

11 Faster, Higher, Stronger (1900–1936)   97

   One Lonely Gold 97
   Hero Etienne Keeps His Job 98
   Canada Gets on a Run 99
   If Only It Wasn't for Jim 99
   As Canadian as Mom, Apple Pie, and a
      Massey Ferguson 100
   From Triumph to Tragedy 101

Ethel and the Jets 102
Gone Hollywood 103
Whacking Adolf with a Paddle 103
Other Stars of the Era 104

12 Pure Amateurism (1948–1968)   107

Taking What You Can Get 108
Second Class Citizens 108
Row, Row, Row Your Damn Boat! 109
How Low Can You Go? 110
Not Too Wild About Harry 111
    The Comeback Kid 112
Roger and George Who? 112
Mighty Mouse 113
Other Stars of the Era 114

13 State-Sponsored T & S (1972–1984)   115

In the Shadow of Greatness 116
From Hero to Bum in 1.5 Billion Easy Steps 116
A Crown Stolen and Never Returned 117
Take That, Dwight Stones 118
Meet Graham Smith 119
Spirit of the West 120
Victor, to the End 120
Anne and Alex 122
Other Stars of the Era 122

14 Back from the Depths of Despair (1988–1996)   125

Ben Johnson, Canadian 126
9.79 127
    Fear and Self-Loathing in Toronto 127
    Kristen Otto Give Them Back 128
Carolyn Can-Do 128
Ring of Fire 129
The Third Baseman's Wife 130
A Troubled Gold 131
Silken 131
And on the Rest of the Lake… 132
The Burning of Atlanta 132
Jobbed Again 133
The Sunny Summary 134
Other Stars of the Era 134

15 The Winter Olympics: In the Arena — 137

- When Canada Ruled the Ice ... 138
  - *First Ripples of a Red Tide* ... 138
- Father Bauer's Boys ... 139
- Beyond the Summit ... 140
- Calgary and Onwards ... 141
- Gold Was in the Bag ... 141
- Figure Skating — The Elusive Gold ... 142
- Stealing a Country's Heart ... 142
- Wow, Can You Believe Their Luck? ... 143
- A Little Bad Timing ... 143
- Brian and Liz ... 144
- It's Enough to Make a Hound Dog Cry ... 145
- Schmirler the Curler ... 146
- Other Stars of the Era ... 146

16 The Winter Olympics: The Great Out (and In) Doors — 149

- A Long Row of Empty Necks ... 150
- The Tricksters ... 150
- Raging Ross ... 151
- Another Ottawa Girl ... 151
- How Greene Was Chamrousse Valley ... 151
- Race and Wait ... 152
- Golden Dreams ... 153
- The Mighty Myriam ... 153
- Into the Teeth of the Wind ... 154
- Out From the Shadow of Eric ... 154
- The View from the Inside ... 155
- In the Land of the Wild and Wooly ... 156
- Still Bobbin' Along ... 156
- Nothing Like Kissing Your Sister ... 157
- Other Stars of the Era ... 157

Part 4: Canadian Football: The Heroes of the Game — 159

17 The Family of Football (1900–1941) — 161

- Blue, Cerise, and Rouge ... 162
- Growing Pains ... 162
- Any Sport Will Do, as Long as the Trophy Says "Lord Grey" ... 163
- Who Has the Cup? ... 163

More Arguments 164
Football as a Teenager 165
From Out of the West They Came...and Lost 165
The Big Train 166
Passing the Torch 167
Importing a Victory 167
Weather Report 168
Other Stars of the Era 169

18 Heroes from Coast to Coast (1942–1969)   171
Amateur only in Name 172
The Grand National Drunk 172
Arrrrgooooos! 173
   "You got any notions, Harry?" 174
Jackie and Sam 174
Holy Mackinaw! 175
Nipping the Tigers in the Bud 175
Russ 177
Weather Report 177
Other Stars of the Era 178

19 From the Penthouse to the Outhouse (1970–1989)   181
Kiicking the Political Football 182
The Underground Railroad 183
A Bone to Pick with the CFL 184
Simply the Best 184
Lord Nelson Loses Trafalgar 185
A Lot to Be Said for Parity? 187
Self-Inflicted Wounds 187
Weather Report 188
Other Stars of the Era 189

20 E Pluribus Unum, Eh! (1990–1999)   191
The Great One, the Funny One, and the Crooked One . . . 192
The Hollywood Influence 193
Larry Smith Takes the Fall 193
A Death in the Family 195
The Diminutive One 196
A Blast from the Past 197
You Can't Keep a Good Game Down 197
Weather Report 198
Other Stars of the Era 198

Part 5: Baseball: Diamonds of the Great White North   201

21 A Tip O' the Cap, and Other Stories (1880–1935)   203
A Line of Greek Goddesses 204
Foxy's Glove 204
At the Turn of the Century 205
Black Balled 206
The Asahis 207
Oh, Brother! 207
On to the Dirty Thirties 208
Trouble in Toronto 209
Other Stars of the Era 209

22 Minor only in Name (1936–1959)   211
Down but Not Out 212
No Goody, Goody Two Shoes 212
Babe 213
Oh, and About Dick... 214
The Girls from the Great White North 214
   Bonnie and Ollie 215
A Love for Jackie Robinson 216
One Lousy Little Pill 217
Doing the Maple Leaf Rock 218
Other Stars of the Era 218

23 Developing Some Reputations (1960–Present)   221
The Yo-Yo Effect 222
Dr. Ron 222
Fergie 223
A Pitchin' Medical Miracle 224
Just a Big, Easy-Going Guy 224
Another Son of Saskatchewan 225
Do You Believe in Miracles? (Junior Division) 226
Not Bad for an Ex-Goaltender 226
Other Stars of the Era 227

24 Triumphs and Tragedies: The Montreal Expos   229
Preventing a Still Birth 230
Fun? Wow! 230
Riding the Roller Coaster 231

Life, the Universe, and Everything 232
Black Monday 233
The Lost Eighties 233
El Presidente is El Perfecto 234
Father Felipe 235
The Darkest Hour 236
Only the Good, and the Ignored, Die Young 236
Other Stars of the Era 237

25 Climbing the Tallest Mountain: The Toronto Blue Jays — 239

Who Is This Guy? 240
Show Us the Money 240
What's a Little Snow? 241
Early Struggles 241
Segap Wolley and a Guy with No Socks 242
Bobby's Boys 242
Sir David 243
Horseshoes, Hand Grenades, and Atom Bombs 244
George and Jimy 244
Sittin' with Cito on Top of the World 245
Touch 'Em All Joe 246
Languishing Through the Nineties 247
Other Stars of the Era 248

Part 6: All the Sports You Can Eat — 249

26 Curling: Hogging the Spotlight — 251

In the Hack 252
Across the Hog Line 252
Into the House of Richardson 253
Wrenched Right into the Button 254
And Now a Word from Don Duguid 254
Shall We Join the Ladies? 255
Other Stars 255

27 Basketball: Just a Humble Peach Basket — 257

Now Here's an Idea 257
Something for Future Secretaries to Do 258
In and Out in One Year 259
A Whole Lot of Almosts 259
Meanwhile 260
The Big, Purple Dinosaur 261

xiii

A Far Less Grizzly Story 262
　　　A Small Base on Which to Build 262
　　　Other Stars 263

28　Racing: The Asphalt Jungle　265
　　　All Eyes Looked to Bowmanville 265
　　　Ain't It Grand, Eh? 266
　　　The Legend of Gilles 266
　　　Earul 267
　　　Back Home Again in Indiana 267
　　　The Invasion of the Continent 268
　　　Let's Go Cart-Racing 269
　　　In Harmsworth's Way 269
　　　Other Stars 270

29　Horse Racing: A Star in the Barn and Other Stories　271
　　　Two Plates Fit for Kings and Queens 272
　　　Horses for Courses 272
　　　The Pumper 272
　　　You Can Call Him Mr. Taylor 273
　　　The Dancer 273
　　　Back in the Sulky Again 274
　　　Ronny and Big Red 274
　　　Fitting Pud with a Halo 275
　　　One Last Kick at the Can? 275
　　　Other Stars 276

Appendices

I　Special Events　279
　　　Don't Look Back (Someone *Is* Gaining on You) 279
　　　The Lady of the Lake 280
　　　The Queen of the Channel 280
　　　All I Need is a Pair of Wheels 280
　　　143 Marathons of Hope 281

II　Other Things You Should Know　283

Bibliography　289

Index　293

Foreword

Malcolm Kelly says he had a great time writing this book. I'm sure he did. Any writer-researcher who dabbles in Canadian sports history soon feels the excitement, the fun, and the pleasure that comes from discovering little-known facts about some of Canada's greatest athletes and passing them along to readers. Even the best-known stories of players and teams making up Canada's rich sporting history become fun in the re-telling.

I must say Malcolm has done a marvellous job in bringing to these pages the incredible deeds and fascinating performances of teams and individuals in pursuit of Stanley Cups, Grey Cups, World Series rings, Briers, Olympic medals, and in some cases, nothing more rewarding than a pat on the back.

All the greats are here—the skaters, runners, rowers, and throwers. Their achievements are awesome, their stories unique. I'll bet you didn't know that Canadian rower Ned Hanlan (344 wins, six defeats) was so beloved abroad that Australia renamed a town after him, calling it Toronto. Or that there's a reason Canadian football teams play with 12 men a side while the Americans prefer 11-man squads.

I pride myself in knowing something about Canadian hockey history but I never knew Aubrey (Dit) Clapper played junior hockey in Oshawa—as a 13-year-old! And I'd almost forgotten that in the mid-1960s, players in the NHL were all-Canadian with one exception: U.S. born Tommy Williams. And, thanks to Malcolm, I now know how many seasons all six Sutter brothers played in the NHL.

Malcolm has covered all the bases, including an account of the first recorded baseball game in the nation, played on June 4, 1838 in a pasture at Beechville, Ontario. In those days, Canadian pitchers differed from their American counterparts by throwing overhand; no underhand lobs like the Yanks preferred and soon abandoned. Not for our boys. He recounts the story of the female hockey player who was kicked out of hockey for life—after attacking both the referee and the linesman in a game. He recalls how sprinter Percy Williams survived rheumatic fever as a youngster, went on to become a great Olympian, and even had a chocolate bar named after him. But Percy was a loner, a recluse who shunned all honours and committed suicide in 1982.

And he reminds us of Montreal mayor Jean Drapeau's famous quote in the 1970s: "The Montreal Olympics can no more have a deficit than a man can have a baby." The cost-unconscious mayor's estimate of $124 million for the games ballooned to $1.5 billion, leaving Quebeckers the rest of their lives to figure out how to pay off the debt.

Stop me, Malcolm, before I reveal most of your best yarns in this little foreword.

Now, wouldn't I feel like an idiot if I did that to you?

Brian McFarlane

Brian McFarlane, author of more than 40 hockey books, including *It Happened in Hockey* and *Stanley Cup Fever: More Than a Century of Hockey Greatness*, is one of Canada's foremost hockey historians. He was a host and colour commentator on *Hockey Night in Canada* for more than 25 years and also hosted games on CBS, NBC, and ESPN. He is a member of the media section of the Hockey Hall of Fame.

Introduction

Welcome to the *Complete Idiot's Guide to Canadian Sports History and Trivia*.

First off, you don't have to be an idiot to get something out of this book. It's really written for a lot of different people:

- For those who love and enjoy reading about sports — any time, any place, any excuse.
- For those who have some knowledge of Canadian sports and want to learn more.
- For those who know nothing about Canadian sports and want to learn (especially young people just discovering them), or those who need a quick primer so they can impress friends, neighbours, dates, etc.
- And for new Canadians, who want to learn something about our culture through its sports history.

The book is meant to be a general view of Canadian sports history, and hopefully it will lead readers to want to learn more through the work of this country's finest writers, many of whom you'll find listed in the bibliography at the back of the book.

Now, a little about this guide. It's divided into six sections plus appendixes.

Part One, "Roots," looks at the beginning of sport in what would become Canada, especially the games of the native people and the early settlers.

Part Two, "Hockey: Our Game," looks at the lifeblood of Canadian sport, its stories, builders, and players. Included is a section on Blacks and women in hockey.

Part Three, "The Olympic Spirit: A New Kind of Drug," focuses on the Olympic Games, including four chapters on the summer games, and two on the winter version.

Part Four, "Canadian Football: The Heroes of the Game," examines the game which for the first 80 years of this century was the second most popular and important spectator sport in the land.

Part Five, "Baseball: Diamonds of the Great White North," discusses a game with roots that go back at least to the 1830s.

Part Six, "All The Sports You Can Eat," takes a look at curling, basketball, auto racing, and horse racing.

The appendices include five important events that didn't fit any of the other categories, 30 other important things you should know, and a personal listing of the top ten greatest events in Canadian sports history.

Extras

Like any *Complete Idiot's Guide,* this one contains other elements designed to make for a more enjoyable and informative read. Watch for them as they appear.

> **Listen Up!**
>
> is a collection of great stories from our sports history.

> **Quote, Unquote**
>
> brings back some of the wonderful quotes in media and books over the years.

> **Know-it-alls**
>
> is a group of over 200 skill-testing questions that test your knowledge of Canadian sports and teach more about the subjects.

Here's hoping you have fun with this book.

Acknowledgments

First of all, I'd like to thank Alan Stuart, curator of Canada's Sports Hall of Fame for recommending me to Prentice Hall to do this book. At PH there's Andrea Crozier (the boss), who was very understanding of a rookie's plight, and my long-suffering editor Paul Woods who put up with my whining, my singing phone messages, visits by Auggie Doggie, and general angst. Thanks also to Greg Ioannou and Wendy Yano for their terrific copy editing. Heartfelt pats on the back to Chris Jones and Scott Burnside of the *National Post* for reading large portions of the manuscript, and a special nod to Mark Askin of Molstar Productions, who corrected mistakes in the hockey portion and made himself available for general arguments over content. John Massingberd of Raceline Radio and George Webster of *Performance Racing News* lent their expertise on the auto racing section, for which I thank them. I'd also like to honour all the authors whose work I stole merrily from — Canada is blessed with exceptional talent, and I used it to the maximum — with especial mention to Brian McFarlane on hockey, William Humber on baseball, Cleve Dheensaw on the Olympics, and Louis Cauz on baseball and horse racing. Thanks especially to Mr. Cauz for inviting me to his house to go over horse racing. And to Noah Richler, books editor at the *National Post*, thanks for guiding me through early negotiations on the contract.

Thanks also to all those who answered questions when I bugged them at all hours of the day and night.

Compressing the entire history of Canadian sports into one volume was a daunting task at times, and many stories and athletes were left on the cutting room floor. To anyone I missed, my apologies.

And finally, this book is dedicated to my wife Barbara, and my son Patrick (who thinks this is really cool, for once), who had to live for six months with me just a rumour hunched over the computer in the basement.

Part 1
Roots

A Native Canadian from 500 years ago plucked from the forests of what's now eastern Canada and dropped on to a local hockey rink would likely recognize the sport right away. Same with a soccer field. And a baseball diamond. Native Canadians invented versions of those games. Football? Been there. Wrestling? Done that. Bowling? Bought the cheaply made, overpriced shirt.

Indeed, the history of sports in Canada does not start at the first recorded organized baseball game in the 1830s or with the whirlwind creation of hockey down east in the early nineteenth century.

It begins on the playing fields of the Iroquois and the Huron, the rocky outcrops of Mi'kmaq fishing villages, and in the west coast forests of the Haida…

Chapter 1

No Autopsy, No Foul?

In This Chapter

➤ The immaculate invention of lacrosse
➤ The games our forefathers and mothers played
➤ The Voyageurs — Playing for keeps
➤ Our first international hero

There has always been this great misconception that any games played by those "savages" found on the other side of the big Atlantic pond must have been uncontrolled, dangerous affairs where blood was regularly spilled in front of screaming crowds hoping for ever more mayhem. But enough about hockey. In truth, the natives were every bit as organized, or disorganized, bloodthirsty or nonviolent, as anyone playing with a ball, club, or bare feet anywhere in the world.

Much as the bow and arrow was discovered by a number of different cultures (all of who quickly invented archery contests to test their skills), sports like soccer and hockey were being played, in different versions, by Europeans and native Canadians alike, long before the former invaded. Some games were rough, and some were not.

We owe much to native people in such areas as architecture, engineering, medicine, mathematics, and, especially, agriculture (where would we be without corn, beans, and potatoes?). Sports too. In this chapter we'll look at sports played before and just after European settlers arrived.

Part 1 ➤ Roots

Lacrosse, or A Guide to Pre-Invasion First Aid

Consider the following: Although there is little recorded interaction between the 150 or so tribes of North America, almost all of them counted an easily recognizable form of lacrosse as one of their most popular sports. As tribes migrated across the continent those many thousands of years ago, they must have brought an ancient version of the game with them, making lacrosse one of the world's oldest sports.

This is not an entirely accepted view, by the way. Some historians, such as Alex Weyand and Milton Roberts, believe that the game actually started among the Huron and Iroquois along the banks of the St. Lawrence River and worked its way west.

Make no mistake, wherever played, lacrosse (or *la crosse*, a French name given by early explorers to a game of many monikers, including *tehontshik aheks*, by the Iroquois, or *Baggataway*, by the Algonquin), was a tough, no-holds-barred, Don-Cherry-would've-loved-it sport. Sides would be chosen within a tribe, or a neighbouring group invited in for what was seen as good training for young fighters.

The most advanced tribes at lacrosse — an early Canada-at-hockey sort of thing — seem to have been the six Iroquois nations. Their stick design is the same one we use today. Although it's not true that the Iroquois League (Cayuga, Mohawk, Oneida, Onondaga, Seneca, and Tuscarora) was founded to compete for the False Face Cup, political and social union did include a lot of inter-tribal sporting rivalry.

Games could last all day, were heavily wagered on, and more often than not led to spilled blood and broken bones. Many writers have described lacrosse as mostly unorganized mayhem, but there is much evidence to suggest that there was a referee of some kind and the rules were institutionalized among the Iroquois, though not written down.

As a test of endurance and reliability in battle, lacrosse was vital for many tribes, especially the Iroquois, who would, of course, go on to force expansion franchises — by burning and pillaging — on the Hurons, who also had a deep love for the game.

The Choctaw, in what's now the southeastern United States, played a highly organized version of the game in which a deerskin ball was tossed between two posts in order to score. Players were not allowed to touch the ball with their hands or use the stick to fight.

> **Listen Up!**
>
> "At the start of a (lacrosse) game, two teams lined up opposite each other in the centre of a field. Then a stuffed deerskin ball was tossed between the teams and the players tried to catch it in the pockets of their rackets. The object of the game was to hurl, carry, or kick the ball between the opposing team's goal posts, but the long-range aim was to test a young man's endurance and potential valor on the battlefield."
>
> — Alex Whitney, *Sports and Games the Indians Gave Us.*

Men and women across the native nations played the game. The women often played as roughly as the men.

It's interesting to note one writer's view of lacrosse, written in the 1960s. He was unable to fathom how the natives were able to create the lacrosse stick, since "they weren't very inventive." Apparently they were inventive enough to create one of the world's great sports, the equipment used to play it, the goal posts used to score into, the referee to watch over it, and a complete system of inter-tribal play.

> **Quote, Unquote**
>
> "It's very pretty to watch."
>
> — Queen Victoria of Great Britain, on viewing a lacrosse game in England.

The Mother of Invention

Native peoples invented their own versions of just about every game played today:

Soccer? Natives across the continent were playing forms of kickball long before the white man arrived. Loved by men, women, and children, each game had its own set of rules.

The men would allow blocking and tackling in their game to prevent or help a ball handler get the orb to the other end — thus inventing the forerunner to American football, which in turn ruined Sunday afternoons in the fall during the latter part of the twentieth century.

Baseball? Out on the prairies, native tribes played a form of dodgeball that suggests the baseball we know. One player was the batter, standing in a small circle, and eight others were the fielders. The bat was a stick of hardwood used to hit the ball. If the ball was caught in the air, the fielder would try to strike the batter in the circle with it. If the batter couldn't get out of the way, he was out. Early baseball, as we know it, used the same rule — if you hit the base runner, he was out.

That was changed when fielders got a little too good at it.

Wrestling? Natives wrestled incessantly, all year round, indoors and outdoors. A number of tribes came up with the intramural wrestling tournament, in which the two smallest members would "rassle" each other. The winner would take on the next largest, and so on, until a champion was declared. "Indian wrestling" involved lying on your back next to your opponent, locking legs and trying to force the other's limb to the ground.

> **Know-it-alls**
>
> Q. What was the west coast Nootka people's most popular sport?
>
> A. Breath holding.

Part 1 ➤ *Roots*

Listen Up!

The man who took the already established native game of lacrosse and adapted it to "modern" rules was Dr. George Beers. A dentist (apt profession for this sport), Dr. Beers published a guide and rulebook for the game in 1860, thus earning the title "The Father of Lacrosse." Though really the game's stepfather, Dr. Beers was the driving force behind establishing the game in eastern Canada, organizing the founding convention of the National Lacrosse Association in 1867. He was also a leading hand behind the Montreal Amateur Athletic Association, which would be a key force in the development of hockey.

Know-it-alls

Q. Where was the first bowling alley in North America?

A. The first alley was found in a Cherokee mound site in Georgia. It is hundreds of years old.

Quote, Unquote

"North American Indians invented all their own games. Their ingenuity and variety were exceptional."

— Henry Roxborough, in *One Hundred-Not Out.*

Shinny Night with the Ottawa

The origins of hockey, as those of baseball, go back many hundreds of years and come from as many different parts of the globe.

Native people played the game we know as shinny all across the continent. In their version, a stuffed deerskin ball or other rounded object was batted across the grass with a 4-foot stick towards the opponents' goal posts.

Pond shinny, or river shinny, was the natural outgrowth of the summer game when ice and snow covered the land. Instead of a ball, archeologists and historians think the players switched to a knot of wood or a small sphere carved out of stone.

When European settlers came to the continent, the native tradition of shinny (also played in many forms as field hockey in Europe) was married to the Dutch invention of skates — and the die was cast for the coming of the great gods of hockey: Gordie Howe, Maurice Richard, and Wayne Gretzky.

Bob, Bob, Bobbin' Along

From the Yukon to Labrador, natives invented and perfected the toboggan — a set of smooth wooden planks curved upwards at the front that would slide nicely down hills. Though it was a hunting and travelling tool, our human competitive nature led, of course, to races. And betting on those races.

Realizing that the sleds would go faster if they went down chutes instead of a flat hill, large logs would be dragged down the slope to form the first bobsled runs.

> **Know-it-alls**
>
> Q. How did lacrosse played by southeastern natives differ from that played by those in what's now eastern Canada?
>
> A. Players used two sticks at once, instead of one.

Twenty-Five Men in a Dugout Canoe

Calling the Voyageurs "athletes" may, at first glance, seem a stretch, but the men who blazed the trails from Montreal through the wilderness as far away as what's now Manitoba and even further to the Mackenzie River (eventually the route stretched 6,500 miles km) were indeed Canada's first non-native athletic performers.

And superb athletes they were. You try paddling a fur-laden canoe hundreds of kilometres a day, tossing it up on your shoulders for a crash through the woods, and paddling on again, from dawn until dusk. Oh, and once in a while, the *coureurs de bois* would have to take up arms with their native allies to fight off incursions from rival traders.

The teams in this sport, after Wolfe defeated Montcalm (on the road in double overtime) at the Plains of Abraham field, were the Hudson's Bay Company and the North-West Company. The latter, based in Montreal, would eventually overreach itself and go out of business. The former, after buying up what was left of its rival, would move its franchise from London, England, to Canada, and start selling underwear and socks at its concession stands.

After the Voyageurs came home with their loads of furs, they often staged canoe races that were extremely popular with the populace, and heavily wagered on.

> **Know-it-alls**
>
> Q. What was the favourite sport of the Inuit in the extreme north?
>
> A. A form of kickball played with a soft ball stuffed with caribou hair, using rules much like modern soccer, though without the nets.

Know-it-alls

Q. How did the Kutchin, who lived in what's now Canada's northwest, often settle family disputes?

A. With wrestling matches.

Deerfoot

The most celebrated native athlete among European settlers in the mid-nineteenth century was a Cattarangua whose name was translated into "Son of the Wind," or Deerfoot. He was this country's first sports hero. A superb distance runner, Deerfoot performed all over the world in races of two miles or more, often with another excellent native runner, an Iroquois named Dibo. According to writer Henry Roxborough, Deerfoot and Dibo toured North America and Europe and were willing to race each other, or any and all comers, for a purse of 50 pounds or more.

Superbly confident in their abilities, they would bet as much as $5,000 that no one could beat them. There is no record that anyone ever did.

The Least You Need to Know

- North American natives already had a strong sporting culture in place before the arrival of European settlers.
- Lacrosse is the natives' gift to the world of sports.
- Natives had their own version of virtually every game played by Europeans.
- Canoe races staged by Voyageurs were among the earliest sporting events of European settlers.
- The first internationally known Canadian athlete was a native runner.

Chapter 2

Roughing It in the Bush, or, Rounders with Susanna Moodie

> **In This Chapter**
> ➤ The bee, and its encouragement of sport
> ➤ Curling — Canada's game in the nineteenth century
> ➤ Other sports popular with settlers
> ➤ Sports in the growing towns
> ➤ Imports and exports

The early European settlers of Upper and Lower Canada spent most of their waking hours fighting to survive. But they didn't do it alone. As writers such as Susanna Moodie revealed, survival was a joint enterprise —barn raisings, quiltings, logging parties and the like were regular occurrences. When our pioneer forebears did find time to celebrate, it was often with sports, games, and other recreations. Fortified by copious amounts of spirits, sports in the early- to mid-nineteenth century produced two inventions that would survive to this day: the Hot Stove League, and repairing to the bar for a brew after a good game. In this chapter we'll look at the sports of the early pioneers.

The Buzz About Bees

Any time a group of settlers would get together to help each other it was called a "bee." The most important from the early days was the logging bee, because so much of the land was covered with stands of timber and removing it by oneself was a lengthy and back-breaking experience. After a bee was over, a celebration, accompanied by food and drink, was called for. At those celebrations, sports began to come into the settlers' lives as a way of working off some aggression and tension.

Not to mention giving the settlers something to bet on and argue over.

Writer Susanna Moodie (whose *Roughing It in the Bush* is a classic of early Canadian literature), perhaps envisioning the weekend hockey or baseball tournaments of the next century, despised bees of all kinds, calling them "noisy, riotous, drunken meetings, often terminating in violent quarrels, sometimes even in bloodshed."

To get the lads to work a little harder on clearing a spot of land, organizers would often split them into two teams and have them compete to see who could clear their parcel the fastest — with the attendant betting, drinking, and swearing going along with it.

Bob's Yer Uncle, and He Can Curl, Too!

Of all the sports imported from across the big pond, or picked up and developed from those the natives played, the Scottish game of curling seems to be the one that grabbed the fancy of settlers the quickest.

The first recorded curling in Canada was in the garrisons of Quebec, around the end of the eighteenth century, as bored soldiers waiting for an American invasion went looking for something to do. The boys in red picked up the game at Kingston around 1820, and it showed up in Muddy York by 1830 — though using shovels instead of brooms to help the stone travel down through the muck wasn't much fun.

The first attempt at organizing a curling club (complete with cash bar and smoky room) was at Montreal in 1807. It didn't take long for the curlers at Quebec City and those at Montreal to start playing each other in challenge matches — the Quebeckers taking the first recorded game 31-23.

Heavy Scottish settlement in western Ontario introduced the game there, often with blocks of wood substituting for stones.

Curling headed west with more settlement, and the first recorded game in Manitoba took place in December 1876, with oatmeal (the prize) distributed among the poor of the local parish by the victorious rink.

Quote, Unquote

"Liquor stores (bottles and kegs) will be limited to six."

— *Toronto Globe*, 1859, hoping to keep the annual Toronto Fair and sports event as sober as possible.

I'll Box Your Ears Off, My Boy!

Wrestling and fighting were two of the most popular pastimes in the bush. A town would often send its best wrestlers to fight against another's, merely for the right to say it was better.

And to have yet another thing to bet on.

Pugilistic activities, and we don't mean boxing here as the Marquess of Queensbury would have it, simply came down to which opponent could beat the tar out of the other long enough that the unfortunate loser could no longer stand.

In the early years of the nineteenth century, the canoeing regatta was hugely popular in summer, as settlers would race against Voyageurs or natives. As many as four dozen canoes would battle across the water with a little money and a keg of spirits on the line. Competitions on the St. Lawrence or Ottawa rivers were common, but there is evidence of racing going on all through the backwoods.

Toboggan racing, picked up from the natives, became a popular pastime and sport. Skating, imported from Holland, was big right away, though girls were considered at first to be too weak of limb and slight of body to participate in this or any other exercise.

Running contests, which would beget more organized meets, were also tremendously popular simply because anyone could do it, it didn't require any special equipment or a stadium, and it was easy to bet on.

Uptown Boys

In the first half of the nineteenth century, Canadian towns in the east began to go from ugly, mud-filled collections of dwellings to established entities where merchants and labourers developed their own fun — not often side by side. With

Know-it-alls

Q. What was the most popular sport in Scarborough (Ontario) in the 1850s?

A. Checkers.

Quote, Unquote

"You fight each other or I'll step aside and let you fight the crowd. Take your choice."

— A legendary Calgary boxing referee named Cappy, trying to get two reluctant brawlers to mix it up in 1883.

Know-it-alls

Q. When was the first recorded curling "bonspiel" in Canada?

A. February 12, 1839, on the Don River, Toronto, with 48 curlers entered.

Part 1 ➤ *Roots*

Know-it-alls

Q. What were non-Scots who took up curling in the nineteenth century called?

A. Barbarians.

Listen Up!

One of the first racecourses in Canada was located in the town of York — what's now Toronto — on a causeway leading to the Toronto islands. It was laid out prior to the War of 1812, which makes it the only track in Canada to be invaded by Americans with more than betting on their minds. So many people wanted to get to the track and the other recreations available on the causeway that it actually led to the building of the first bridges over the Don River. Even then, politicians had their priorities straight.

gentlemen of means, military officers, and government bureaucrats involved, whatever was played would be handled with a certain amount of aplomb, as compared to the rabble in the bush.

Popular sports included horse racing, football (an early version of it), cricket, and skating.

Horse racing, the sport of kings, princes, and anyone with a bob or two to put down on a nag's head, bred its first tracks in the late-eighteenth century, offering purses of 20 guineas or less. Speaking of breeding, jockeys weren't that small back then — the listed minimum weight limit at one meet of the time called for not less than 150 pounds carried. Today's horses, used to a maximum of 126 pounds, would be shocked and appalled.

Steeplechase was an especially popular sport with the gentry — some of whom would develop large stables of horse flesh with which to compete. And with the unfortunate number of breakdowns and fence crashes suffered by the animals in that endeavour, those large stables were needed.

Racing in the backwoods was not quite as refined. Rowdiness was commonplace, and, because money was hard to come by, bets would be placed using whatever was available to barter — "A barrel of pork on number 3 to win, eh."

Lawn tennis (as lah-de-dah a game as you could imagine) and court tennis (sort of like racquetball today) were also popular among the richer folk in the latter part of the century, with private clubs opening first in Montreal and Toronto. When the Prince of Wales visited in 1860, he is said to have played a game of court tennis in Toronto.

Imports and Exports

Rounders was a game Susanna Moodie would have known from her own childhood in England (played mostly by girls, by the way, with the runners going the opposite direction to modern baseball). It was brought to the new world and slowly developed its own rules, influenced by cricket, another English import, and native games. Eventually, that amalgamation would grow into the game we know today as "America's Pastime."

Chapter 2 ➤ Roughing It in the Bush with Susanna Moodie

As we shall see ahead in Chapter 3, baseball grew up in Canada in much the same way it did south of the border.

Lacrosse was an easy pick-up from the natives.

Association football (soccer) was imported, but was quickly altered by the addition of rugby, Irish football, and other rougher endeavours to create North American football.

And hurley and field hockey, combined with the native's shinny and the Dutch invention of skates, begat ice hockey.

Only basketball, created by James Naismith in 1891, was specifically invented as a game we play today by one of that new breed of people known as Canadians.

> **The Least You Need to Know**
> ➤ Settlers played much of their sport as part of bees.
> ➤ Curling arrived here around 1800.
> ➤ Wrestling and fighting were very popular.
> ➤ Horse racing was strongly supported everywhere.

Know-it-alls

Q. Where was the first YMCA opened in North America?

A. Montreal, 1851.

Listen Up!

According to writer Henry Roxborough, an athletic meet in the 1850s would include short and long running races, light or heavy sledgehammer throws (14 or 21 pounds), light or heavy stone puts (16 or 24 pounds), caber tosses (a high pole), and forms of high jump and long jump. Organizers would also add a greasy pig contest (the first to catch it, kept it) and the very difficult greased pole climb.

Know-it-alls

Q. Why was the Manitoba parliament called off one day in 1844?

A. Most of the members were off curling.

13

Chapter 3

Towards the New Century

In This Chapter

- ➤ Hockey, the new national sport
- ➤ Baseball, north of the border
- ➤ Football, the all-Canadian game
- ➤ The 1896 Olympics

The sports our ancestors played were eventually supplanted by new ones, developed out of familiar games and made our own. Hockey started out east and headed west with a vengeance. Baseball began in Upper Canada and fanned out across the new country in the same way. As the new century, the last of the millennium, dawned, those sports together with football began to compete for the attention of Canadian sports fanatics with established activities such as rowing, curling, and running. The construction of railroads in the 1840s also had a great impact on sport because enthusiasts could now take their games to other areas. But we still had a distance to go as an organized sporting country. And we weren't ready by 1896 to be caught up in the rush of the new Olympics. In this chapter, we'll look at these issues.

Part 1 ➤ *Roots*

From Windsor, by Way of the Mi'kmaq

Cooperstown, New York, was identified as the birthplace of baseball by Albert Goodwill Spalding, because he wanted a truly "American" background for the Grand Old Game. It isn't true, of course, and neither is it so that Abner Doubleday laid down the first rules.

Windsor, Nova Scotia, on the other hand, can fairly lay claim as the place where all the disparate elements of ice hockey — field hockey, hurley, shinny (called *Oochamkunutk* by the local Mi'kmaq natives), cricket, and many others — were brought together in the game we now recognize as ours.

Yes, the Bluenoses are the hockey bluebloods.

Hockey began around 1800 and really gained its popularity on the grounds of King's College (est. 1789) in Windsor. The boys there were rich, and because they had money they could afford the equipment and the time needed to become enthused in sports, almost full-time. They loved hurley, an Irish game imported into Nova Scotia, and refused to put it down even when the ice and snow covered the fields. Thus was born ice-hurley.

Innovators all, the King's College boys began to take what they liked from cricket and other sports and use it in their new game.

Listen Up!

Hockey has its own A. G. Spalding in James Thomas Sutherland, called hockey's "legend maker." Sutherland claimed he played in the first organized game, at Kingston in 1886, which isn't true, and he spent his life creating and passing on the legend that Kingston was the source of hockey. It was a crock. Organized club hockey had seen its birth 10 years previously in Montreal, and the game had grown up in Nova Scotia. Sutherland was so good at passing the bull, Kingston was known for years as the "birthplace of hockey."

Enter the Mi'kmaq, who already had a version of the sport and wanted to play too. The games were melded, and, *voilà!* Hockey was born.

Nova Scotians, native and settler alike, gave us much more than just the game itself. The Mi'kmaq, practically wiped out as a people by the newcomers, held their grudge long enough to become the chief inventors and innovators of the hockey stick. They then happily stood back as their invaders learned to whack each other with it.

Their superb craftsmanship created the stick as we now know it, and MicMac brand sticks made by native workers remained popular until the 1920s. The puck was also refined down east. The Starr Manufacturing Company of Dartmouth created the first quality skates for hockey, inventing the rockered blade and the innovation of rounding its front and back.

And, the Bluenosers created the net as we know it, though some historians credit Montreal sportsman W. A. Hewitt.

Hockey — Nova Scotia's gift to the world.

A Young Game Goes West

Whether or not the game was actually named for one Colonel Hockey, who had his troops in Nova Scotia play the game to keep in shape while waiting for invasion, hockey eventually began to spread across the country.

Slowly.

Soldiers took hockey to other posts, especially Kingston, where bored military men played it on the St. Lawrence in winter.

James Creighton, educated at Dalhousie University in Halifax, brought the game to Montreal as a 22-year-old in 1875, where he taught hockey, and the Halifax Rules for it, to engineering friends. There, he quickly took the game indoors out of the freezing weather.

The sport jumped from province to province, arriving in Victoria in 1890, where the western islanders took to it so quickly they were back east challenging for the Stanley Cup in no time.

Three Yards and a Kick in the Head

In 1823, so the story goes, a boy by the name of William Webb Ellis picked up a round football (soccer ball to you colonials) on the playing fields of Rugby School in England, and took off up the middle for the totally illegal, but very popular, first run from scrimmage. That was both the supposed birth of rugby and the faint beginnings of North American-style football.

The first football club, playing rugby rules of course, was formed in Montreal in 1868, but an event that occurred six years later set North America on a course that would ruin Sunday afternoons for many — and cause Las Vegas to flourish.

Some of the boys from McGill University in Montreal were asked to get it on with the gentlemen at Harvard University, because the latter couldn't find anyone in the Ivy League willing to play rugby-football with them. So off they all went to Cambridge, Massachusetts, where, on May 14 and 15, 1874, the first true football games were played.

Know-it-alls

Q. What year was the rubber hockey puck invented?

A. 1872.

Listen Up!

Three Ways to Decide the End of a Hockey Game:

➤ When one team scores three goals.

➤ When the men have to return to barracks.

➤ When a player falls through the ice and is in danger of drowning.

Hockey rules in nineteenth century Kingston, from Brown and Fairbairn, *Pioneer Settlement in Canada.*

Part 1 ▸ Roots

Quote, Unquote

"Don't do it!"

— Walter H. Perram, former McGill player, pleads with football officials not to adopt American (Harvard) rules for the game.

Know-it-alls

Q. What was the first indoor hockey rink in Canada?

A. Victoria Rink, Montreal, 1870s.

The Harvard players loved the sport so much that they quickly convinced their snobby Ivy League brethren to give up on soccer (association football) and work on this new game instead. It was the colleges that gave impetus to the great game south of the border.

Back home, however, McGill was snubbed for playing such a rowdy match (and let's be honest, before the outlawing of straight-arm blocking to the head and other nastiness, people were occasionally getting killed), so universities didn't really pick up on the sport until the turn of the century.

So it was up to private clubs to push the game, especially the Toronto Argonaut Rowing Club and the Hamilton Amateur Athletic Association. They got together with clubs from Port Hope, London, Stratford, and Guelph and formed the first recognizable football league in Canada.

By 1882, the Ontario and Quebec rugby football unions had formed.

However, the colleges were still holding informal games with their American neighbours, and the game of football continued to develop. Canadian universities finally gave way to the inevitable and formed their own intercollegiate group in 1898.

The game was also spreading west with a vengeance, and by the turn of the century, the seeds of what we know today as the Canadian Football League were starting to grow.

Buy Me Some Peanuts and Back Bacon, Eh!

"Good Afternoon, Ladies and Gentlemen, and welcome to the pasture out back of Enoch Burdick's store, here in Beachville, Ontario, for today's first recorded game of Base between the Beachville 11 and the visitors from Zorra. Yes, this June 4, 1838, is an exciting day, sports fans. The knockers have all brought their favourite clubs along and are ready to circle those byes at blazing speed..."

Yep, the first recorded game of baseball in this country actually dates a full year before A. G. Spalding claimed ol' Abner laid out the sport for his buddies in Cooperstown. Not that you should blame General Doubleday, of course — he had no idea he was going to be tabbed as the "inventor" of baseball in 1905. After all, he was already dead.

Chapter 3 ▶ *Towards the New Century*

Listen Up!

If you've ever wondered why American football plays with 11 men and the Canadian version with 12, here's the deal. When McGill University went down to play Harvard University in the first real football game back in 1874, studies and illness meant they only took 11 of their normal 15 players. The Harvard side agreed to play with that number, and liked it so much they kept the 11-man version and began introducing it to other colleges across the U.S. But the Canucks came home and went back to 15 men. It was only when Thrift Burnside, captain of the University of Toronto Blues, suggested a cut from 15 to 12 players in 1900, that our game began to go in that direction. Thus, 11-man football is an accidental Canadian invention.

Baseball, in all its forms including rounders, had been played for centuries. But it was Alexander Cartwright and his friends who, by founding the New York Knickerbockers club and working things out on the famous Elysian Fields across the river in New Jersey, really organized the game.

The sport developed in Canada alongside the United States, with a significant difference. Baseball, and its new rules, was spread far and wide in America because of the Civil War (1861–65). Army life during a war has been described as nearly endless periods of boredom, occasionally punctuated by a few minutes of stark terror. Those down times led to much playing of the game by boys, North and South, who would then take it back to their hometown after the war ended.

Know-it-alls

Q. When was the first international baseball game played?

A. In the 1860s, between the Woodstock Young Canadians and the Atlantic Club of Brooklyn, New York. The Canadians lost 75-11.

Here, baseball moved a little more slowly out of Ontario. In 1869, Woodstock hosted a huge tournament that brought in 5,000 spectators, and in 1876, the Canadian Base Ball Association was formed. The group included the London Tecumsehs, who had the temerity to beat up on the Chicago White Stockings, champions of the new professional National League, in an exhibition game.

Baseball arrived on the west coast in the mid 1880s, with teams playing mostly American clubs.

We'll get into the early Canadian professional stars in Part Five, but Canadian clubs were in on the beginnings of pro leagues. The London Tecumsehs and Guelph Maple Leafs both joined the International Association — baseball's first minor league — in 1877, knocking heads with Pittsburgh, Columbus, Lynn, Massachusetts, Rochester, and Manchester, New Hampshire.

And we do mean knocking heads. Baseball in the later nineteenth century was often a party and gambling sport. The athletes played and partied hard, and were often in the pockets of professional bettors.

A number of sports historians, including Robert Barney of the University of Western Ontario, have turned up an interesting fact about the baseball game played in Beachville, Ontario in 1838, by the way. Unlike south of the border, the pitchers in the Canadian contest threw overhand. It was only after the influence of the Civil War on baseball that Canucks went back to submarining the ball, only to switch back again in the 1870s, when the Yankees went top-side.

Canadians, you see, were ahead of the game.

> **Quote, Unquote**
>
> "The trouble is caused by the unlooked-for illness of several printers following a ball game."
>
> — *Pictou Standard*, 1880s, on why the paper was late — too many injuries on the field.

Around the Canadian Bases

Quebec and the Maritimes began to host touring American sides in the 1880s, and with cricket fading in popularity, and betting growing, baseball was a natural.

As the game itself grew and the rules developed (underhand pitching and "plugging" a player by hitting the runner with the ball were both removed — rule makers always take the fun out of sports), so did Canadian involvement in it.

Toronto had a team in the Canadian League in 1885, but was looking to the south for its future. That came in 1886, when Toronto and Hamilton joined the new International League. Though names would change, Toronto would be part of that group until 1967, except for five years in the 1890s when the team sat on the sidelines while organized baseball brawled with itself over players' rights and with new competitors to the existing National League.

The Toronto club built the first park constructed entirely for baseball, and a brilliant history was begun.

Montreal's entry in the International League was a fiery one — literally. The Rochester franchise was struggling along financially and its stadium burnt down in 1892. Out of the league until 1895, they built another park, only to have that one go up in flames as well. The owners lent the franchise to Montreal for 1897, but when Rochester had a new park ready a year later, the Quebeckers refused to give it back.

Rochester interests bought the Scranton club instead, but couldn't make a go of it and actually lent the team to Ottawa. That club they actually hung on to (fool me twice, shame on me), and our nation's capital lost its club for the next season.

In 1901, the Baltimore Orioles were asked to leave the new American League. So, the Orioles' owners bought the Montreal Royals and moved the club to Baltimore. Undeterred, Montreal inherited the Worcester team in June.

Anybody Seen the Canadians?

What if you held an Olympics and no Canadians showed up?

That's precisely what happened in 1896, when the Olympic movement was reborn through the visionary eyes of Baron de Coubertin, a Parisian nobleman who wouldn't take no for an answer. Actually, it was a German, J. C .F. Guts-Muths, who first came up with the idea of bringing the ancient games to modern times, almost 40 years before the Baron pulled it off. But de Coubertin gets the "Father of" moniker because of his success in convincing the city of Athens to host the games, Crown Prince Constantine of Greece to fund it, and 81 athletes from 12 countries to join the 230 from Greece at it.

But, no Canadians.

> **Quote, Unquote**
>
> "Let us export oarsmen, runners and fencers. That is the free trade of the future."
>
> — Baron de Coubertin, 1892, gives future Prime Minister Brian Mulroney an idea.

> **Know-it-alls**
>
> Q. How many medals did Canada win in the first modern Olympiad in 1896?
>
> A. None. We weren't there.

Canada would not officially send a team until 1908, though the country grabbed its first medal in 1900 and was represented in 1904 — stories for Chapter 11. Back in North America, the first Olympic Games caused nary a stir among the sports fans or newspapers of the time. That would begin to change over the next decade, but at the beginning, the Olympic movement was simply a bore.

The Least You Need to Know

- Hockey as we know it was developed in Nova Scotia.
- James Creighton of Montreal brought hockey west in 1875.
- McGill played Harvard in the first intercollegiate football games, 1874.
- The first recorded baseball game in Canada happened one year before Abner Doubleday supposedly invented the sport.
- Canada did not compete in the first Olympic Games, 1896.

Chapter 4

My Canadian Can Beat Your (Fill in the Blank) Anytime!

In This Chapter

➤ A new country rows to glory

➤ Ned Hanlan, our first superstar

➤ Hanlan vs. Trickett

➤ Louis Cyr, Canada's fair-haired boy

➤ Other heroes

When the Fathers of Confederation gathered in Charlottetown to forge a new nation in 1867, they were also forging the beginnings of a new player on the world sporting stage. It was one thing to be an athlete from a British colony, quite another to be representing your own country. From the time they threw out the first protester from the House of Commons in Ottawa, Canadians did their new country proud. Or rather, male Canadians did it proud. To this point, despite the fact native culture had encouraged women and girls to be involved in sports, and overlooking the salient point that women had wielded axes, dragged out stumps, and ploughed fields right along with their pioneer hubbies, the "weaker sex" was not allowed to compete. In this chapter, we'll look at the early heroes of the new country.

Part 1 ➤ *Roots*

On the Waterfront

Picture this scene. The snobby gentry at the 1867 Paris Regatta are watching the crew from the newly minted country of Canada unload its equipment by the River Seine, in preparation for one of Europe's most prestigious races.

Barely concealed snickers greet the crew — Robert Fulton, George Price, and Samuel Hutton, all New Brunswick fishermen, and Elijah Ross, a lighthouse keeper — who are resplendent in pinkish sweaters and caps. The snickering turns to laughter at the sight of the lime-green boats that weigh over a hundred pounds more than the nice shells of Oxford and the like.

The laughter lasted only until the Canadians, without a coxswain (that little guy in the bow who yells a lot), beat the tar out of the competition and made themselves into the fledgling country's first sports heroes.

Okay, they used to argue all the time, and they weren't the classiest looking crew on the water, but they could fly.

A year later they won a big race against an American crew, but were stopped in 1870 when an English foursome whupped 'em good.

A rematch was scheduled for the Kennebecasis River in New Brunswick where the English, led by their famous captain James Renforth (alright, New Brunswickers, we know you know what's coming), were favoured. But halfway through the race, trailing by a long way, the English captain suddenly fell dead, at 29 years old.

"Confusion reigned," writes Marsha Boulton. "Rumours spread, with some accounts suggesting that Renforth's last words had been 'Oh Harry, I've had something.' English newshounds rushed to the conclusion of murder most foul — by poison!"

Listen Up!

The good people of Saint John, New Brunswick, knew a good bet when they saw one. And in the Paris Crew of Price, Hutton, Fulton, and Ross, they saw a chance to make a big killing. So, they banded together and came up with $4,000, and then put the squeeze on the province to come up with another $2,000 (thus creating the first provincial lottery). Off to Paris went the four, accompanied by a Sheriff Harding who was carrying a huge bankroll in his belongings to bet on the Saint John rowers. The investment paid off when the Paris Crew came home the winners. And a good thing too, because if they had lost, the good Sheriff might not have let them come home at all.

So, the body was sent off to Boston for autopsy. The cause of death was either heart failure or asphyxia, and foul play was no longer suspected.

The people of New Brunswick honoured the English captain by renaming a small town on the river, Renforth.

After the race, no one would accept a challenge from the Canadian foursome, now known as the Paris Crew, ending their career.

The Talent Coming up Behind

Canada quickly developed other water-borne heroes.

> **Quote, Unquote**
>
> "Perhaps nothing since Confederation has occurred which so thoroughly brings home to the broad mass of our people that our bold Maritime friends are now our fellow countrymen in name and in fact."
>
> — *Toronto Globe,* on the Paris Crew.

George Brown, another fisherman (something about racing in with your catch to beat everyone else to the dock), had already earned honours three years before Confederation by taking a local Halifax championship called the Cogswell Belt, which he would hang on to for four consecutive seasons.

Turning pro in 1873, the native of Herring Cove, Nova Scotia, saw a way to maximize his earnings a year later, but it would also take a maximum of belief in his own talents to do it. Just before a match-race against William Scharff, an American, for the U.S. singles title, Brown withdrew his life savings and bet it on his own head. He went out and won the battle by six seconds.

Perhaps overstressed by that experience, Brown dropped dead of a stroke later in the same season while training for a race against world champion Joseph Sadler.

Joe Wright could do it all, but it was his rowing career, which spread far into the twentieth century, that earned him the most laurels. A boxer, wrestler, runner, baseball and football player, Wright led the Toronto Argonauts eight to a U.S. national win in 1885, did it again at the famous Henley Regatta 20 years later and, at 42 years old, won the Grand Challenge event in England for good measure.

Wright's son, Joe Jr., won the Diamond Sculls, emblematic of the world championship, in 1928. Coached by dad, of course.

And then, there was the incomparable Ned.

The Boy in Blue

Rowing was the western world's largest, most well-attended sport by the late nineteenth century. It attracted huge crowds, the biggest prize money, and the most newspaper coverage. The best rowers were feted everywhere they went. And in that big-time world of rowing, there was no one bigger than Ned Hanlan. He was Canada's first superstar.

Ned Hanlan was born July 12, 1855, to poor Irish immigrant parents who settled in a shanty town at Mugg's Landing, on the Toronto Islands. The senior Hanlan set about making something of himself by building what would become a popular hotel there, employing young Ned to help out.

In his spare time, Ned built himself a rowing shell by sharpening 2-inch wide planks of wood at both ends and adding a seat and oarlocks.

A star on the Ontario scene in the early 1870s, Hanlan showed up in Philadelphia in 1876 for the Centennial Cup meet, honouring America's 100th birthday, and turned heads by beating North America's best oarsmen.

After winning the Canadian title in 1877 over Wallace Ross of New Brunswick, and the U.S. crown in 1878 over Evan Morris, Hanlan hopped a ship for England (he didn't row himself, but one gets the idea he could have, if necessary), where he sailed to an 11-length defeat of William Elliot for that country's crown.

The English were aghast. Here was a tiny (5' 8", 155 lbs.) Canadian, of Irish immigrant stock, no less, beating everybody in sight.

A master at the newly developed sliding seat in the boat, Hanlan liked to stake himself to a lead and hold on from there. He was so smooth on the oars that one observer said his shell looked as though "it were pulled by a string."

All of his talents led up to one of the nineteenth century's most anticipated sporting events…

Know-it-alls

Q. For whom is Hanlan's Point on Toronto Islands named?

A. For Ned Hanlan's father John Hanlan, who erected a hotel there, not the great rower himself.

A Match Race Made in Blue Heaven

Edward Trickett, reigning world champion in the only sport that really mattered in 1880, agreed to meet Ned Hanlan in a match-race on the River Tyne in England, a piece of news that set off the nineteenth-century version of today's pay-per-view specials.

The betting public (almost everyone) was desperate to put a few bob, dollars, francs, or whatever on the race, and the favourite had to be the Aussie champ. After all, he stood 6' 4", weighed over 200 pounds and was "strong like bull."

While Trickett went into hiding to prepare for the race, shunning press and public alike, Hanlan arrived in England as modest, open, and accessible as he'd always been. The people loved it. By race time, thousands lined the river, or jostled around telegraph stations to pick up word of the event.

As was his style, Hanlan blasted out to an early, two-length lead, exerting almost no effort. Whenever the lead became too much, the Canadian would glide along, take a drink, wave to the crowd, and keep going. Trickett was soundly beaten, officially by seven seconds, but in actuality, into a pulp.

Chapter 4 ➤ *My Canadian Can Beat Your (Fill in the Blank) Anytime!*

People went crazy. When Hanlan visited the London Stock Exchange a few days later, trading was stopped while he was paraded around on the shoulders of the money men. In New York, where the thrilled public, and gleeful bettors, gave him a public welcome at Madison Square Garden, and in Toronto, where a holiday was declared, Hanlan was a true hero.

Ned's Legend

Hanlan defended his world title six times, eventually making the unprecedented move of travelling to Australia (where he was so beloved a town renamed itself Toronto in his honour), where he was beaten in 1884 by William Beach.

The Boy in Blue died on January 4, 1908, at the age of 53, with a career record of 344 wins against just 6 losses.

In 1920, a group of rowing enthusiasts erected a 20-foot statue in his honour on the grounds of the Canadian National Exhibition. The city itself named a tugboat in his honour (there's now a Ned Hanlan II in service).

A motion picture, *The Boy in Blue*, was made in the 1990s of Hanlan's life.

If ever there was a Canadian hero whose story all schoolchildren should know by heart, it's Ned Hanlan.

> **Know-it-alls**
>
> Q. What excellent Toronto athlete would go on to compose Canada's first national anthem, "The Maple Leaf Forever"?
>
> A. Alexander Muir, who starred in athletics in the 1840s and 1850s.

One Big, Fair-Haired Boy

One can only imagine the reaction of his mother when Noe Cyprien Cyr arrived on the scene on October 10, 1863 in the village of St.-Cyprien-de-Napierville, south of Montreal.

All 18 pounds, or 8.2 kilos, of him.

Mrs. Cyr went on to have 16 more children, which either meant the first birth wasn't that bad, or she took her religious and societal duties of the time a little too literally. Young Noe, meanwhile, went on to become one of the most famous Canadian athletes of his age.

It could be said that Louis Cyr (his mom talked him into changing his name to Louis so the Anglos could pronounce it when the family moved to Lowell, Massachusetts in 1878), whose long, curly blond locks were almost as famous as his feats, was stronger than an ox, simply because he could lift one. A career policeman in Montreal who could restore order in a drunken crowd simply by arriving, Cyr's displays of strength were legendary.

In 1895, 18 men, who together weighed 4,337 pounds (they weren't fat, they were big boned), piled onto a platform that Cyr backlifted (all 1,967 kilos of it) off the ground. It's still considered the greatest weight ever lifted by one man.

No steroids, no androstenedione, just pure muscle.

Cyr won his first Canadian strongman title in 1882, when he was just 19, by defeating David Michaud at Quebec City thanks to a lift of 522 pounds — the weight of the boulder that was the final test. According to writer Marsha Boulton, Michaud had his eye on the woman Cyr was to marry — Melina Comtois — so there was more to this match than the title.

> **Quote, Unquote**
>
> "I can defeat any man in the world, but no man can defeat this elephant."
>
> — Swedish strongman August Johnson, on Louis Cyr.

Cyr took the unofficial world title in 1896 by beating August Johnson of Sweden in a three-hour tour de force. He toured the globe, leaving spectators awed at every turn. In England he once lifted a 250-kilo weight with one finger.

Unfortunately for Little Louis, he loved food almost as much as he loved Melina, and wound up eating himself into Bright's disease by the age of 37. After that, his diet was straight milk. His last match was at 44, and he died at 49, a larger-than-life Canadian hero to the end.

A Procession of Giants

Out of the wilds of Canada came a succession of strongmen, led by Louis Cyr.

Right behind was George Gray, who appeared in Toronto at the age of 20 with hopes of entering the shot put. Officials let him in, and then stood back and marvelled as he threw the 16-pound shot (really a cannon ball) 41 feet, 5 inches, beating the best from around the world. He was immediately judged world champion.

Every athlete dreams of retiring undefeated — Gray actually pulled it off. Until 1902, Gray was the world's best, winning 188 consecutive times.

He was never touched.

> **Quote, Unquote**
>
> "The Greatest Aquatic Event the World Has Ever Seen."
>
> — Toronto organizers get a little carried away promoting a rowing event in 1881.

Then there was George Dixon, who lost his mind and decided to become a bareknuckle boxer (kidding!). In 1888, Dixon won the world title as a bantamweight, and fought off two challenges to it afterwards.

Fought is the word here. In those days, there was no two-knockdown rule, or 12-round bouts, or doctors at ringside except to revive the half-dead. Fights went on until one man could no longer get up.

Dixon put on some weight and, in 1891, went for the featherweight crown against Cal MacCarthy. He won that too, defending three times before losing a 20-round match in 1897. Undeterred, he won it back the following year.

You Want Ice? We've Got Ice!

With all of this ice around, it was natural that many Canadians entered the world sporting stage on this platform.

Louis Rubenstein, known as the father of Canadian figure skating, travelled to St. Petersburg, Russia, seat of the Czars, for the unofficial world championships in 1890. Artistic impression was the name of the game back then (none of this quadruple jump stuff), and Rubenstein had the artistry down to an, um, art form.

He won.

Rubenstein would stay involved with figure skating in Canada, founding and then serving as president of the Amateur Skating Association. He died in 1931.

A little less artistic, but quicker, was Norval Baptie who was only 16 when he won the world speed skating title. Hardly overcome by the sophomore jinx, Baptie broke every existing record, both amateur and professional, and in a 25-year career won nearly 5,000 races.

Baptie also was responsible for one of the first professional ice shows, touring around North America.

Two years after Baptie, there was Jack McCullough, one of the best speed skaters of the nineteenth century. He won five Canadian championships of differing lengths in one memorable 1891 afternoon. He became world champion in 1897 before turning professional.

McCullough was also a fine roller skater, bike racer, gymnast, and hockey player.

> **Know-it-alls**
>
> Q. What's the oldest, continuously run sporting event in Canada?
>
> A. The Quidi Vidi regatta in Newfoundland, run since 1820.

A Couple of All-Arounders

Donald Bain just couldn't make up his mind which sport in which to compete, growing up in Belleville, Ontario. So, he did them all.

When the family moved to Winnipeg when Bain was 13, they remembered to take him with them, and he returned the favour by winning the three-mile roller skating championship there. That was followed by Manitoba titles in gymnastics and bicycling.

Apparently easily bored, Bain took up a gun and began blasting away at clay pigeons with such skill he was acclaimed Canada's best crack shot.

Part 1 ➤ Roots

Listen Up!

George Duggan was a master yachtsman, boat designer, and builder. A Montreal civil engineer, Duggan constructed 142 craft in his career, including five for a shot at the Seawanhaka Cup — a small boats' America's Cup — in 1896. One of those boats, Glencairn I, with Duggan on board as skipper, won the event over 17 Canadian and U.S. challengers. Almost 90 years later, an argument would spring up as to whether race car driver Jacques Villeneuve was really an athlete when it was his car supposedly doing all the work. The same could be said for Duggan. Let's see...manhandling a big boat, in a huge wind across open water, with all that pulling, cranking, and hoisting of sails, and one slip and you could drown. Sounds pretty athletic from here.

Know-it-alls

Q. What was the most expensive trophy donated for a sport in Canada prior to 1900?

A. The Prince of Wales trophy, to the Royal Canadian Yacht Club, which cost a princely $500 in 1860.

Then there was pairs figure skating. And lacrosse.

Oh, did we happen to mention he won two Stanley Cups (1896 and 1901) as a member of the Winnipeg Victorias?

That was in his spare time.

The victorious Victorias, by the way, beat the unvictorious Montreal Victorias in that 1896 spring cup classic (and people picked on the Canadian Football League for having a Rough Riders and a Roughriders!).

Montreal's team included Hartland MacDougall, another all-arounder.

MacDougall could rub noses with the upper class — he was captain of the Montreal Polo club ten times — and also get down with the hogs, playing football for the Montreal Amateur Athletic Association and four years of hockey with those Victorias, who won three Stanley Cups.

He was also one of the key figures in financing and building the Montreal Forum and in operating the Montreal Maroons of the National Hockey League.

The Least You Need To Know

➤ The Paris Crew blew the competition out of the water at an 1867 regatta in France and became world famous.

➤ Ned Hanlan was the best rower Canada ever produced.

➤ Louis Cyr became known across the globe for his immense strength.

➤ Louis Rubenstein won the first unofficial world figure skating title.

➤ Donald Bain was a superb all-around athlete.

Part 2
Hockey: Our Game

Jacques Barzun once wrote: "Whoever would understand the heart and mind of America had better learn baseball, the rules and realities of the game."

Those words could have been written about Canadians and hockey. It is our game. It is our passion. It is the only sport that truly fills our souls and matters to us, not just as fans, but as a people. In the same way baseball defines an American, or association football defines an Italian, hockey defines a Canadian. It is our one true love. It is, disgusted academics aside, the only truly binding force from sea to sea. A sporting dream that is…

Sorry. Got carried away there. Dramatics aside, in this section, we'll trace the growth of the game and how it has become the passion of Canadians old and new.

Chapter 5

We'll Take Your Puck and Start Our Own League (1890–1919)

In This Chapter

- ➤ The origin of the big silver bowl
- ➤ Early Stanley Cup battles
- ➤ The Pacific Coast League
- ➤ The birth of the National Hockey League
- ➤ Stars of the era

As we've seen, modern hockey began down east and spread westward during the nineteenth century, arriving in Montreal by 1875 and the west coast by 1890. The true nurturing ground for the sport was in Montreal, however, where James Creighton brought the game as a 22-year-old. It was there, and in towns within reasonable travelling distance, that the first successful club teams were born — exclusively, by the way, in the Anglo community, which would have control over the game until a visionary Irishman decided French Quebeckers needed their own heroes. And what a team that would turn out to be. From the awarding of the first Stanley Cup until the tragedy of 1919, hockey's first era was a rollicking, experimental, Darwinian exercise in development. In this chapter, we'll trace hockey's growth into the new century, and on up to the end of the Great War.

Part 2 ▸ Hockey: Our Game

Listen Up!

There is a photo in the National Archives that shows a number of women, in ankle-length skirts, playing hockey in front of Rideau Hall in Ottawa, around 1890. It is said that Lord and Lady Stanley had a rink in the yard at Rideau Hall, home of Canada's governor general, from the time they arrived here in 1888. On that rink, both boys and girls, men and women, played. One of Lord Stanley's daughters, Isobel, played for a Government House team that met a group of Rideau ladies in the first recorded women's game in Canada.

Know-it-alls

Q. Who is the only man in the Hockey Hall of Fame who never saw a Stanley Cup game, owned a club, or played a game?

A. Lord Stanley himself.

A Fifty Dollar Investment in the Future

When Lord Stanley of Preston arrived in Canada to take up his post as the new country's sixth governor general, he instantly fell in love with hockey, seeing it as the perfect tool for tying together the vast plot of land over which Britain still held an arm's-length dominion. Such a great game, however, needed a proper reward. "I have for some time been thinking that it would be a good thing if there were a challenge cup which should be held from year to year by the champion hockey team in the Dominion of Canada," wrote his lordship.

Actually, his hockey-crazy sons and daughters had bugged him so much he finally gave in and sent a message to a London silversmith, who, for a little less than $50, created a nice little bowl with his lordship's name on it and shipped it back.

And just in time too, because this being 1893, his lordship's time in Canada was running out, and he was heading back "over 'ome" for retirement, a trip that came sooner than expected when his brother died.

A Scalper's Dream

Since the Montreal Amateur Athletic Association team had just won the Amateur Hockey Association championship, Stanley awarded the trophy to them on the proviso that the silver mug be open for challenge by any club in the dominion, as long as the club was agreeable to trustees Sheriff Sweetland and P. D. Ross, a couple of Bytown sports fanciers.

Ottawa, angry they weren't awarded it as Ontario champs, emerged as the first challenger — and a game was set up with the Montreal Hockey Club (new name of the AAAs), for March 22, 1894, in Montreal. About 5,000 people came into the cold and plunked down anywhere from two-bits (a quarter) to a dollar to see Billy Barlow score two for a 3-1 Montreal win in a dirty little affair.

The Stanley Cup would stay in that city (and, until 1917, be won by Montrealers a whopping 14 times) until February of 1896, when another group of Victorias — this one from Winnipeg — came east for a Valentine's Day battle with the Montreal Victorias. The home team, shockingly, lost 2-0. The defeat was made even worse when referee Alex Martin called back a Montreal goal in the early going.

Madder than heck, Montreal went back to Winnipeg in December and won the mug back in a huge game for which speculators were getting over $12 a ticket (a month's rent on a big house).

Give That Man a Pacifier

It would be nice to say that the invention of the Stanley Cup meant hockey travelled a straight path towards the creation of the National Hockey League in 1917, and from there to today. Actually, our game staggered back and forth over the timeline like a drunk at a weekend men's tournament.

Ontario formed its hockey association in 1890, Manitoba had organized leagues by 1892, followed by the prairie not-quite-provinces-yet, and then all the way up in the Northwest Territories and the Yukon, which at that point was still overwhelmed by the gold rush, Dangerous Dan McGrew, and 10 months of winter.

> **Quote, Unquote**
>
> "The referee forgot to see many things."
>
> — *Montreal Gazette*, writing on the 1894 Stanley Cup game, throws out the first referee complaint.

> **Know-it-alls**
>
> Q. Name the only small-town team to win a Stanley Cup.
>
> A. The Rat Portage (Kenora) Thistles, in 1907.

It was a rough, dirty game in which arguments off the ice were usually as prevalent as those on it.

In early 1895, in Quebec City, the referees became so disgusted with the crowd and the players they took off for the train station. They were headed off at the pass by an angry mob, which herded them back to the arena and demanded a game with Ottawa be declared a tie, instead of a loss. The police had to intervene.

Under-the-table payments to players became commonplace as competition for their services began to grow.

The 1899 cup game saw referee J. A. Findlay hand out a two minute penalty for a slash by a Montreal player on a Winnipeg victim. Winnipeg left the ice, and after a huge argument, so did Findlay, who dressed and went home. He was persuaded to come back after an hour, but by then a number of the Winnipeg players had taken off to party in Montreal bars and the team couldn't continue.

Stories like these abounded.

Part 2 ➤ Hockey: Our Game

> ### Quote, Unquote
>
> "The worst exhibition of butchery ever seen on ice."
>
> — *Montreal Star* on a huge stick swinging fight between Montreal and Ottawa in 1907 that resulted in three arrests and two players being fined in court.

> ### Know-it-alls
>
> Q. Who was the first goaltender to wear pads in a game?
>
> A. A man named Merritt, Winnipeg, 1896 Stanley Cup.

> ### Quote, Unquote
>
> "You try it Frankie, and I'll knock your other eye out."
>
> — Montreal Wanderers Pokey Leahy to One-Eyed Frank McGee, after the latter threatened to flatten him.

In 1902, the rush to get into the Winnipeg Arena for a Stanley Cup challenge by the Toronto Wellingtons was so bad that four men were crushed into unconsciousness. They were revived and stayed for the contest, won by Winnipeg.

In 1903, Rat Portage (in the process of being renamed Kenora — wonder why?) tried a crafty move. They put two goalies in against the Ottawa Silver Seven in a cup match. The rulebook didn't say they couldn't. The pair spent the game bumping into each other and Ottawa bombed them.

That trick was nothing compared to 1905, when the Kenora Thistles were back at it with Ottawa. They won the first game with the Bytowners, 9-3, and seemed on the verge of taking the mug. That is, until the rink rats put two inches of water on the natural ice surface — with the temperature well above freezing — which meant the slick passing, fast skating (they were using the new thin-bladed tube skates) Thistles were helpless in a 4-2 loss that evened the series. The ice was back in decent shape for game three, but the Thistles were still a little freaked. Ottawa, behind Frank McGee's winner, won 5-4.

After the Gold Rush

A bunch of the boys were apparently whooping it up at the Malamute Saloon in 1904, when they hit on this great idea. Why not pack up our little Dawson City hockey team here, take it down there to Ottawa, and challenge the two-time defending cup champion Silver Seven for Lord Stanley's mug?

"Great idea, Bo! Let's do it!"

With 17-year-old goalie Albert Forrest in tow, the players went by train to Alaska where they waited three days for a ship to Seattle, hopped a train there to Vancouver, then the transcontinental from the coast to Ottawa. That would be 23 days. Frosty the Snowman had an easier time trying to get back to the North Pole.

Silver Seven officials turned down the Dawson City request for a few days rest (the rats), and the two game series went 9-2 and 23-2 — Ottawa's way. The second game featured a record 14-goal performance by Frank (One-Eyed) McGee, against the spirited, but shell-shocked, Forrest.

Les Canadiens sont là (Here Come the Canadiens)

The best way to trace the beginnings and growth of pro hockey in Canada (the first pro league was actually started by a Canadian in Michigan — J. L. Gibson) is to look at the roots of our greatest pro hockey franchise. No, not the Winnipeg Jets. The Montreal Canadiens.

Let's go back to 1909, when the Eastern Canadian Hockey Association wanted to divorce itself of the Montreal Wanderers' franchise because that team played in the Jubilee Rink, and the ECHA wanted the bigger gate receipts of the Westmount Arena. The sneaky owners disbanded the ECHA and started the Canadian Hockey Association without the Wanderers.

Along comes J. Ambrose O'Brien, who already owned a couple of teams (Cobalt and Haileybury) in the Temiskaming league. He finds his way to the Windsor Hotel looking for a franchise in the CHA for Renfrew, but gets "laughed at in room 135," O'Brien told hockey writer Andy O'Brien (no relation) years later.

Outside the room, J. Ambrose runs into the general manager of the leagueless Montreal Wanderers, who suggests that O'Brien's three teams join with his to form a new league — the National Hockey Association.

Quote, Unquote

"As the Wanderers have been able to obtain a goalie with outstanding credentials, we will not require your services in the game tonight against the Shamrocks."

— Fake message sent to Wanderers goalie Henri Menard before a big game in 1906, almost causing him to miss it.

Listen Up!

Hockey has its own version of Babe Ruth's famous called-shot home run in baseball. On February 12, 1910, Cyclone Taylor may, or may not, have purposely scored a goal while going backwards. Playing for Renfrew, Taylor came in on Percy LeSueur of Ottawa, spun around and rifled a backhander to the top corner. Some witnesses said Taylor simply turned his back at the last minute, but others insisted it was a goal going backwards. Taylor went to his grave at the age of 95, refusing to say, either way.

> **Know-it-alls**
>
> Q. How much was Cyclone Taylor paid to play for Renfrew of the NHA?
>
> A. $5,250 — a huge sum in 1910.

Better yet, says J. Gardner, the Wanderers' GM, why don't you toss some money at a guy I know named Jack Laviolette, and he can put together a French Canadian team in Montreal that would be the perfect rival for the Wanderers.

Into room 129 the pair goes, and not too long after the NHA is a go, with five franchises (four of which would be owned by O'Brien). Cobalt, Haileybury, Renfrew, and Wanderers would be joined by a new club — Les Canadiens. That team was to be run by French Canadian sportsmen in Montreal.

The Canadiens played their first game in January 1910, featuring Didier Pitre at cover and Newsy Lalonde (who would become a legend) at rover. It was a win (naturally), 7-6 over Cobalt. It took Les Canadiens six years to win a championship. They would never look back.

Three Patricks on the Left Coast

> **Know-it-alls**
>
> Q. What defenceman holds the all-time record for goals in a major pro game?
>
> A. Frank Patrick, six goals in a PCHA contest, 1912.

Joseph Patrick made himself a few million by cutting timber on the west coast. This would have relegated him to a mere footnote in B.C. history if he hadn't also sired two stallions that would have a huge influence on the early years of the NHL, and on hockey in general.

Lester and Frank Patrick loved hockey and were determined to make it their careers, both as players and executives. Using their dad's nickel, the Patricks formed the Pacific Coast Hockey Association in December of 1911, built around the Vancouver Millionaires, Victoria Aristocrats, and New Westminster Royals, and immediately set out to challenge the Eastern pro leagues for players and innovation.

> **Know-it-alls**
>
> Q. What trophy became the symbol of the best senior men's team in Canada, starting in 1908?
>
> A. The Allan Cup.

Lester became player-coach with Victoria, and Frank did everything for the Vancouver club. Nice to have a hobby and the money to back it up! Nice to have a building to play it in, as well — in this case the new Vancouver Arena, opened in 1911 with 10,000 seats, artificial ice and a 200 x 85 foot surface, which would become the standard for pro hockey.

Chapter 5 ➤ *We'll Take Your Puck and Start Our Own League (1890–1919)*

The Patricks headed east to raid the National Hockey Association and came home with enough high-priced beef to get the ball rolling, including all seven of Victoria's starting lineup. The PCHA lasted until the early 1920s, leaving a legacy that kept hockey thriving on the west coast for the rest of the century. Two of its clubs — the Millionaires of 1915 and Seattle Metropolitans of 1917 — would capture the Stanley Cup.

> **Know-it-alls**
>
> Q. What was the first professional league in Canada?
>
> A. The Ontario Professional Hockey League, founded in 1908.

What was perhaps as important were the rule innovations that the Patricks, especially Frank, brought to the game. The PCHA was the first league to use the blue lines, which divided the rink into three equal zones. They were the first to allow goaltenders to sprawl to make a save. They initiated the forward pass in the neutral zone, and came up with the penalty shot for players tripped from behind on a breakaway.

Both Patricks would be heard from much more in the 1920s.

Up the Vimy Ridge, Boys!

In August 1914, the Great War broke out in Europe, and the first trips by hockey players to the old countries were with gun in hand, rather than a stick.

Many of the men who joined the army wound up in military teams on both sides of the pond. Junior and senior aged players, their coaches, team officials, and referees mustered in, leaving shortages in the leagues.

The Winnipeg 61st Battalion team headed for France in 1916 after winning the Allan Cup — emblematic of the senior championship of Canada. The Winnipeg Falcons all joined the 223rd battalion and went overseas in 1917. Three Falcons paid with their lives — Olie Turnbull, Buster Thorsteinson, and George Cumbers.

One-Eyed Frank McGee, who was 32, found a way to pass his physical with perfect eyesight, despite being blind in one of them. McGee wound up on the Somme, where in September of 1916, he fell to German fire.

Gordon Southam, of the Southam newspaper family, formed the Sportsman's Battery, which included a University of Toronto hockey captain by the name of Conn Smythe. That group played in the OHA while waiting shipment. Buoyed by about $10,000 in party money won in a bet on a game, the battery got to France and wound up part of the attack on Vimy Ridge in 1917 that would see the Canadians take both the height of land and the first major step to helping the country become a true nation of its own.

Southam would not come home — he was killed by shellfire.

Canadian Stanley Cup Winners of the Era

- 1893 Montreal AAA
- 1894 Montreal AAA
- 1895 Montreal Victorias
- 1896 Winnipeg Victorias (February)
- 1896 Montreal Victorias (December)
- 1897 Montreal Victorias
- 1898 Montreal Victorias
- 1899 Montreal Shamrocks
- 1900 Montreal Shamrocks
- 1901 Winnipeg Victorias
- 1902 Montreal AAA
- 1903 Ottawa Silver Seven
- 1904 Ottawa Silver Seven
- 1905 Ottawa Silver Seven
- 1906 Montreal Wanderers
- 1907 Kenora Thistles (January)
- 1907 Montreal Wanderers (March)
- 1908 Montreal Wanderers
- 1909 Ottawa Senators
- 1910 Montreal Wanderers
- 1911 Ottawa Senators
- 1912 Quebec Bulldogs
- 1914 Toronto Blueshirts
- 1915 Vancouver Millionaires
- 1916 Montreal Canadiens

Out west, the Victoria Arena was turned into an armoury by the government, which forced the Victoria club to move to Spokane, Washington until after the war.

In the National Hockey Association, Scotty Davidson of the Toronto Blueshirts, winners of the cup in 1914, went to France and was killed a few months later in June of 1915.

It Was All Because of Eddie

The National Hockey League was formed because everybody hated Eddie Livingstone.

Eddie was a Toronto sports reporter who bought the Ontario franchise in the NHA and renamed them the Toronto Shamrocks. A year later, he annexed the Toronto Blueshirts, causing the league executive to break into a screaming fit. Apparently, it was all right for J. Ambrose O'Brien to own four teams because they were in different cities, while Livingstone's were in the same burg.

That storm died down when the Pacific Coast league raided most of the players on the Blueshirts, but the other league owners were decidedly out to get old Eddie.

Move ahead to 1917, when the owners (forgetting they had formed themselves because the CHA didn't want them), decided to start a new league with the expressed purpose of keeping Livingstone out of it.

So, back in the Windsor Hotel on November 22, the National Hockey League was born, with Montreal Canadiens, Ottawa Senators, Montreal Wanderers, and Toronto Arenas.

Trouble started right away. On January 2, 1918, the Westmount Arena in Montreal burned to the ground. Convenient, really, since the Wanderers weren't drawing flies and were in a huge debt. That left three teams, though the Canadiens were sitting pretty because Joe Malone of the Wanderers — the hated Joe Malone — became a member of the bleu, blanc, et rouge.

Influenza

After a brutal, violent series, the Canadiens beat Ottawa in 1919 to earn a chance against the Seattle Metropolitans, the Pacific Coast champs, in a five-game series for the Stanley Cup.

With the series 2-1 (and one tie) for Seattle, hockey took a back seat to real life.

"Cully Wilson of Seattle fell to the ice complaining of dizziness and fatigue," in game five, writes Brian McFarlane, "and Montreal's Bad Joe Hall, also very ill, could not continue playing. He was rushed to hospital with a temperature of 105 degrees."

The black-flu epidemic, which swept the continent after the war and killed tens of thousands of people, had hit hockey. Officials cancelled the series. Hall, one of hockey's heroes in that period, died in hospital. George Kennedy, the Montreal manager, beat the grim reaper at that time, but died two years later of a connected illness.

Hockey headed for the Roaring Twenties on a downer.

Other Stars of the Era

- Edouard "Newsy" Lalonde was born a travellin' man, playing for 10 clubs in a career that stretched from Cornwall to the New York Americans. A terrific lacrosse player, judged the best in that sport in the first 50 years of this century, he scored 441 hockey goals in his career. The nickname came from his job in a newsprint factory as a boy.

- Joe Malone had the face of an angel, but was as tough as a ten-cent steak. The best puck handler of the era, he had 379 professional goals spread between Quebec, Montreal Canadiens, Quebec again, and the Hamilton Tigers. He was the NHL's first leading scorer in the 1917–18 season. His seven goals against Toronto in a 1920 playoff game is still the NHL record.

- Fred "Cyclone" Taylor, from Tara, Ontario, played for Ottawa and Renfrew before becoming one of the key players copped by the new Pacific Coast League in 1912. He starred for the Vancouver Millionaires until 1923. A prodigious scorer, Taylor once had 32 goals in just 18 games. He won Stanley Cups with Ottawa in 1909 and Vancouver in 1915.

- Georges Vezina, the Chicoutimi Cucumber (he was cool under pressure), was the best goalie of his era, and possibly one of the greatest ever to strap on the pads. He played 328 consecutive games for the Canadiens, starting in 1910, in an era when goalies weren't allowed to fall down to make a stop. He died on March 26, 1925 of tuberculosis, four months after pulling himself out of his final game. The trophy for best goaltenders in the NHL is named in his honour.

The Least You Need to Know

- Lord Stanley of Preston provided the Stanley Cup.
- Hockey developed into the modern game in Montreal.
- Any club could challenge for the Cup in its early days.
- The Montreal Canadiens were founded in 1909.
- Pro hockey was strong on the west coast in this era.

Chapter 6

Blood Sport (1920–1939)

In This Chapter

- Franchises rise and fall like dominoes
- Howie Morenz enters the scene
- Conn Smythe and the birth of the Maple Leafs
- Ace Bailey takes it on the head
- Radio takes centre stage
- Other stars of the era

Hockey had come a long way since those early days when there were seven players for each club on the ice, they wore little equipment, there were no boards, and artificial ice rinks were unknown. But the game still had a reputation for violence. This was the era when one famous player would end another's career with his stick, and still be allowed to compete. When dropping the gloves instead of wielding the lumber had not yet become accepted

Know-it-alls

Q. What goalie had 22 shutouts in just 44 games in 1928–29?

A. George Hainsworth, Montreal Canadiens.

practice. And when the phrase "If you can't beat 'em in the alley…" was the siren call of the game. But it was also the era when a slick skating young man from Stratford, Ontario would come to epitomize everything that was right in the sport. And it was a time when all Canadians would be able to follow the fortunes of their favourite NHL club through the new medium of radio. In this chapter we take hockey from the Roaring Twenties to the eve of World War II.

The Disappearing-Reappearing Canadian Franchise Boogie

Follow the bouncing puck, and sing along with us:

The Quebec Bulldogs joined the new NHL as a plank owner in 1917, but because of financial trouble did not play until the third season — 1919–1920. After winning a whopping 4 games of 24, and despite the heroics of Joe Malone, the franchise transferred to Hamilton and became the Tigers. Quebec City would not have NHL hockey again until 1979.

Hamilton's NHL run lasted five seasons, four of which ended out of the playoffs. The fifth, when the Tigers found themselves as 1925 regular season champions, ended in disaster when the players went on strike just before the post-season and were suspended. Bill Dwyer bought the franchise and moved it to New York as the Americans.

Meanwhile, the NHL began expansion to the United States by awarding a franchise to Boston.

Listen Up!

Labour unrest in sports is not a modern phenomenon. Baseball had strikes in the nineteenth century. And hockey, right in the labour steeltown of Hamilton, had one all the way back in 1925 that wound up costing that city its NHL franchise — which the good burghers there have desperately been trying to get back ever since. Though in first place, the Tigers were unhappy. The ownership was cheap, games had been added without extra money paid, and the players wanted $200 more each. They refused to play in the playoffs, and Frank Calder, the NHL president, suspended the club. After the season, the Tigers were sold to New York and became the Americans. To add insult to injury, all the Tigers' players were told they had to apologize before being allowed back in the league. They did.

Chapter 6 ➤ Blood Sport (1920–1939)

Montreal Wanderers lasted just six games in the NHL's first season. Depleted by the war and financial trouble, the club gave up the ghost in January of 1918 when its arena burned down due to "unknown causes."

Montreal's Maroons joined the NHL in 1924 as a club designed to appeal to the English-speaking section of the city. But it was a French Canadian, Donat Raymond, who was the force behind building the Montreal Forum that would house both the city's clubs. The Maroons were an excellent team, winning two Stanley Cups, and over 14 seasons would feature goaltender Clint Benedict, Nels Stewart (Old Poison), Lionel Conacher, and Jimmy Ward. Owner Tommy Gorman, a notorious tightwad among a legion of notorious tightwads, was blamed for the fall of the Maroons' talent base in its final season, 1937–38, which led to declining attendance. The team took a year off, and then decided they would not operate further.

> **Quote, Unquote**
>
> "Down in their hearts they should feel that they can beat the opposition in the alley as well as on the ice."
>
> — Montreal Canadiens' owner Leo Dandurand, not Conn Smythe, coins a famous hockey quote.

Bytown had their Ottawa Senators in the NHL from the get-go, and for 13 years they thrived. But with box office receipts falling off, the club began selling off its talent, especially King Clancy to the Leafs in 1930, and the team that won four Stanley Cups since the league began, became non-competitive. The Senators took a leave of absence in 1931–32, and came back for two seasons before being transferred to St. Louis. NHL hockey would not return to Ottawa until 1992.

The Victoria Cougars of the Western Hockey League (formerly the PCHL) had the honour of folding and providing all the players for the brand new Detroit Cougars (later the Red Wings) in 1926, including superstars Frank Fredrickson, Jack Walker, and Frank Foyston, plus goaltender Happy Holmes. Frank and Lester Patrick, holding one big garage sale for WHL players, found another taker in Major Frederic McLaughlin of Chicago. The Western league's Portland players wound up there. No fire sales for Lester, however. When the expansion New York Rangers fired general manager, Conn Smythe, before the 1926 season began, old Lester wound up running the Broadway Blueshirts.

By the start of the 1939 season, with the Pacific Coast/Western League long dispatched to history, Canada was down to just two big league teams — Les Canadiens de Montreal, and the Toronto Maple Leafs.

You may now all take a seat and rest.

Quit Yer Cryin' Howie, You're About to Be a Star

It would not be hyperbole to say that Howie Morenz was as important to hockey as Babe Ruth was to baseball in the 1920s.

Part 2 ▶ *Hockey: Our Game*

> ### Quote, Unquote
> "He was as fast as a bullet and had a shot to match. He could stop on a dime and give you five cents change."
> — King Clancy, on Howie Morenz.

> ### Know-it-alls
> Q. Who was the first goalie to wear a mask regularly?
> A. Elizabeth Graham, Queen's University, starting in 1927.

But he almost didn't make it out of Stratford, Ontario, because of the biggest bout of homesickness in NHL history.

Morenz would score 270 goals in 546 regular season games — totals unheard of for that era — and he did it despite the fact that for his first four years, from 1923, players were still not allowed to make forward passes behind the opposing team's blue line.

He was the player who made hockey in New York. Tex Rickard saw him play, fell in love with hockey, and instantly wanted a franchise for his new Madison Square Garden.

Morenz was, by far, the greatest of his era. And he almost didn't make it to Montreal.

With Toronto sniffing around the Stratford flash, the Canadiens tossed $850 in small bills at the youngster in the summer of 1923, and he went for it. But Toronto launched a campaign at the kid, in and out of the press, for abandoning Ontario. A local man of the cloth thought it sinful for Montrealers to woo young Morenz away from his home.

Morenz caved in and sent the money back, with apology.

Actually, Howie didn't really need the money because he was getting lots, illegally, from the Stratford OHA club (an "amateur" outfit), and the Canadiens threatened to tell all. So, off to Montreal Howie went, where he pleaded with owner Leo Dandurand to let him out of the contract, even breaking down in tears.

Dandurand smelled a Toronto rat behind the stressed-out Morenz' pleas, but decided to use the famous Canadiens' players to convince him. That worked. Despite some shaky times in training camp, Morenz stayed and became an instant, fast skating star.

Ironically, the Montreal fans decided they had no more use for their hero when his legs started to go, and Dandurand reluctantly sold him to Chicago, which later shipped Morenz to New York, all during the 1935–36 year. Montreal got him back that summer.

Killed by a Broken Heart

On January 28, 1937, at the Montreal Forum, Howie Morenz tried to dipsy-doodle past Earl Seibert of the Chicago Black Hawks, fell hard into the boards, skates first, and wound up with a double fracture. His career was over.

Morenz was in hospital until March 8, when he suddenly died of cardiac arrest. Brian McFarlane speculates that, realizing his career was over, Morenz may have died of a broken heart. And who's to argue?

Writer Andy O'Brien says the impact on Montreal was similar to that on the United States when President John F. Kennedy was assassinated in 1963. Thousands passed by Morenz' casket on centre-ice at the Forum, and when he was laid to rest, the Canadiens retired the number 7 sweater he had worn so famously.

> **Know-it-alls**
>
> Q. On St. Patrick's Day, 1934, what player showed up in a green jersey?
>
> A. King Clancy. The New York Rangers made him take it off after one period.

The Maple Leafs: Conn's Emblem Dear

To review: Conn Smythe came out of the Sportsmans' Battery in the Great War, and went into the gravel business where he made a ton of money. He stayed in hockey as a coach of the University of Toronto Varsity Blues, and eventually landed the job to build the New York Rangers, which because of his fiery temper lasted all of a couple of months.

Not easily put off was young Mr. Smythe. So, being a gambler, Smythe put money on some big games, won a decent amount, and bought the Toronto St. Patricks franchise in the NHL for $160,000. He immediately renamed them the Maple Leafs for the 1926–27 season.

Smythe's first order of business was to build a decent team — which he did. But his real dream was to construct a hockey palace, a place that would be known far and wide as the Taj Mahal of the sport. And to do this, he needed more than money. He needed a star.

Enter Francis Michael (King) Clancy, as Irish as the Blarney Stone (and he obviously kissed it, too), and a horse named Rare Jewel.

Ottawa wanted $35,000 for Clancy, and Smythe didn't have the extra $10,000 above the amount the Leafs' board of directors were willing to pay for him. "Get the money yourself," he was told.

Smythe was empty of pocket, but he did have this very average nag of a horse bought for $250, which had finished well down the track in most of her outings. Smythe entered her in a big

> **Quote, Unquote**
>
> "Somebody sneaked in and put sand on the floor."
>
> — Conn Smythe accuses the Canadiens of dirty tricks — trying to dull the players' skates — in 1937.

Quote, Unquote

"Well, I'll be a son of a bitch if you ain't one smart busher."

— Leafs' trainer Tim Daley to a cocky 19-year-old Harvey Jackson in 1930. The name "Busher" stuck.

Know-it-alls

Q. What player played all six positions in an NHL game?

A. King Clancy, 1923.

stakes race and bet practically everything he had on the mare, who went off at 106-1. In what had to be one of the biggest upsets in racing history, Rare Jewel turned it on this one time and came home a winner.

That bagged Smythe $11,000, and he bought Clancy.

Star in place, the only thing left was that new arena.

Spinning Gold Out of Straw

When the Depression hit, Conn Smythe's dream seemed dead. Unwilling to give up, however, he went around town, practically on his knees, and put together enough backing from the Bank of Commerce, Sun Life Insurance, and a local businessman named Alf Rogers that he could keep going.

Smythe convinced the T. Eaton Co. to sell him a plot of land at Carlton and Church streets, got Frank Selke to convince the labour unions that their members could take 20 percent of their pay in arena shares, and got Maple Leaf Gardens up in just six months. The building held over 13,000 fans, with room to expand. It would, with the help of radio, become the most recognized landmark in Canada outside of Niagara Falls and the Parliament Buildings in Ottawa.

Ace Bailey is Crowned in Boston

To understand the Ace Bailey incident, it's first necessary to understand that hockey in the '20s and '30s was a violent, often blood-soaked endeavour where sucker punches were a regular occurrence, vendettas were common, and using the stick as a weapon far from unheard of.

Misguided souls of the late twentieth century would often complain that hockey had "become" too violent and dangerous. They truly had no idea.

Okay. Ace Bailey was one of hockey's greatest stars of this era. He was a member of the Toronto St. Patricks when Conn Smythe bought the team and turned it into the Maple Leafs. In Toronto, he was revered, right up there with Clancy, Charlie Conacher, Joe Primeau, and the other blue and white stars.

On December 12, 1933, the Leafs were in the Boston Garden to face the Bruins and to stage the renewal of a black hatred between Clancy and Boston's star defenceman Eddie Shore. Clancy hit Shore hard on a play, and when the puck went back up ice with Toronto killing a two-man disadvantage, the Irishman was carrying it.

Bailey, a forward, trailed behind to fill for Clancy and had his back turned when Shore got up off the ice and came at him. The dirty blindside stick move sent Bailey down, and his head hit the ice and fractured in two places.

All hell broke loose. Toronto's Red Horner went after Shore and knocked him out with one punch. Smythe was heckled at the wrong time by a fan and the Leafs' owner punched him out, getting arrested for the effort.

It took surgeons hours to save Bailey's life, but his career was over.

As Brian McFarlane writes, Bailey's father headed for Beantown with a gun to get Shore, but luckily "he was intercepted in Boston by Leaf officials, who spiked his drink and placed the groggy father of the stricken star on a train to Toronto."

The NHL and its players held an all-star game — the first ever — before the end of the season as a fundraiser for the stricken Leaf, and Bailey and Shore shook hands.

But, all Shore got for ending the career of, and almost murdering, another human being was a month's suspension. In that era, you really could get away with almost anything.

Hello Canada...

Basil Lake, an editor at the *Toronto Star*, may never have known how important he was to the history of his country. In March 1923, Lake did something that would change the way two following generations would live their lives.

As the radio editor of the daily newspaper, Lake had an idea. Why not send someone out to do a broadcast of a hockey game that could run on the fledgling station the Star itself

Listen Up!

Women's hockey developed a solid base through this period. Individual clubs sprang up across the land, and the game caught on at the University level, especially at McGill in Montreal and at the University of Toronto. A three-team league, with Queen's University, ran for about 10 years in the '20s and '30s. Women's hockey stars included Marian Hilliard and Phyllis Griffiths of U of T. At Queen's there was Charlotte Whitton, who in later years became mayor of Ottawa. And organizers such as Marie Parks in Toronto did all they could to push the game. Out west, Calgary and Edmonton had strong programs, many women playing in "church leagues." The era's most dominant team was the Preston Rivulettes, in Ontario. The most dominant players in the 1930s were Bobbie Rosenfeld, an Olympic champion sprinter, and Hilda Ranscombe.

> **Quote, Unquote**
>
> "He shoots, he scores!"
>
> — Foster Hewitt hits a winning phrase in his first broadcast.

> **Know-it-alls**
>
> Q. What team accidentally left the Stanley Cup on the side of the road when they stopped to fix a tire?
>
> A. The Montreal Canadiens, in 1924. It was still there when they went back.

owned? Looking around, he noticed 18-year-old Foster Hewitt, a cub reporter on the same broadsheet his famous father, W. A., was serving as sports editor. Lake sent a dazed Hewitt out to the Mutual Street Arena with a nickel in his pocket for a hot dog and not the slightest idea of what to do.

In a tiny, glassed-in booth, Hewitt made radio history (though some claim he was beaten to the punch by nine days by Pete Parker, who called a Western Canada Hockey League game in Regina on March 14). He would call games, off and on, for a few years, until Smythe got a hold of him and realized what a gold mine having the Leafs' games on the radio actually was.

When the new Gardens was built, Smythe gave Hewitt carte blanche to choose a location in the building from which to broadcast. Foster went down the street to the Eaton's department store where he leaned out of windows on different floors to find just the right height from which to do a game. Back at the Gardens, he had the now-famous "gondola" built above the ice. Hewitt's call, "Hello Canada, and hockey fans in the United States and Newfoundland," would ring from coast to coast and make Saturday night with the Leafs a ritual.

The Canadiens were not far behind, and their broadcasts became as important in Quebec, Eastern Ontario, and New Brunswick, as Hewitt's were to the rest of the country.

Hockey became a radio star.

Other Stars of the Era

- Aubrey "Dit" Clapper, from Newmarket, Ontario, was just 13 when he made the Oshawa junior club, playing against young men up to 8 years older. At 19, he was in Boston, where he stayed for 20 seasons, scoring 228 goals. His number 5 was retired with him.
- Charlie Conacher, from a family of exceptional male and female athletes (brother Lionel was the athlete of the half century), joined the Leafs in 1929 where he was put on the famous Kid Line with Joe Primeau and Busher Jackson. In 12 seasons with Toronto, Detroit, and the New York Americans, Conacher scored 225 goals and took two scoring titles. As a coach, he took the Oshawa Generals to the

Chapter 6 ➤ Blood Sport (1920–1939)

Memorial Cup junior crown in 1944, and led the Chicago Black Hawks for three seasons.

➤ Little Aurel Joliat was a star football player who turned to hockey. A native of Ottawa, Joliat signed with Montreal where he played with Howie Morenz and Billy Boucher. A left winger, Joliat tipped the scales at around 135 pounds, but still found his way to the net 270 times and won three Stanley Cups. He was so tough that in 1963, at a banquet, he got into an argument with Punch Broadbent over a fistfight the two had back in the 1920s, and they wound up on the floor, trading blows in their sixties.

➤ Eddie Shore was the toughest, meanest son of a Saskatchewan farmer ever to play the game. He joined the Boston Bruins in 1926, exhibiting superior rushing skills in an era of stay-at-home defencemen. He would fight at the drop of a hat, often without dropping his stick. Four-time Hart Trophy winner as most valuable player, he helped win two Stanley Cups. After hockey, Shore took to coaching and team ownership in the American Hockey League, where his antics, his cheapness, and his ability to hold a grudge all made him a legendary dark figure. However, Shore developed more future coaches for the NHL than almost any other man.

➤ Nels Stewart had a strange skating style, a stranger stick, and an uncanny ability to put the puck in the net. Described as using "short, toddling steps," and a stick with such a flat lie "he had to play the puck almost between his legs," Stewart was nonetheless a brilliant player, joining Babe Siebert and Hooley Smith on the Montreal Maroons' S-Line. He was the first NHLer to hit the 300-goal mark, playing for Montreal, Boston, and the New York Americans.

Know-it-alls

Q. Who was the first goalie to wear a mask in the NHL?

A. Clint Benedict, Montreal Maroons, February 20, 1930. He took it off after a period.

Canadian Stanley Cup Winners of the Era

➤ 1920 Ottawa Senators
➤ 1921 Ottawa Senators
➤ 1922 Toronto St. Pats
➤ 1923 Ottawa Senators
➤ 1924 Montreal Canadiens
➤ 1925 Victoria Cougars
➤ 1926 Montreal Maroons
➤ 1927 Ottawa Senators
➤ 1930 Montreal Canadiens
➤ 1931 Montreal Canadiens
➤ 1932 Toronto Maple Leafs
➤ 1935 Montreal Maroons

> **The Least You Need to Know**
> - Hockey in this era was violent and often uncontrolled.
> - Canada lost five NHL teams.
> - Howie Morenz was the greatest star of the era.
> - Conn Smythe founded the Maple Leafs in 1926 and built Maple Leaf Gardens in 1931.
> - Ace Bailey almost lost his life due to a dangerous tackle.

Chapter 7

An Original Six (1940–1967)

In This Chapter

- A black-eyed Quebecois
- The pride of Saskatchewan
- The troubles of Terry
- Big Jean
- The Golden Jet
- Punching out the Big M
- Other stars of the era

The title Original Six is a baby-boomer fantasy, of course. With the exception of the Montreal Canadiens, who were in the NHL when it began in 1917, there was nothing original about the six teams who made up the NHL from the war years until expansion in 1967. Toronto, Boston, Chicago, Detroit, and the New York Rangers all came along in the 1920s. The era from the war until the late '60s is still thought of most fondly by aging fans (the mind goes as you get older) who long for the days when the league was a proprietary, regional, closed club; owners still ruled with iron fists; the players were underpaid; and the minor leagues were filled with hundreds of

> **Know-it-alls**
>
> Q. Who was the second player to score 50 goals in a season?
>
> A. Bernie "Boom Boom" Geoffrion.

mostly Canadian men hoping to make a living wage. Canada looked only to Toronto and Montreal — out west they had NHL dreams that wouldn't come true for most until an upstart league came along and challenged the big boys at their own game in the 1970s. What this period mostly featured was some of the most memorable players to come along — Canadians all — who defined what the era meant, and what those who remember it hold most dear in their hearts. In this chapter, we'll look at six of those men, the impact they had on the fans who adored them, and how the era swirled around them.

An Unstoppable, Unforgiving Rocket

English Canada went off to war again in 1939, to finally put a stop to Hitler and the Nazis. But while the conflict was supported whole-heartedly outside Quebec, the French Canadians were far less committed. Many felt the war belonged to the Europeans, and, after Pearl Harbor was attacked by the Japanese on December 7, 1941, to the Americans. As the war went on, ever more Canadian soldiers were required and shortages began to appear. That resulted in conscription in Canada — and a huge crisis. Many Quebeckers were appalled by the forced drafting of their sons, and a political and social upheaval that spread the first, hairline roots of Quebec nationalism was spawned.

Out of this atmosphere blasted a young man who would be the best pure goal scorer and the most volcanic individual in NHL history — Joseph Henri Maurice Richard.

Ironically, Richard would have gone into the army, if it had wanted him. But the boy had chronically bad ankles, having broken both of them within the previous two years.

After trying to trade Richard to the New York Rangers, the Canadiens finally settled on him, especially since they were short of bodies with the war on.

Imagine Rocket Richard as a Ranger!

Canadiens coach Dick Irvin switched Richard to the right wing in the youngster's second season of 1943–44, and a true scoring genius was born. He would be the first ever to score 50 goals in a season.

Montreal had been a so-so club for years until Richard came along, but it was instantly transformed into a contender. With Elmer Lach at centre, Toe Blake at left wing and the man they were now calling The Rocket, on the right side, the Habs won the 1944 cup.

Richard would play until 1960, score 544 goals, adding 82 in the playoffs, win eight championships and make the all-star team 14 times.

That, as they say, was only half the story, however. There was something different about this man — something that burned inside him. There was a distinct and palpable hatred for the Anglo seigneurs in Quebec.

Chapter 7 ▶ An Original Six (1940–1967)

There was, writes Mike Ulmer, "a natural rage, an instinctive need to overcome whatever obstacles were put in his way. He poured resentment toward his bosses into his play, and regarded the shadows who followed his every move as necessary stage-hands for his greatness."

Richard constantly raged at manager Tommy Gorman and at league president Clarence Campbell, and, silently, at the English elite.

Know-it-alls

Q. Who was the first player ever given all "three stars" in a game?

A. Rocket Richard, 1944. Wayne Gretzky, in his last game, is the only other.

That Richard, He's Such a Riot

It all came to a head in the spring of 1955, when the Richard Riot broke out in Montreal.

Richard had been taking shots at Campbell, accusing him of anti-French bias, in a ghost-written regular column for a French-language Montreal weekly. Campbell got Canadiens' manager Frank Selke on the carpet and gave him hell, and one week later Richard "retired" as a columnist — effectively gagged by Campbell.

So much for freedom of the press.

The following season, after striking an official in a game while trying to get at an opponent, Richard was heavily fined — he was already the most fined player in league

Listen Up!

Since the end of the First World War, the best teams in Canadian junior hockey have fought each spring for the Memorial Cup. The trophy was named to honour players who had sacrificed their lives in the Great War, and especially for John Ross Robertson, a former Ontario Hockey Association president, who died in 1918. The first final, in March 1919, featured the University of Toronto Schools vs. the Regina Patricias, won easily by the eastern champs. Since then, junior hockey loops have prospered across the land, but the major players became teams from the Quebec major league, the Western major junior loop, and the Ontario major junior ranks. NHL teams owned or sponsored junior teams for many years, using them as direct farm clubs. In the late 1960s, however, a junior draft was initiated which made young players available to all clubs in the growing NHL ranks.

Part 2 ▶ Hockey: Our Game

Quote, Unquote

"I have often seen Rocket Richard fill the Forum, but that's the first time I've ever seen him empty it."

— Montreal coach Dick Irvin on the Richard Riot, 1955.

history — and that just got the Rocket madder. Late in the season, Hal Laycoe of Boston hit the Rocket on the head with his stick and an on-ice riot broke out, during which Richard managed to break his stick across Laycoe's back, and punch official Cliff Thompson in the head.

Campbell threw the book at him and suspended the Rocket for the remainder of the season.

Fuelled by a hysterical media, French and English, trouble exploded on the last day of the season at Montreal, March 17, 1955. Not wanting to cave in to death threats and intimidation, Campbell, a former military officer, showed up at the game and took his regular place. He was showered with eggs and garbage during the first period, and a fan tried to attack him at intermission. A tear-gas bomb went off, and the building emptied out onto Rue Ste. Catherine as the game was forfeited.

That was when the mob took over. Mostly hoodlums, they began by smashing store windows and car windshields on the street, beat up passersby, and looted as they went up the street. 137 people, of whom 100 were juveniles, were arrested. Calm was only restored when Richard went on television and radio and begged for a stoppage.

It worked.

Ironically, that riot, and the hiring of Toe Blake as coach, were the harbingers of five-straight Stanley Cups for the Canadiens, who would dominate like no other team ever had.

There, But for the Grace of the Hockey Gods

Gordie Howe. Mr. Hockey. Old Number Nine. Old Elbows. Played 33 seasons as a professional, including 26 in the NHL and 6 in the World Hockey Association. Retired at 52 years of age. Led the Detroit Red Wings to four Stanley Cups in the 1950s.

Lucky to be alive.

Let's take you back to 1950, when the pride of Floral, Saskatchewan was still settling into a stellar NHL career that began at 18 in 1946. Opening night of the playoffs. Detroit Olympia. Toronto Maple Leafs the opponent.

Ted "Teeder" Kennedy, a great Leafs captain, streaks up the ice where young Howe cuts in front of him. Though Kennedy brakes to try and avoid contact, the two collide and slide heavily into the boards. Teeder gets up. Howe doesn't. He's bleeding from the head. Howe is taken off. Kennedy stays. Game, and series, turn very ugly.

Luckily for Howe, famed brain surgeon Frederic Schreiber just happens to be in town. Ninety minute surgery. Fluid taken off brain. Howe recovers.

Chapter 7 ➤ An Original Six (1940–1967)

What if that had been the end? One of Canada's greatest sporting heroes would never have survived to take his place among the very best the country has produced.

Howe went on to score 801 regular season goals and 68 more in the playoffs (NHL stats only — there were 174 markers in the WHA), appear on 21 NHL all-star teams, and win 12 league trophies.

He would retire in 1971, but return to make more history by playing in the WHA with his sons, Mark and Marty. And then, at 52, there was one more year in the NHL with Hartford.

> **Know-it-alls**
>
> Q. Whose season scoring mark did Gordie Howe break in 1951, with 86 points?
>
> A. Herb Cain's.

Along the way, he survived the monarchical reign of Jack Adams as Detroit general manager (who solved an abortive attempt by captain Ted Lindsay to organize a players' association by trading him to Chicago); played with superb teammates such as Lindsay, Red Kelly, and Terry Sawchuk; saw the rise and fall of the World league; and scored more goals after he turned 30 than before.

Though a gentleman off the ice, on it, next to Eddie Shore, he may have been the meanest player ever. His elbows scared away and broke the jaws, noses, and teeth of numerous opponents.

If You Won't Sign with Us, Big Jean, We'll Buy Your Whole League

Imagine the look on Montreal management's visages when Jean Beliveau, who because of the system in place in the 1950s had to sign with them if he ever wanted to play in the NHL, said no.

No? He didn't want to play with a team that featured Maurice Richard? That was loved throughout Quebec? That would put him in the big time?

Actually, Beliveau — tall, spirited, humble, thoughtful, talented — was already making a nice living playing junior for the Quebec City Citadels, and was loved by that city more than any other athlete. So, he turned down the Canadiens and signed with the senior, semipro, Quebec Aces. For two years, arenas were packed wherever Big Jean and the Aces went.

The Canadiens had had enough. If Les Gros Bill (named for a legendary folk hero) wouldn't sign, they'd buy the whole darn league and make it professional, which meant Beliveau would belong to the Habs whether he liked it or not.

He signed, after picking general manager Frank Selke's pocket for a $20,000 bonus and more than $100,000 over five years — huge money.

Listen Up!

One of the most famous ghosts in hockey is that of Bill Barilko. A star defenceman on the Leafs, Barilko joined the big club from the minors in 1946 after serving in the air force during World War II. In the spring of 1951, Barilko scored the Stanley Cup winning overtime goal by charging in from the point. A few weeks later, Barilko and a friend climbed into an aircraft for a fishing trip in the northlands. The aircraft disappeared. It remained a mystery for 11 years until the plane was finally found, with Barilko and his friend still aboard. Barilko was honoured, late in the 1990s, in a song by the Tragically Hip — 50 Mission Cap.

Know-it-alls

Q. Until Scotty Bowman broke his record in 1984, who had been the winningest coach in NHL history?

A. Dick Irvin, 690, with Toronto and Montreal.

Know-it-alls

Q. Who was the first hockey player on the cover of *Sports Illustrated* magazine?

A. Jean Beliveau, 1956.

"I simply opened the Forum vault and said 'Help yourself, Jean,'" said Selke afterwards.

Money well spent. Beliveau played 18 years, missing the playoffs just once. Over 1,125 regular season games he had 507 goals and won 10 Stanley Cups. He was captain for 10 years.

It was Beliveau who took the Canadiens into the expansion years when they would go on another spree and win three straight cups from 1968–70.

When he retired, Beliveau worked for the organization, and as an ambassador for hockey and Canada. In 1994, Ottawa offered him the post of governor general, which would have closed the circle with Lord Stanley of Preston and the cup Beliveau fought so hard for.

He politely turned the offer down.

The Troubles of Terry

When Brian Kendall was researching his biography of Terrance Gordon Sawchuk, he came across a quote from Joe Falls, former sports editor of the *Detroit Free Press*, who had covered the brilliant goaltender from Winnipeg during his Red Wings' career.

Chapter 7 ➤ *An Original Six (1940–1967)*

"He was the greatest goalie I ever saw," wrote Falls, at the time of Sawchuk's funeral in 1970, "and the most troubled athlete I ever met."

Dogged with injuries throughout his career, not the least of which was a terrible elbow problem in his teens that resulted in surgery and a left arm two inches shorter than his right, Sawchuk would go on to post the most remarkable numbers in goaltending history. His 103 shutouts may never be touched. His five straight years of a less than 2.00 goals against average, and creation of the crouch style used by all goalies today, are a testament to his skill. His 20 seasons for five teams, achieved despite arthritis, constant bone chips in his elbow, severed wrist tendons, a herniated disk — all tributes to his courage.

But Sawchuk had troubles, with a capital T.

Driven down by demons, drinking, personal troubles, domestic violence, and inescapable depression, Sawchuk had a rocky relationship with his teammates, a rotten one with the press, and a tragic one with himself, despite four Stanley Cup wins.

His career, and life, came to an end in the spring of 1970, when a tussle with Rangers' teammate Ron Stewart, on the front lawn of a Long Island home they shared, wound up with Sawchuk falling over a barbecue pit, sending him to hospital with internal injuries. A blood clot moved from his liver to a major artery during surgery, causing a massive coronary that killed him.

Terry Sawchuk was 40 years old.

The Golden Jet? How Did They Know?

His name was Robert Marvin Hull, and when he came out of Pointe Anne, Ontario, by way of Belleville, Hull turned hockey on its ear. With

> **Canadian Stanley Cup Winners of the Era**
> ➤ 1942 Toronto Maple Leafs
> ➤ 1944 Montreal Canadiens
> ➤ 1945 Toronto Maple Leafs
> ➤ 1946 Montreal Canadiens
> ➤ 1947 Toronto Maple Leafs
> ➤ 1948 Toronto Maple Leafs
> ➤ 1949 Toronto Maple Leafs
> ➤ 1951 Toronto Maple Leafs
> ➤ 1953 Montreal Canadiens
> ➤ 1956 Montreal Canadiens
> ➤ 1957 Montreal Canadiens
> ➤ 1958 Montreal Canadiens
> ➤ 1959 Montreal Canadiens
> ➤ 1960 Montreal Canadiens
> ➤ 1962 Toronto Maple Leafs
> ➤ 1963 Toronto Maple Leafs
> ➤ 1964 Toronto Maple Leafs
> ➤ 1965 Montreal Canadiens
> ➤ 1966 Montreal Canadiens
> ➤ 1967 Toronto Maple Leafs

Know-it-alls

Q. Who was the first NHL goalie to earn 100 shutouts in a career?
A. Terry Sawchuk, 1967.

59

blond locks flowing as he sailed at 30 miles an hour down the ice on one of his patented end-to-end rushes, Hull's nickname The Golden Jet seemed so apt.

None knew just how apt.

Hull scored 610 NHL goals, mostly with the Chicago Black Hawks with whom he won a Stanley Cup.

But, already constantly at odds with management over his worth, already with four 50-goal seasons in the bank, already famous beyond belief, Hull would take the ultimate step in 1972 by signing with the Winnipeg Jets of the World Hockey Association.

Hull's 118 mph slapshot, offered off a radically curved stick that would make the puck rise and dip unpredictably, was just part of the makeup for an on-ice gentleman who had trouble containing an off-ice temper.

He called owners idiots, coaches incompetent, and players inept, often right to their faces. Hull was also the first player to hit the $100,000 mark in yearly salary, but it took a bitter holdout in 1968 to get it.

And, he would continue an NHL legacy that already included brother Dennis, by fathering Brett Hull — the Golden Brett — one of the greatest scorers of a later generation.

A Man Not Named Maholovich

Punch Imlach just couldn't stand Frank Mahovlich. Which seemed only fair, since Mahovlich hated Imlach with a passion. The two were thrown together on the Toronto Maple Leafs for one of the worst coach-player relationships ever seen in the NHL.

A lot of hockey people have praised Imlach for his brilliant handling of the Leafs — changing them from the moribund team of the late 1950s, to a club that won four Stanley Cups in the 1960s. He would then go on to more glory in building the expansion Buffalo Sabres in the 1970s, before ruining his reputation with a pathetic last kick at the can with Toronto.

Imlach, some felt, could be cruel and thoughtless, and was driven to win no matter how many young men he stomped on along the way.

One of those young men, and the one who deserved it least, was the son of a Timmins miner —a quiet, friendly, thoughtful man who would score 533 goals in 17 seasons.

All Mahovlich did, after coming in from the Toronto St. Michael's juniors, was score 42 goals in his first two seasons, and make a run at becoming the only Leaf to that point to get 50 in one year. He scored with 48. No matter what the man they called The Big M (his younger brother Peter would have a long career of his own and be naturally known as The Little M) did on the mainly defensive-minded Leafs, Imlach was critical.

The coach wouldn't even call him by his real name — bastardizing it to "Maholovich" when speaking to the press.

Following Imlach's lead, the fans at Maple Leaf Gardens began to boo him unmercifully, and, by the age of 30, Mahovlich was in hospital on the verge of a nervous breakdown. Traded to Detroit, and two seasons later to Montreal, Mahovlich blossomed.

"It was," he would say, "like a giant weight had been lifted off my shoulder."

Mahovlich is now a member of the Canadian senate.

Other Stars of the Era

- Bernie "Boom Boom" Geoffrion, born in Montreal, was the second man to score 50 goals in a season, after Rocket Richard. He notched five in a game in 1955 and wound up with 393 goals for Montreal and New York. He went on to coach the Rangers, Atlanta Flames, and the Canadiens.
- Glenn Hall, "Mr. Goalie," came out of Humboldt, Saskatchewan, to the Detroit Red Wings, and later led the NHL in shutouts for six seasons as a Chicago Black Hawk. Hall earned 84 career donuts, and had a playoff goals against average of 2.79. He went to St. Louis in the expansion and took the Blues to three straight Cup appearances.
- Red Kelly was born in Simcoe, Ontario, in 1927, and grew up to be one of the classiest players ever. He first was an all-star defenceman for Detroit, and when traded to Toronto in 1960, moved to centre. He won the first Norris Trophy as best defenceman, and played on eight cup winners with the Wings and Leafs. While playing in Toronto, he also spent three years as a member of

Quote, Unquote

"Imlach wore us down at practice and at the negotiating table."
— Frank Mahovlich.

Listen Up!

Women's hockey took a dive in popularity in the 1950s and 1960s, partly because women themselves were shoved back into the kitchen with their shoes off after the Second World War. Some young girls found a way, however. Chief among those was Abby Hoffman, who in 1955 joined the Toronto Hockey League as "Ab" Hoffman. No one had thought to check her birth certificate, and Hoffman, 8, went on to be an all-star that year. Eventually, the mistake was noticed, but after originally kicking her out, THL officials let her stay — a much happier ending than for many other girls who tried the same thing. Hoffman quit hockey after two seasons and concentrated on other sports, winning an Olympic track medal in the 800 metres for Canada in 1972.

Part 2 ➤ *Hockey: Our Game*

> **Quote, Unquote**
>
> "We want her to stay with us. She's really good!"
>
> — Russ Turnbull, 8, teammate of Abigail "Ab" Hoffman, 1955.

> **Quote, Unquote**
>
> "He's as strong as an ox, and hits with terrific force."
>
> — John Ferguson, Montreal Canadiens, on star defenceman Tim Horton of the Leafs.

federal parliament. Coached in Los Angeles, Pittsburgh, and Toronto after his playing career was over. Kelly's strongest expletive was "dang."

➤ David Keon played 22 seasons in the pros, including 18 in the NHL and 4 in the WHA. He's considered the best checking centre in the history of the game, and also one of the most gentlemanly. He had only a handful of fights in his career, so shocking Foster Hewitt one night in Boston when he hammered into a Bruin that the venerable play-by-play voice was left speechless. Keon captained the Leafs, won the Conn Smythe trophy in 1967 as playoff MVP, but eventually left Toronto in 1975 in a dispute with Harold Ballard.

➤ Jacques Plante had a two-part career. A brilliant goaltender with Montreal in the 1950s, he led the Habs to five straight cups. Retiring in 1964 after two seasons in New York, Plante came back in 1968 to join Glenn Hall in St. Louis, and amazingly played with the Blues, Leafs, and Bruins, until 1973, when he finally retired for good at 46. Plante was the first goaltender to wear a mask regularly in games. A noted extrovert, Plante kept himself calm by knitting.

The Least You Need to Know

➤ Hockey's so-called "Original Six" period, featuring Toronto, Montreal, New York, Chicago, Detroit, and Boston, lasted from 1942 to 1967.

➤ Montreal dominated the second half of the 1950s, and Toronto the first half of the 1960s.

➤ Goalies began to wear masks regularly in this time.

➤ Owners still held all the cards over the underpaid players.

➤ Television, especially Hockey Night in Canada, exploded onto the scene.

Chapter 8

Expansions, Explosions, and a Kid Named Bobby Orr (1967–1980)

In This Chapter

➤ Expansion first excludes Canada, but Vancouver finally makes it back

➤ The greatest of all time (Part One)

➤ The World Hockey Association

➤ Paul Henderson

➤ The brutality of the 1970s

➤ An ending, and a beginning

➤ Other stars of the era

Many of those Canadian hockey players stuck in the minor leagues during the era of the "Original Six" were sprung in the summer of 1967, when the National Hockey League expanded to 12 teams. All six of those new clubs were in the United States. For most Canadian fans, getting pro hockey meant latching on to the new World Hockey Association, which put clubs into seven cities north of the border, three of which would survive to join the NHL at the end of the decade. But, more than for the brutality of play on the ice, more than for the Stanley Cup run of the Montreal Canadiens and their coach, Scotty Bowman, Canadian fans remember the 1970s for two players and what they achieved — Bobby Orr and Paul Henderson. In this chapter, we'll chart hockey as it moves from the garbage bins in the back alley where brawling took precedence, to a new understanding, helped by a European invasion and games with the Soviets, of what true artistry could be on ice.

The Wrong Left Coast

Realizing that provincialism was going to kill it, the National Hockey League finally voted to expand in 1965, and by the spring of the following year announced the six cities that would be allowed to pay a ton of money and join the club. As anyone who can read a map will tell you, none of those six — San Francisco, Los Angeles, Philadelphia, Pittsburgh, Minnesota, and St. Louis — was located in the Great White (Dying for NHL Hockey) North.

What happened?

Really, the only Canadian city the league was interested in was Vancouver, and that didn't work out because of squabbling over building an arena, and who would own the team.

So, Vancouver missed the first expansion.

But, an arena — the Pacific Coliseum — was built by 1968. A new ownership group bought the Western League's Vancouver Canucks to put into the building, and finally the Canucks were accepted, along with the Buffalo Sabres, for the 1970–71 season.

The Greatest, Part One

What can you say about Bobby Orr? That he was one of the two greatest players ever? That he changed the way hockey in his era was played? That he did things on defence that no other player ever had, or has since?

That he had horrible knees?

All of the above is true. Robert Orr, native of Parry Sound, Ontario, became Boston Bruins property in 1960, when he was just 13. The Bruins saw him and immediately became a sponsor of the Parry Sound team, which under the rules of the day tied Orr to the Boston club for the rest of his life.

Ignoring that he was supposed to be an indentured servant, Orr hit Boston at 18, but not before his young lawyer, R. Alan Eagleson, had forced the Bruins to pay $25,000 a season for the youngster, which was about $17,000 more a year than other rookies got.

Orr would go on to score 270 goals and 645 assists in nine injury-riddled campaigns, leaving a plethora of

> **Know-it-alls**
>
> Q. Who was the first player to score 100 points in a season, twice?
>
> A. Phil Esposito, Boston, 1969 and 1971.

Chapter 8 ➤ Expansions, Explosions, and a Kid Named Bobby Orr (1967–1980)

admirers in his wake. He could skate rings around the fastest skaters. He could shoot as hard as anyone. He was as good a puck handler as the game had seen — once killing a two-minute penalty against Toronto all by himself, keeping the puck the entire time. He was tough as nails.

Nine times an all-star, 16 individual trophies to his name, two Stanley Cups — the first coming on his own overtime goal against St. Louis in 1970 that created a moment captured for all time: Orr stretched right out in the air, arms raised in triumph.

But Orr, like Achilles, had his heel. Only in this case, it was a left knee first injured when Marcel Pronovost checked him into the boards in his rookie season of 1966–67. Two knee operations in the following year, and two more about 10 years later, left him with bone moving against bone. No cartilage. No tendons. No hope.

After performing miracles in the 1976 Canada Cup, Orr was about done.

Bobby Orr retired at just 31. His legend will play forever.

> **Know-it-alls**
>
> Q. Who were the first brothers to play goal against each other in the NHL?
>
> A. Ken and Dave Dryden, Montreal and Buffalo, 1971. Ken won.

> **Know-it-alls**
>
> Q. Who coached Team Canada, 1972?
>
> A. Harry Sinden.

Coming In on Left Wing and a Prayer

Laugh at it all you want, but the World Hockey Association, born in 1972, died in 1979 when the last four teams were gobbled up by the NHL, did more than anything else to further the cause of top-level professional hockey in Canada.

Before the birth of the WHA, there were three NHL clubs north of the border. When the radical league folded up, there were seven (Atlanta moved to Calgary, jumping into a gap the World league had left open).

At the same time, the average salary of a big league hockey player went up many fold, the first European influences on "our" game were solidly felt, and the unquestioned control of pro hockey by a few rich owners was ended.

Not bad for a league most pass off as bush.

A little history: In 1971, Dennis Murphy and Gary Davidson, co-founders of the American Basketball Association (which went into competition against the existing

65

National Basketball Association with the idea of forcing a merger), came up with basic plans to found a new league that would rival the NHL.

Edmonton businessman "Wild" Bill Hunter got involved almost right away, seeing a chance to bring pro hockey to the prairies. That November, the WHA announced 10 franchises, with three for Canada — Alberta Oilers (Edmonton), Calgary Broncos, and Winnipeg Jets — and three weeks after that a team was awarded to an as-yet unnamed Ontario town that would turn out to be Ottawa (Nationals). By February, the San Francisco group sold to Quebec City, and the Nordiques were born.

That made five Canadian clubs.

Doug Michel, original owner of the Nationals, would pen an excellent book on the league's founding, *Left Wing and a Prayer*, and that title about summed up what some of the financial details behind the WHA were really based on.

But it also spoke to how the league earned instant credibility by pooling its resources to sign the game's greatest left winger, Bobby Hull, out from under the nose of Chicago Black Hawks' owner Bill Wirtz — a legendary cheap owner. Hull's signature on a Winnipeg Jets' contract cost $2.75 million over 10 years and made him, truly, the Golden Jet. That deal set off a signing frenzy of NHLers and teams that didn't cough up the money to keep players wound up devastated — especially the Toronto Maple Leafs, who were finally coming back to respectability.

Their owner, Harold Ballard, didn't believe the league would survive, and he lost almost half of the roster over the next few years.

> **Listen Up!**
>
> The WHA was known for everything from coloured pucks to the last maskless goalie, to incredible bench-clearing brawls. It was the home of Steve and Jeff Carlson, and their friend Dave Hanson, who starred in the movie *Slap Shot* as the bespectacled, goon trio "The Hanson Brothers." It was the league in which Toronto goalie Gilles Gratton "streaked" naked through a practice. In which the ice at Cherry Hill, New Jersey was tilted. Where the signing of the 17-year-old Wayne Gretzky helped changed the face of drafting rules in pro hockey forever. Where the Toronto Toros snuck Vaclav Nedomansky across the Czech border to freedom. Where a beer league player named Derek Haas came out of Trail, B.C., to make the Calgary Cowboys. And where more than one team arrived at the dressing room to find the local sheriff had seized all their equipment for unpaid bills.

Hull would play for six seasons, most of them with dynamic Swedish stars Ulf Nilsson and Anders Hedberg as linemates. The WHA, you see, also changed perceptions about Europeans.

What Do You Mean, You Can't See the Puck?

Despite such short-lived innovations as red and blue pucks (good for television, lousy for players' eyesight), the WHA became known as much for its franchise disasters as it did for its players — who themselves ranged from has-beens, never-weres, and dreamers, to

Chapter 8 ➤ *Expansions, Explosions, and a Kid Named Bobby Orr (1967–1980)*

legitimate stars such as Hull, Gordie Howe (who came out of retirement to play with his sons in Houston), Marc Tardif (71 goals, 77 assists in 1976 for Quebec), Frank Mahovlich (Toronto Toros), and a 17-year-old sensation by the name of Wayne Gretzky (Indianapolis Racers, Edmonton Oilers).

Back to the franchise boogie, again:

Calgary quickly folded. Vancouver picked up the Philadelphia Blazers, who stayed a couple of seasons and then moved to Calgary to become the Cowboys, and folded. Ottawa made the playoffs in the first year, but moved to Toronto before the post-season began, where they became the Toros, lasted a few years and wound up in Birmingham. Ottawa got a team back for about a month when the Denver Spurs became the Civics in 1976, and then promptly shut down.

> **Know-it-alls**
>
> Q. What ex-player was made head coach of Edmonton (WHA) in 1977?
>
> A. Glen Sather.

But, thanks to strong ownership and excellent players, when the league itself folded in 1979, Quebec, Edmonton, and Winnipeg made it into the NHL fold.

Add the Calgary Flames, who had moved from Atlanta when that expansion NHL franchise failed to make a go of it deep in the heart of Dixie, and Canada hit the 1980s with six clubs.

God Bless You, Paul

Where were you in September of 1972? Off school with a rotten cold, thank you, and never has a cold been more welcomed.

For 27 days that month, while most of the rest of the world was reeling from the Munich Massacre of Israeli athletes at the Olympic Games, Canada and the Soviet Union turned to the most anticipated sporting event in either country up to that time.

Finally, after years of complaining that the Soviet "amateurs" were no more amateur than our NHLers, and after claiming for two decades that "We could easily beat those Commies if we had our best players," the chance arose.

Eight games. Winner take all. Best against best (minus Bobby Hull who was not allowed to play by NHL bosses for bolting to the WHA, Bobby Orr, who was injured, Gordie Howe, in the middle of a short retirement, and Jean Beliveau, also retired that year). Bragging rights, forever.

What actually happened was that our own concept of hockey was indelibly altered. Our game became more wide open. Unconscionable violence slowly became unacceptable. European players became sought-after commodities.

And, in those September days, one Paul Henderson, number 19, scored three goals that made him the most famous athlete ever in this country.

Listen Up!

The strangest, most tragic incident in the NHL of the era happened off the ice. Brian Spencer, a rookie with the Toronto Maple Leafs, from Fort St. James, B.C., was to be interviewed by Hockey Night in Canada during the 1969–70 season. His father, Roy, had just been made a grandfather by his son's wife two days previously, and desperately wanted to see the interview. But CBC switched to the Vancouver–Oakland game from the Toronto–Chicago one, and the elder Spencer lost it completely. He took a rifle and drove to the CBC station in Prince George, B.C., where he stormed into the building and ordered staff to switch it back. They couldn't do it. Spencer went back to the parking lot where he made the mistake of pointing the rifle at RCMP officers, who shot him dead, while his son was on the air.

Quote, Unquote

"I would have killed someone to win that series. I mean it."
— Phil Esposito, Team Canada 1972.

The story in short: Foster Hewitt out of retirement to call the games. Soviets surprise Canada with big win in game one at Montreal. Goalie Vladislav Tretiak is superb for the visitors. Country stunned. Canada bounces back in game two, thanks to Peter Mahovlich (unforgettable short-handed goal). Series tied. Stays so after draw in Winnipeg. Canada awful in loss at Vancouver. Crowd boos. Assistant captain Phil Esposito gives the country hell on TV.

Series shifts to Moscow. Canada loses again. Needs three straight wins to take series. Valeri Kharlamov killing us. Bobby Clarke goes out and purposely breaks the Soviet star's ankle. At the time, everyone cheers. Now, everyone embarrassed to remember that.

Enter our Paul, who to that point had been a party guy, little worried about the future. Kind of the shallow type.

Henderson scores the winner in game six. Canada's still alive. He scores the winner, while flat on his face, in game seven. Go to game eight. Canada must win. Trailing 5-3 into the third period of game eight, with 12 million Canadians watching on television, schools closed, or students watching in gyms and classrooms. Canada gets two to tie it up.

With a minute left in the Moscow arena, Henderson jumps on the ice without being told to go, joining Esposito and Yvan Cournoyer. "Henderson takes a wild stab for it and fell," screams Foster, while his colour guy, Brian Conacher, tries to keep him from falling out of the booth. Henderson down behind the net. Gets up and heads for the front. Esposito steals the puck, passes it to the goal. Henderson takes one whack, then…"He scores! Henderson scores for Canada!"

Celebration. Huge national party. Total relief. Gradual realization the game could never be the same.

And Henderson? He came home a changed man, found God, and settled down to what is still a happy, fulfilled existence.

Bless you, Paul.

The Gruesome, Violent Seventies

Hockey had always been a tough, dirty game, and before we get too far into this, it must be said that nothing that happened in the 1970s was quite as bad as the stick-swingin' Roaring Twenties and the decades that directly followed.

But in the 1970s, our perception of what was violent and unacceptable began to change. Hockey was late catching up.

> **Quote, Unquote**
>
> "It was like being shot at, and missed."
>
> — Ken Dryden, writing in *The Game*, on the 1972 Summit Series.

It all got off to a rough start three months before the 1970s even began. In an exhibition game at Ottawa, September 21, 1969, Wayne Maki of St. Louis lost his head and almost separated Boston's Ted Green from his, bringing the lumber crashing down on Green's skull at the end of a stick swinging duel both had been involved in. Green went through five hours of brain surgery, and in a subsequent operation had a steel plate put into his skull. Maki was suspended just 30 days — 13 games. And the joke of it was, that was the harshest suspension for direct violence in NHL history (Rocket Richard, remember, was kicked for being violent, and being an overall bad boy).

Both men were arrested, and both exonerated. Ironically, Maki would be dead a few years later — of a brain tumour.

Giving In to the Bullies

The Philadelphia Flyers of the mid decade were known as the Broad Street Bullies (named for the street that ran by their arena), and with good reason. Coach Fred (the Fog) Shero had a lineup that defied writers of dictionaries everywhere to come up with new meanings for the word dirty. Led by Dave "The Hammer" Shultz, "Hound Dog" Bob Kelly, and numerous teammates, the Flyers beat their foes into submission while winning two Stanley Cups.

Across Canada, players from the youngest ages began emulating them, and anarchy threatened to rear its ugly head and forever doom our game to a dark, bloody future. The European influence, led in the NHL by Toronto's Borje Salming and Inge Hammerstrom, and Nilsson and Hedberg in Winnipeg, had not had time to change thinking. The lessons learned from the Russians through the Summit Series and the Canada Cup of 1976—a creation of Alan Eagleson ostensibly designed to fatten the coffers of the NHL Players' Association, but which also helped fatten his own bank account (see Chapter 9)—had not taken hold.

Terrorism was the in thing.

Governments, seeing a great public relations opportunity, felt compelled to do something about it. They held investigations, published recommendations, and, on a few occasions, actually pressed charges against players.

All Hell Breaks Loose

In a 1976 WHA playoff game, Rick Jodzio of the Calgary Cowboys hit the ice, skated 80 feet at full speed, and cross-checked the superb Marc Tardif of Quebec right in the face. Dropping his gloves, Jodzio then tried to beat the stuffing out of Tardif, who was already unconscious on the ice. A brawl broke out that was so out of control, 20 Quebec City police had to come on the ice to restore order. Tardif had a severe brain contusion and missed the rest of the season. Jodzio was arrested and charged with assault, eventually earning a $3,000 fine.

Tardif was never the same. Jodzio was kicked out and told to stay out.

1976. Leafs–Flyers playoff game. Maple Leaf Gardens. The Flyers waited until the Leafs had five non-aggressive players on the ice, and sent out their goons to get Borje Salming, the future hall-of-fame defender. Mel Bridgeman jumped him in front of the net and gave him a terrible beating. Blood and fights everywhere. In the penalty box, Joe Watson is spat on by a fan, and he goes after the expectorator with his stick. A policeman grabs the stick and he and Watson wrestle for it. Don Saleski and Bob Kelly get involved. An usherette is accidentally crowned with the lumber. Ontario Attorney General Roy McMurtry, himself an ex-athlete of some repute, decides he's seen enough. Bridgeman is charged with assault causing bodily harm for attacking Salming; Watson gets common assault, assaulting a police officer, and possession of a dangerous weapon (his stick); Saleski gets two charges of common assault; and Kelly a charge of assault.

Quote, Unquote

"Those Penguins are done like dinner."

— Dave "Tiger" Williams, Toronto Maple Leafs, 1975. Leafs won the series.

Colour commentator Brian McFarlane called it the hardest hockey game he'd ever had to cover.

The charges against Saleski and Bridgeman were eventually dropped. Watson and Kelly pleaded guilty to lesser charges in 1977 and were fined.

These were not the only incidents. Leagues everywhere began to realize they had to do something, or governments would do it for them. Rules were changed, bench clearing brawls were severely dealt with, and the instigator rule brought in (if you start a fight, you get an extra penalty). But what really changed everything for the better was the late-decade dominance of one team, the Montreal Canadiens, and the arrival of one player — Wayne Gretzky.

Chapter 8 ▸ *Expansions, Explosions, and a Kid Named Bobby Orr (1967–1980)*

Les Habitants sont là, Again

You must thank the Gods of Hockey for Scotty Bowman and the Montreal Canadiens of the late '70s.

Led by Bowman, who would go on to become the winningest coach in league history, and featuring a wonderful lineup of players such as Guy Lafleur, Steve Shutt, Jacques Lemaire, Serge Savard, Guy Lapointe, Larry Robinson, Bob Gainey, and goaltender Ken Dryden, the Habs captured the cup in the spring of 1976, and kept it for four years. In the 1976–77 season, the Canadiens lost at home just once, on the way to posting a 60-8-12 mark.

They could play it tough if you wanted to, and they couldn't be intimidated, but mostly Montreal controlled and dictated the play.

It was the Canadiens who brought the speed and beauty back into the game.

It was the Canadiens who showed that grace, honour, and hard work were what won games in the end.

It was the Canadiens who played in what's considered one of the most exciting games ever — a 1976 New Year's Eve contest with Moscow Central Red Army and goaltender Vladislav Tretiak, in which they showed the Soviets how to put our game together with their game and come up with something a level above. Tretiak had to be brilliant to earn a tie.

And, it was the Canadiens who laid the groundwork for the next two teams to follow — the New York Islanders, who would dominate the early 1980s, and the Edmonton Oilers, who would completely control the middle part of the next decade.

Quote, Unquote

"I died on May 10, 1979; at 11:10 p.m. to be exact."

— Donald Stewart Cherry after two late Habs goals won the Stanley Cup over his Bruins.

Know-it-alls

Q. Who set a record for consecutive games with at least a point, in 1978?

A. Guy Lafleur, 28 games.

And So...

And so, as the decade came to an end, a new style of hockey was beginning to emerge. It would flower and grow in a number of players, but the best and brightest would be a skinny little kid from Brantford, Ontario, who would become known as The Great One.

Other Stars of the Era

- Bobby Clarke came out of Flin Flon, Manitoba, with a chip on his shoulder, and a black mark on his resumé. Clarke suffered from diabetes, but never allowed it to dull his competitive edge, or his skills. At once one of the most respected, and most hated, men to ever play the game, he captained the Philadelphia Flyers to two Stanley Cups. No one ever played with more heart. He had a reputation, right or wrong, for starting fights and then letting the Flyer goons handle it. It was also Clarke that tipped the balance of the 1972 Summit Series with the Soviets when, following orders, he purposely broke star forward Valeri Kharlamov's ankle.

- Marcel Dionne, Le Petit Castor (the Little Beaver), never won a Stanley Cup in 16 seasons, but captured the hearts of fans everywhere with his scoring skills (731 goals, third all-time) and endless energy for the Detroit Red Wings, Los Angeles Kings, and later the New York Rangers.

- Goaltenders have always been unusual, and Ken Dryden fit that mould perfectly. He won the Conn Smythe Trophy as playoff MVP in 1971, despite having come up to the Montreal Canadiens only late in the season. The next year he took top rookie honours. Won six Stanley Cups, but retired in 1979 at just 31 to pursue a career in law.

- Phil Esposito was one of the most gifted natural goal scorers in history. He potted 76 in 1970–71, while leading the Boston Bruins to the Stanley Cup. The heart and soul of Team Canada in 1972. Played for Chicago, Boston, and New York Rangers before becoming a coach and general manager. He wound up with 717 goals.

- Marc Tardif was another natural, who spent his most productive years with Quebec of the World Hockey Association. Scored 71 goals in 1973–74. He was never the same after Rick Jodzio almost killed him in a 1976 game.

- Guy Lafleur, The Flower, earned such acclaim, his fame and fans carried across the nation from sea to sea. An elegant, instinctive player, Lafleur was a member of Montreal's four straight cups in the late '70s, and eventually scored 518 goals in the bleu, blanc, et rouge. Retired for four seasons and then came back to finish his career with the New York Rangers and Quebec, retiring for the second time in 1991.

- Gilbert Perreault went to Buffalo in 1970 when the expansion Sabres won a coin flip with Vancouver for first pick. Out of Victoriaville, Quebec, Perrault joined with Rick Martin and Rene Robert on the French Connection line, and took the Sabres all the way to the Stanley Cup final in 1975.

Know-it-alls

Q. Who was the first NHL rookie to score 50 goals in a season?

A. Mike Bossy, 1978.

Chapter 8 ➤ *Expansions, Explosions, and a Kid Named Bobby Orr (1967–1980)*

➤ Darryl Sittler captained the Toronto Maple Leafs to a resurgence in the late 1970s. Played for 11 seasons, before being traded to Philadelphia, and then Detroit. Won the hearts of Toronto fans by standing up to a fading Punch Imlach in 1981, which eventually saw him traded. Scored 6 goals and 10 points on February 7, 1976, tying the modern record for goals set by Red Berenson of St. Louis, had 5 in a playoff game later that season, and the winner in the 1976 Canada Cup.

Canadian Stanley Cup Winners of the Era

➤ 1968 Montreal Canadiens
➤ 1969 Montreal Canadiens
➤ 1971 Montreal Canadiens
➤ 1973 Montreal Canadiens
➤ 1976 Montreal Canadiens
➤ 1977 Montreal Canadiens
➤ 1978 Montreal Canadiens
➤ 1979 Montreal Canadiens

The Least You Need to Know

➤ NHL expanded to 12 teams in 1967, but ignored Canada.
➤ Vancouver was added to the NHL in 1970.
➤ World Hockey Association inflated salaries and broke control of NHL owners.
➤ Bobby Orr dominated the era.
➤ Goon hockey predominated.
➤ In 1972, Paul Henderson became the greatest Canadian sports hero of all time.

Chapter 9

The Great One, The Magnificent One, and the International Pastime (1981–Present)

In This Chapter

- ➤ The greatest of all time (Part Two)
- ➤ Mario
- ➤ A question of money
- ➤ The international influence
- ➤ Reactionaries and crooks
- ➤ Wayne says goodbye
- ➤ Stars of the era

It would be tempting to turn this entire section over to a discussion of just two players — one a skinny kid from Ontario who flipped the era on its ear, and the other a monster of a man from Montreal, whose shyness off the ice belied his ferocity on it, and whose courage enabled him to rise above cancer. But there's so much more to the most recent era of hockey in Canada, and the world, not the least of which is the globe's contributions to the game as a whole. In this chapter, we'll look at the era's two greatest stars, how money, or the lack of it, has affected Canada's recent hockey history, and some of the reactionary forces within the sport.

Part 2 ▸ Hockey: Our Game

Know-it-alls

Q. What defenceman holds the record for most NHL teams played for?

A. Michel Petit, nine.

Know-it-alls

Q. Name the only player in NHL history to take penalty shots for two different teams in the same season.

A. Mark Recchi, 1995, Montreal and Philadelphia.

Quote, Unquote

"I was sure I was right. He had that sparkle in his eyes where others have glass."

— Glen Sather, on what he first saw in Wayne Gretzky.

The Great One

The story is now a Canadian legend. Walter Gretzky, a hard-working Bell Canada employee in Brantford, Ontario, floods his back yard and sets four-year-old Wayne down on the surface with an oversized hockey stick in his hand, and thus alters forever the history of our game.

Best part of that story, of course, is that it's true.

No one, save for Michael Jordan in basketball, has ever dominated his or her sport the way Gretzky has dominated hockey. Almost every offensive record in the book belongs to him. Every trophy imaginable has come his way. *The Hockey News* polled 50 experts and they unanimously chose Wayne Gretzky as simply the best.

Gretzky was a Canadian phenomenon before he was 10 years old. He actually started skating at two, on the Nith River, hard by his grandparents' farm. Eight years later, he scored 378 goals and 120 assists as an atom. He was already in the limelight. When Gretzky went to the famous peewee tournament at Quebec City, the 12-year-old was blitzed by autograph seekers and pre-teen hangers-on.

A junior at 14, a major junior at 15, he was signed to a personal services contract with Nelson Skalbania and the Indianapolis Racers in the World Hockey Association at 17.

That deal lasted just a few months as Skalbania, always in it for a buck, sold him to the Edmonton Oilers for 1.5 million of them.

When the WHA merged with the NHL in 1979, the Oilers kept Gretzky and brought him to the NHL. His quickness and ability to see the play as though separated from his body and viewing it from above made him an instant star.

Critics said he couldn't skate very well. But no one could lay a hand on him. They said he wasn't big enough. But no one could line him up and find out.

"Gretzky sees a picture out there that no one else sees," said Boston general manager Harry Sinden. "I've never seen the game he's looking at."

Chapter 9 ➤ *The Great One, The Magnificent One, and the International Pastime (1981–Present)*

Records began to fall like forgotten Hollywood stars. In 1981, Gretzky did the unthinkable, scoring 50 goals in just 39 games — a mere 11 contests faster than it had ever been done before. Teamed with the likes of Mark Messier, he continued to outdo himself, finishing that season with 92 goals and 120 assists. That 212-point mark may be as unreachable as Joe DiMaggio's 56-game hitting streak is in baseball.

The Oilers, pushed by coach/general manager Glen Sather, won four Stanley Cups in five years during the 1980s, and it looked as though Edmonton would dominate for as long as Gretzky could stay healthy and continue.

But money, or the need for it, reared its ugly head, and it would not be.

He Did What?

On August 9, 1988, Edmonton owner Peter Pocklington traded Wayne Gretzky. Traded the best player ever! Traded the heart of the city to Los Angeles, along with Marty McSorley and Mike Krushelnyski, getting Jimmy Carson, Martin Gelinas, three first-round draft picks, and $15 million (U.S.) in return.

Pocklington has never been forgiven.

Gretzky played eight seasons in L.A., and wasn't quite able to take a talent-drained (remember those first round picks?) club to a Stanley Cup, though they did make the finals once, losing to Montreal. After spending 18 games with St. Louis, he signed with the New York Rangers as a free agent in 1996.

His NHL work wasn't all, either. Through numerous Canada Cups, world championships (the Canadian team in recent years has been made up of players who missed the NHL playoffs), a World Cup, and the 1998 Olympics, Gretzky has given himself to the rest of the planet. Other than Muhammad Ali and Jordan, there isn't a more recognizable sports name anywhere.

"I love it," said Gretzky, of hockey — the same sentiment that Bobby Orr had for it, by the way. "I love every part of it. Skating, playing, joking around with the guys in the dressing room."

> **Quote, Unquote**
>
> "They all knew that eventually they would make it to the top, and the Stanley Cup would move for a while to Edmonton."
>
> — Peter Gzowski, on the young Oilers.

> **Know-it-alls**
>
> Q. When Wayne Gretzky scored his 77th goal in 1982, whose goal scoring record did he break?
>
> A. Phil Esposito's.

> **Know-it-alls**
>
> Q. What family has sent the most sons into the NHL?
>
> A. The Sutters — six.

Part 2 ➤ Hockey: Our Game

Know-it-alls

Q. How many shifts into his first game did Mario Lemieux score his first goal?

A. One.

Listen Up!

Viking, Alberta may just be a spot on a very detailed map to most people, but to Canadian hockey fans it has become hallowed ground. For out of that tiny community came seven Sutter brothers, six of whom made it to the NHL. There was Brian (12 seasons with St. Louis), Darryl (8 with Chicago), Duane (8 with New York Islanders and 3 with Chicago), Brent (18 seasons with the Islanders and Chicago), and the twins Rich (13 seasons with seven clubs) and Ron (17 seasons and counting with six clubs). Brian and Darryl also coached in the NHL.

Imagine how anybody who has played with him, or who has imagined playing with him, must have felt being in the dressing room themselves — with The Great One.

Magnificent Mario

As Good as Gretzky. That was the title hung on Mario Lemieux while he was still playing junior hockey in Quebec, where in his final season at Laval he had 133 goals and 382 points. Totally unfair. No one would be Wayne Gretzky.

And no one may ever bring to the game what Lemieux did. Strong, with a huge reach, among the best goal scorer's instincts ever (possibly only Rocket Richard was better), an ability to bull through you, stick handle around you, or simply pull up and blast the puck by you, Lemieux was considered by many to be the best pure talent to put on blades.

But, there is something of Lemieux the man that the public and press were never able to put a finger on. His shyness. His controlled emotions. His need to be alone, with his family and out of the spotlight as much as possible. His matter-of-fact approach to everything he did was fascinating and confusing for fans.

If he chose not to go to the world championships, Lemieux was criticized. But when he scored the winning goal in the 1987 Canada Cup against the Soviets, he was lionized.

He scored 85 goals and assisted on 114 others in 1988–89, and people were left wondering if it should be more.

Back problems began to plague him. Pittsburgh, which at least was starting to draw decent crowds, still hadn't won a Cup with him. But, in 1991, he took the Penguins to the Stanley Cup, six years after arriving. The club did it again the next year.

They were trying for a third one, when, in January of 1993, Lemieux was diagnosed with Hodgkin's Disease, a form of cancer. He missed two months for radiation treatments, came back and won the scoring race, but had to sit out the following season when back surgery and weakness from the cancer treatments made it impossible to continue.

Chapter 9 ▸ *The Great One, The Magnificent One, and the International Pastime (1981–Present)*

Two more seasons of hard work, constant hacking and holding, and losing efforts in the playoffs, were enough. Mario Lemieux retired.

Bring Us Your Tired, Your Hungry...

In the mid 1960s, the six-team NHL featured only one non-Canadian, Tommy Williams of the Boston Bruins, who was American.

By the 1970s, Swedish players, and a few Finns, were beginning to find their way legally to the NHL. Those who couldn't get out of Europe, snuck out in the dark of night, chief among those being the Stastny brothers of Czechoslovakia, Peter, Anton, and Marian, who signed with the Quebec Nordiques.

Not much of an onslaught. But by the late 1990s, Canadian players made up just over 60 percent of all players in the league. The Americans won the World Cup in 1997. The Czechs won the Olympics, the first games to allow NHLers, in 1998. A look at the top ten scorers for the 1998–99 season shows Jaromir Jagr (Czech Republic), Teemu Selanne (Finland), Peter Forsberg (Sweden), and Alexei Yashin (Russia) all in there.

> **Quote, Unquote**
>
> "I never saw anyone outcoach him."
>
> — Guy Lafleur on Scotty Bowman, who won cups with Montreal, Pittsburgh, and Detroit.

> **Quote, Unquote**
>
> "The day off helped me a lot."
>
> — Mario Lemieux, explaining his five-goal game on December 31, 1988.

The first Soviet to play was Victor Nechaev, who had a cup of coffee with Los Angeles in the 1982–83 season cup. But he had gotten out legally, having married an American. A harbinger of what was truly to come was the 1983 amateur draft, in which 144 Canadians were chosen, but 63 Americans and 35 Europeans were also picked up. Brian Lawton of the U.S. was chosen first overall.

A lot of teams were spiriting players out from behind the iron curtain, and in 1987 the Soviets began to make overtures to the league that, for money, they might be willing to let some of their older players out to play. When Calgary signed Sergei Priakin a year later, it looked like that rumour might be true.

Not that Priakin was any good, mind you, but more would come. As a matter of fact, by the following season, with the Berlin Wall crumbling, the five top players in the Soviet Union — Igor Larionov, Vladimir Krutov, Sergei Makarov, Viacheslav Fetisov, and Alexei Kasatonov — were all in the NHL.

Since then, the number of players from anywhere but Canada has continued to grow.

The Truly Unthinkable

If Peter Pocklington could sell the greatest player ever to the Los Angeles Kings (and make no mistake, it was a sale), then anything could happen. But Canada losing whole teams to the United States?

Believe it. All through the 1990s, teams in Edmonton, Calgary, Winnipeg, and Quebec City began to suffer badly due to the rapidly shrinking Canadian dollar (as matched to its U.S. counterpart) and arenas that were falling behind the times. Even Calgary, with its beautiful Saddledome, built for the 1988 Winter Olympics, was finding it could use a few more private boxes and suites to attract the corporatti.

But surely, it would work out. Hadn't the NHL agreed to come to Ottawa, where the Senators would be reborn, as part of the two-team expansion announced in 1990?

This is Canada, darnit. This can't happen!

In Quebec, the government made the fatal error of not kicking in to help build a new arena to replace the ancient Collisee. Revenue streams had dried up, taxes were killing the Nordiques, and ownership was warning it couldn't continue.

It didn't.

In 1995, the Nords were sold to COMSAT Entertainment Group, and on July 1, it was announced the team was moving to Denver to become the Colorado Avalanche.

No more life-or-death struggles with the Montreal Canadiens.

A loss of revenue in the lockout-shortened year of 1994–95 only made things worse for the Winnipeg Jets, who played in an old barn of a building that couldn't provide the money needed to keep going. In Manitoba, the government did toss in some money, but it wasn't enough. A new arena was needed, and owner Barry Shenkarow didn't have the funds.

No more was forthcoming from the province.

Community groups tried to raise enough money to pull it off, but that was whistling past the graveyard. In the summer of 1996, after one more year of trying to make it, the Jets were packed up and flown to Phoenix to become the Coyotes.

Deaths in the family.

At this writing, the remaining teams are still struggling to make ends meet, in all but Toronto. They are attempting to get tax breaks and financial help from the federal government. The days of three Canadian entries in the NHL may not be that far off.

> **Quote, Unquote**
>
> "I don't know if it's a storybook ending or not. But it's a hell of a way to write the final chapter."
>
> — Lanny McDonald wins the Stanley Cup in 1989 with Calgary, scoring in his last ever game.

Chapter 9 ➤ *The Great One, The Magnificent One, and the International Pastime (1981–Present)*

Bite Him, Blue! Bite That Bad Man!

If there was one man Don Cherry's famous dog Blue (and her successor, Blue Two), would have loved to bite, it was R. Alan Eagleson.

First, a little explanation of the dog's owner.

Donald S. Cherry moved from a long career as a minor league defenceman, to coaching the Boston Bruins and the old Colorado Rockies, to a new gig on Hockey Night in Canada's Coach's Corner.

There may not be a more recognizable face in the nation now. Though his views are decidedly right wing and xenophobic (he wouldn't even let Europeans play on his junior hockey team when it started in Mississauga in 1998), Cherry's between-period rhetoric, his made-for-media bombastic tone, and his nose for publicity, all made him a 1990s pop icon in Canada.

Love him or loathe him, Cherry's heart is 100 percent in the game of hockey.

Then, there was Alan Eagleson, international hockey Czar, head of the NHL players' union, agent for untold individual players, member of the Hockey Hall of Fame and Sports Hall of Fame.

And a crook.

Alan Eagleson was as powerful a man in hockey as there has ever been. He controlled the union that he had founded with an iron fist, trading off free agent rights for agreements for even more international hockey, which in turn meant more money for the pension fund and himself.

Things, as they usually do in these cases, began to unravel slowly. But with ex-players picking incessantly at the hanging thread, Eagleson was eventually laid out naked.

Here's how:

➤ In 1980, Bobby Orr, Eagleson's first client and the man for whom he had obtained a big first contract, fired the Eagle. It was later revealed Orr had retired with barely a dime in his pocket and that Eagleson had kept an offer from the Bruins from him to make sure he signed with Chicago.

➤ In November 1991, the FBI launched an investigation of Eagleson, looking for financial conflicts of interest and other matters. A month later, the Eagle quit as head of the players' association.

Know-it-alls

Q. Who was the first goalie to actually shoot and score a goal in the NHL?

A. Ron Hextall, 1987.

> **Part 2** ➤ Hockey: Our Game

Know-it-alls

Q. What team holds the record for most consecutive overtime playoff victories?

A. Montreal. Ten straight in 1993.

➤ March 1994 found a United States Grand Jury in Boston indicting the Eagle and issuing arrest warrants charging him with theft of union funds, and a year and a half later, some former players launched a law suit in Philadelphia.

➤ January 1998 and the trap was fully closed as Eagleson agreed to plead guilty in both Canada and the United States, pay a $1 million fine and serve 18 months (he served five) in a Canadian jail.

It was all over for Alan Eagleson. He resigned from the Hockey Hall of Fame, was kicked out of Canada's Sports Hall of Fame, and was broken as a public figure.

Goodbye to The Greatest One

As if to give the century a fitting end, Wayne Gretzky hung up his skates for the last time on April 18, 1999, after 21 seasons of pro hockey. His last year in New York was filled with injuries and self-doubt about his own abilities. He scored but 9 times and had 61 points.

Tired of the grind, and with a growing family (three children) and wife Janet, who had given up a promising acting career for him, Gretzky called a news conference for April 16 at New York's Madison Square Garden and told everyone that Sunday afternoon against Pittsburgh would be his last game.

The NHL announced it was retiring the number 99 permanently. In his last contest, that 99 was painted behind both nets — indicating Gretzky's "office," where he had set up so many goals in the past. The Hockey Hall of Fame decided to waive the waiting period for getting in, and would induct him on November 22, 1999.

"Of course I'm sad," said Gretzky to the press. "I've played hockey for 35 years, since I was three. I hate the fact I have to retire in a lot of ways."

But, as he said a number of times in the press conference, there came a realization that "I'm done."

A classy human being took a classy exit from a game he changed forever.

Other Stars of the Era

➤ Mark Messier, the son of a minor leaguer, signed with the Indianapolis Racers in the WHA at 17, quickly moving to the Cincinnati Stingers, and was drafted at 18 by the Edmonton Oilers. He was a key figure in the Oilers Stanley Cup run, winning his fifth there after Gretzky was traded to Los Angeles. A heart of fire hidden

Chapter 9 ➤ *The Great One, The Magnificent One, and the International Pastime (1981–Present)*

Listen Up!

L'affaire Lindros began when Eric was still with the Oshawa Generals of the Ontario Hockey League — a team he had chosen to play for, rather than accept the standing convention of being drafted. Even though they were warned ahead of time that Lindros would not sign with Quebec (both because of Quebec's French-only language laws, and the fact it was an NHL backwater as a bad team in a small market), the Nordiques took the big centre first overall in 1991. True to his word, Lindros wouldn't sign and became the most hated player in the province. After sitting out the season, Lindros found himself peddled to the Philadelphia Flyers in a huge nine-player deal that put him in the City of Brotherly Love. Ironically, many of the pieces sent from Philly to Quebec were used to build the Nordiques, and when they moved to Colorado, were a key part of the Avalanches' Stanley Cup win.

behind a scowling, dark visage, Messier scored over 600 times before the end of the century. In 1994, he helped the New York Rangers win their first cup since 1940.

➤ Raymond Bourque is a lifetime Boston Bruin, turning down a free agent opportunity to go elsewhere to stay with the club he loves. With Paul Coffey, he is one of the two highest scoring defencemen in NHL history. Steadily spectacular.

➤ Denis Potvin played 15 years in the NHL. A native of Ottawa, he was a member of the New York Islanders on their four-year run of Stanley Cups. A complete player, often compared to the great Doug Harvey, Potvin had 310 goals and 742 assists.

➤ Mike Bossy played with Potvin on the Islander teams. Out of Montreal, Bossy was one of the greatest pure scorers in the game, grabbing 60 or more goals five times and putting together nine straight 50-goal years. Retired at 32 after his back gave out. Softest hands in hockey history (meaning, he could handle the stick like no one else).

Quote, Unquote

"Sometimes you'd see him on the ice and you'd think his mind was at Newport Beach watching the waves come in."

— Sather on Mark Messier's first season.

Quote, Unquote

"Guts, pride and desire. We refused to be licked."

— Wayne Gretzky on Team Canada, 1987.

Canadian Stanley Cup Winners of the Era

- 1984 Edmonton Oilers
- 1985 Edmonton Oilers
- 1986 Montreal Canadiens
- 1987 Edmonton Oilers
- 1988 Edmonton Oilers
- 1989 Calgary Flames
- 1990 Edmonton Oilers
- 1993 Montreal Canadiens

- Paul Coffey is the other top scoring defender in league annals. Won four Stanleys with the Oilers. Played for Edmonton, Pittsburgh, Los Angeles, Detroit, Hartford, Philadelphia, Chicago, and Carolina. Superb on the offence, not so hot defensively.

- Patrick Roy. Born in Quebec City, Roy was the first in a long line of spectacular goaltenders to come out of the Quebec Major Junior League. Won three Vezina Trophies as top goaltender and three Stanley Cups. Has played for Montreal and Colorado.

- Mike Gartner's rise to the top ten of all-time scoring may have been the quietest ever. In his first 14 years, for four teams, his lowest goal total in that span was 33. Scored 613 goals overall. Considered one of the fastest skaters to strap on the blades.

- Eric Lindros was drafted by the Quebec Nordiques, but refused to report, sitting out the year instead and forcing Nords management to trade him to the Philadelphia Flyers. Scored 360 goals in his first six seasons, but over that time was unable to take the Flyers to a Stanley Cup.

The Least You Need to Know

- Wayne Gretzky became the greatest player ever.
- Mario Lemieux fought a bad back, became a superb player, and beat cancer.
- A falling dollar and aging arenas forced the Winnipeg and Quebec teams to move south.
- Don Cherry became a pop icon.
- Alan Eagleson was disgraced.
- Gretzky retired at the end of the 1999 season.

Chapter 10

The Dispossessed

In This Chapter

- ➤ Blacks in the NHL
- ➤ Grant Fuhr makes them forget
- ➤ Women get it together
- ➤ Manon Rheaume breaks the glass ceiling
- ➤ Us vs. Them

We've now spent five chapters talking about how men did this, and men did that. Mostly, it was white men who did these things, partly because there was not a large Canadian Black population, but also because the same racism that kept Blacks out of baseball existed, to a lesser degree, in the NHL. Women struggled to get their own hockey back on track in the post-war years, but get it back they did. By 1990, Canada hosted the first official world championship, and just eight years later, women were playing grudge matches in the Olympics. And then there was Manon Rheaume, who did something no one ever thought possible. In this chapter, we'll look at these issues.

Casting a Shadow on the Game

Hockey was actually played by the tiny Black population in Canada from before the turn of the century, especially in Ontario and down in Atlantic Canada. There was, as a matter of fact, a Coloured Hockey League that played in the Maritimes beginning in 1900, with teams in Africville, Dartmouth, Halifax, Truro, and Amherst. Unfortunately, one of the things the white crowds wanted was to see some clowning along with the hockey — it must have been hard to tap dance on skates.

In the early part of the century, Fred "Bud" Kelly played on Frank Selke's 118th Battalion hockey team in London, Ontario, which competed in the Ontario Hockey Association. Reportedly an excellent player, Kelly almost made it to the NHL Toronto St. Pats but didn't play well when scouted at a game in Toronto. Kelly faded into hockey history shortly afterwards.

George Barnes came along in Ontario after Kelly, and starred for Cayuga in the OHA during the 1920s. In the late 1930s, the St. Catharines Orioles, an all-Black club, played in the Niagara District League. It seemed semi-professional hockey in Canada was quite open to Black players.

The NHL was a different story.

Ignoring Jackie Robinson

Herb Carnegie was a superior player who came out of Toronto into junior hockey as the 1940s began. He caught the eye of Conn Smythe, the Leafs' owner, but Carnegie wasn't signed. It was said later that Smythe had said, "If only he wasn't black, I'd sign him right away." Whether that's true or not, and Smythe never said, it did fit into the general feeling among NHL owners.

Carnegie earned a place in the Quebec Senior League — home to some of the best hockey on the planet outside the big show — and he even won that loop's most valuable player award one year. Carnegie played with Jean Beliveau, among others, on the Quebec Aces, and earned a call to camp with the New York Rangers in 1947.

As writer William Humber points out, 1947 was the year Jackie Robinson broke baseball's colour barrier with the Brooklyn Dodgers, and the Rangers may have been jumping on the bandwagon.

New York wanted to send Carnegie to the minors, but money was good in Quebec, and Carnegie went back to the Aces, where he finished his career.

O'Willie!

On January 18, 1958, the NHL's colour barrier was finally broken by Willie O'Ree, who suited up with the Boston Bruins.

This was quite amazing for two reasons. One, the fact he made it. Two, the fact he made it in Boston, a city renowned for its racist attitudes, and home to the Red Sox, who were the last American League baseball team to sign a Black player.

O'Ree, out of Fredericton, New Brunswick, had superb speed, but was also cursed by an inability to finish — something hockey people call "stone hands." A graduate of the Kitchener Rangers junior team, he also made a stop with the Quebec Aces, but got the call to the big club where, in 45 games over two seasons, he had four goals.

After that second year, 1960–61, O'Ree found his way to the west coast and played for Los Angeles and San Diego in the WHL.

O'Ree always claimed that racism had nothing to do with his short stay in the NHL, but he also had to put up with a few nasty incidents on the ice and from the stands.

"I didn't face any of the real problems [Jackie] Robinson had," said O'Ree. He also said, however, "Somebody was always saying something about my colour. I felt it was my duty to stand up for myself."

If They Don't Want Him...

After Willie O'Ree, it was almost 20 years before another Black player made it to the NHL, and then it was two.

Mike Marson and Bill Riley both played for the Washington Capitals in their first few years in the NHL in the mid '70s, and performed steadily but not spectacularly. Marson appeared in 196 games and scored 24 times, while Riley had 31 goals in 139 games.

> **Quote, Unquote**
>
> "I wanted dearly to be just another hockey player, but I knew I couldn't."
>
> — Willie O'Ree, first Black to play in the NHL.

There still had not been an outstanding Black player, however.

That all changed when Sarnia, Ontario's Tony McKegney burst onto the scene in October of 1978. Ironically, McKegney had jumped from a superb junior career to the Birmingham Bulls in the spring of that year, but owner John Bassett, Jr. reneged on the deal when he received a few calls from local bigots, threatening to cancel season tickets. Bassett caved in (he later apologized), and the young forward went on to be the first pick in the NHL draft of the Buffalo Sabres.

> **Quote, Unquote**
>
> "I'd never run into anything like that in my life."
>
> — Tony McKegney, on being released by Birmingham (WHA) because he is Black.

Good choice.

McKegney played five years with the Sabres, in two of which he had 36 and 37 goals, then packed his bags and went to Quebec, Minnesota, New York Rangers, St. Louis, Detroit, back to Quebec, and then to Chicago for his last nine games. In 912 contests over 13 seasons, he had 320 goals with 319 assists, finding the net 40 times for St. Louis in 1987–88.

Filled with Sound and Fuhry

Tony McKegney was the first Black star in the NHL, but Grant Fuhr was the league's first Black superstar.

Fuhr grew up in Spruce Grove, Alberta, as the adopted son of white parents, and fit right into the hockey mad community. Dynamic, aggressive, assertive, and superbly talented, Fuhr's job was to hold the fort for the offence-crazy Edmonton Oilers during their long Stanley Cup dominance. With everyone up ice looking for goals, Fuhr and the occasional offensively confused defender were often the only ones back when the puck headed their way.

Fuhr could not have come to a better team, socially. The young Oilers were enormously close in the dressing room, and they stuck together on the ice as well. Fuhr played 10 seasons with Edmonton, winning a Vezina Trophy and five Stanley Cups.

After an injury-plagued year and a suspension for substance abuse, he went to Toronto, Buffalo, Los Angeles, and St. Louis. He was still playing at this writing.

By the turn of the century, there were still just two handfuls of Blacks in the NHL, but the number grows every year. Boston's Anson Carter, Edmonton's Mike Grier, Calgary goaltender Fred Brathwaite and forward Jarome Iginla, Vancouver's Donald Brashear, and the Rangers' Rumun Ndur were among those Blacks who joined Fuhr on active rosters.

We Got Puck!

It's not as though women stopped playing hockey in this country in the decades after the Second World War (it had been growing rapidly in the '20s and '30s), but organized opportunities, not to mention ice time, were difficult to find.

Growth began again in the 1970s, but it was the early 1980s when a veritable explosion took place.

The federal government began to kick in money and sponsors began to appear. 1982 saw the first women's national championship (playing for the Abby Hoffman Cup), held that year in Brantford, Ontario, and the Canadian Amateur Hockey Association got around to

Listen Up!

In 1990, at the first sanctioned Women's World Hockey Championships, held in Ottawa, Canada showed up in familiar jerseys — similar to the ones the men had worn for a number of years. Except, instead of red and white, they were pink and white. Writer Jane O'Hara called them "the wussiest uniforms you've ever seen. As a team colour, pink stinks." Brian McFarlane points out that "others disagreed" and that many thought the uniforms were pretty cool. Whatever, the city went pink nuts, as bars and restaurants featured pink specials, and ushers wore pink bow ties and carnations, and even the players put pink ribbons in their hair. The "wussy" faction eventually won out, and Canada switched back to red and white for future tournaments.

putting together a women's hockey council. The Ontario Women's Hockey Association and a woman named Fran Rider were front and centre in pushing a game that many young girls and older women began to turn to in increasing numbers.

Growth was steady, but needed a major kick to put the fire to the wick. That boost came along in 1987, courtesy of the first women's World Hockey Tournament. An "unofficial" world championship because the International Ice Hockey Federation wasn't ready to sanction a global tournament yet, the Toronto-based event drew two teams from Canada, plus Australia, China, Norway, the United Kingdom, and West Germany.

> **Know-it-alls**
>
> Q. Who captained Canada to the gold medal in the first official world championships, 1990?
>
> A. Sue Scherer.

Canada won, and, in fact, would win every world championship up to this writing.

By March 1990, the first sanctioned world tourney was held in Ottawa (Canada winning again), an event whose final drew 9,000 paying fans, and over a million in a national television audience.

That tournament was interesting for another reason. Canadian and U.S. women did not use body contact in their games, but the Europeans did. Sensing a chance to gain an advantage, the Euro teams pushed for checking in the first worlds, forgetting that many of those North American players had grown up playing with the boys. It only took a half-minute of play against the Canadian women for the Europeans to realize they had made a mistake.

No more checking.

Canada's Dawn McGuire earned MVP honours in the gold medal game.

The 1990 tournament provided a huge boost — the CAHA reported that registered women playing in Canada went up 75 percent in the following year. In Ontario, almost 9,000 women were signed up for 1990–91.

Word that women's hockey would be a medal sport in the Olympics for 1998 gave it even more of a push.

Canada's talented teams at the world level meant that young girls, and not a few boys, had new heroes to look up to. Cathy Phillips, Nancy Drolet, Danielle Goyette, Cassie Campbell, grizzled (can you say grizzled?) veteran France St. Louis, Angela James, Geraldine Heaney, and more became household names in a lot of hockey households.

One name, however, would stand above the rest and reach a fame that would take her to worldwide recognition.

Look Dad, There's a Girl in Goal

There have been only a handful of players in our history who are recognizable by first name, or nickname — Wayne, Gordie, Boom Boom, The Rocket, Mario — the list is not a long one.

Ask hockey fans to identify "Manon," and they will. Easy.

Manon Rheaume had already made enough history as a woman goaltender before the fall of 1992 to become fairly well known. She was the first woman to play in a major junior A game, battling through 17 minutes as an injury replacement for the Trois-Rivieres Draveurs, and six games for a Tier II (next level down) club in her home province of Quebec.

But after backstopping Canada to a gold medal at the world championships in the spring of 1992, Rheaume was invited to training camp with the Tampa Bay Lightning of the NHL, a team run by hockey legend Phil Esposito.

Okay, it was something of a publicity stunt. But the 20-year-old Rheaume decided to take the invitation seriously and trained faithfully throughout the summer, showing up for camp in the best shape of her life. Lightning coach Terry Crisp was so impressed, he sent Rheaume out for the first period of an exhibition game against the St. Louis Blues — making Manon the first woman to appear in any of the major sports.

Rheaume gave up two goals on nine shots and earned a professional contract with the Atlanta Knights of the International League. Shortly, she found herself in the East Coast Hockey League with Nashville and Knoxville, playing occasionally and appearing for the national women's team in world championships and major tournaments.

In the mid 1990s, there were three women goaltenders in pro hockey.

Rheaume's accomplishments, followed as they were by those of American Erin Whitten, helped stimulate another boom in women's hockey registration.

For Manon, it became a lucrative deal. Some reports had her making over $500,000 a year, most of it from endorsements, and keeping her wits about her at the same time.

Quote, Unquote

"They're actually going to pay me to play hockey. I can't believe it."

— Manon Rheaume signs her first men's pro contract.

Quote, Unquote

"I'm just so happy about our sport today that I'm almost bursting."

— Mickey Walker, pioneer women's player, speaking in 1993 at 75 years old.

Know-it-alls

Q. Who did Manon Rheaume face in her one period of NHL hockey?

A. St. Louis Blues.

Gail, Justine, and the Big Question

Let's go back and take this one step at a time:

Many (not all) men were against allowing girls to play with boys because they were worried about injuries, how to take care of dressing and toilet facilities, and simply because a few of them were chauvinist pigs.

Many (not all) women wanted girls to play with the boys because, hey, if they can, they should, and that's what liberation is all about.

Simple, right? Hardly.

The issue of whether girls should play with the boys came to a head in the late 1970s, and is still being argued about on both sides. Many men think girls should play with boys if they can, especially in the under-13 groupings where boys' physical stature hasn't yet started to show. Many women have been against girls playing with the boys because it would make women's hockey seem second rate.

These arguments were spurred along by two young girls and court battles that sprung up around their simple desire to play hockey wherever they wanted.

Back in 1977, an 11-year-old budding hockey player named Gail Cummings was told she couldn't tend the nets for a boys' team in Huntsville, Ontario — a community that didn't offer high-level hockey for girls.

That one wound up in front of an investigative commission, which found in her favour. Appeals were launched, and in 1978 the Ontario Supreme Court overturned the ruling, and nine months after that the Ontario Court of Appeal overturned that ruling.

Jump ahead to 1985 and Justine Blainey, a 12-year-old in Etobicoke, now part of Toronto. She appealed to the human rights commission in Ontario for the right to play on a boys' team if she were good enough, whether there was a strong girls' program or not.

After four years, hundreds of thousands of dollars in legal fees, and a visit to the Supreme Court of Canada, Blainey was allowed to play.

> **Listen Up!**
>
> Brian McFarlane offers proof that women aren't as "wussy" as some might think. In fact, some of them can be as downright insane as male players. In a 1988 summer league game in Windsor, a woman named Trudy Banwell, 24, and a nurse to boot, lost her head on the ice and tackled referee Angela James. Not done, Banwell than went after linesman Barbara Jeffrey, and that striped shirt wound up with a separated shoulder. Banwell was arrested, convicted on assault charges, got two years' probation with 200 hours of community service, and was kicked out of women's hockey for life.

"Allowing girls to leave girls' hockey simply because they want to only stigmatizes the female game as second-rate," said Fran Rider, head of women's hockey in Ontario.

"The best way to advance female hockey opportunities is through unified efforts to develop a parallel stream for girls and women of all ages."

As writer Brian McFarlane points out, there was a "tremendous irony" to all of this. When Blainey was playing for the University of Toronto women's team in 1993, school fathers decided to drop the program despite the fact it cost all of $11,000 to run. Blainey and her teammates went to war, and, with the help of Rider's OWHA, successfully forced the obviously over-testosteroned men to back off.

In most Canadian communities nowadays, girls can freely play on boys' teams up to the age of 13, and above that if they wish and are good enough.

The argument, however, continues.

A Touch of National Angst

How could it be? How could the "Star Spangled Banner" be playing in the arena at Nagano, instead of "O Canada"? How could that be the American flag being raised? How could those gold medals, those beautiful, 1998 Nagano Winter Olympic gold medals be around the necks of women wearing red, white, and blue, with USA emblazoned across the front?

Well, it could. And, it was.

Coach Shannon Miller, a Calgary police officer on a leave of absence to take Canada's first Olympic women's team to an expected gold, wound up without a job as critics opened fire, both barrels, on her coaching skills and especially her preparation for the big tournament.

Imagine that? The media caring enough about women's hockey that they turned lots of space and airtime over to discussions of Miller and her handling of the club? It was unprecedented.

Know-it-alls

Q. Who was the first woman named head coach of the women's national team?

A. Shannon Miller.

The Americans had been slowly catching up to our women over the previous few years, and when the U.S. played well in a 13-game exhibition series leading up to the Olympics (bad strategy for our side to play those, the critics said), they were ready to pull the upset.

It didn't help that long-time star Angela James, cut from the team before Nagano, questioned her relationship with Miller, in the press. Heck, the Canadian Hockey Association even held an investigation into whether Miller had had a sexual relationship with one of her players.

Chapter 10 ➤ *The Dispossessed*

She hadn't. But, can you imagine that happening in men's hockey?

By the time the Olympics rolled around, the Canadians were on edge, having lost a pre-Christmas tournament to the U.S. Losing 7-4 to the Americans in the round-robin portion at Nagano, despite having led 4-1 in the early going, didn't help.

Gold medal game time came and you never saw a more nervous, uptight bunch of players than Canada's. Concentrating on a physical game, the Americans led 2-1 late in the third, withstood a Canadian onslaught, and scored into the empty net to cement it.

It will probably turn out to be one of the best things that could have happened for the women's game, worldwide, as a whole. But what agony for Canada.

The Least You Need to Know

➤ Willie O'Ree was the first Black in the NHL, 1958.

➤ Blacks and other visible minority players are slowly making their way into the pros in greater numbers.

➤ Women's hockey began to grow quickly in the 1980s.

➤ Canada dominated women's hockey for most of the last 20 years.

➤ The United States upset Canada to win the gold medal in the first Olympic tournament for women, 1998.

Part 3
The Olympic Spirit: A New Kind of Drug

The modern Olympic movement was already six years old and had two summer games officially in the books before Canada joined the fraternity. And a fraternity it was, at first — no women were allowed. Before the Second World War, Canada was quite strong at the games, but afterwards our performances dropped in quality until government money and better programs began to pay dividends in the 1980s. In 1988, a Canadian nicknamed Big Ben would bring us to the pinnacle of excitement and drag us back down just as quickly. It would be an omen for what would overcome the entire Olympic movement. In this section, we'll spend four chapters looking at the summer games and two at our winter performances.

Chapter 11

Faster, Higher, Stronger (1900–1936)

In This Chapter

- Hey, that's our medal!
- Strong like Ox
- Kerr to Hodgson to Thomson to no one
- Chariots of tragic gunfire
- The women make their mark
- Hilda makes the co-ed final
- Other stars of the era

When Canada did finally jump into the Olympic movement, it was with both feet. Almost every games created a new Canadian hero in this era, especially when women were allowed to compete starting in 1928. In this chapter, we'll look at the early heroes and what happened when women first went for gold.

One Lonely Gold

If Canada had actually sent a team to the Paris Olympics in 1900, the resulting 72-year controversy over George Orton's gold medal would never have happened. But the nation had not jumped on the Olympic bandwagon for the first games in 1896 at Athens and missed it when it went by the second time four years later.

Part 3 ➤ *The Olympic Spirit: A New Kind of Drug*

George Orton didn't, however. The Toronto resident was already something of a middle-distance running star in the 1890s at the University of Toronto when he went off to the University of Pennsylvania for his graduate studies and added 15 U.S. championships. When the U.S. put together a team of college kids for Paris, Orton was chosen to go along, and he made the most of the chance, winning the 2,500 metre steeplechase and adding a bronze in the 400 metre hurdles.

Of course, Orton's medals were credited to the American team and it stayed that way for the next 72 years. According to writer Cleve Dheensaw, it was then that researchers such as David Wallechinsky began to list our George as the Canadian champion he truly was. The International Olympic Committee finally got on board, and those two medals are now on Canada's tab sheet.

Listen Up!

Writer Cleve Dheensaw uncovered one of the most fascinating teams ever to represent Canada at the games. In 1904, the Six Nations Reserve, near Brantford, Ontario, helped preserve the memory of where lacrosse actually had come from by sending an all-Mohawk team to St. Louis, where it joined two others (including another Canadian outfit) to fight over the three medals. The Mohawks finished a distant third, taking the bronze. Among the competitors were Snake Eater, Black Hawk, Black Eagle, Rain in Face, Almighty Voice, Flat Iron, and Spotted Tail, which at the time many thought a rather humorous lineup, but the Mohawks did themselves proud, white man's conceit aside.

Hero Etienne Keeps His Job

Off to St. Louis in 1904 went Canada's first official entry, to take part in what's considered the worst organized affair in Olympic history. Yes, worse than Atlanta. St. Louis really didn't want the games that much, but organizers of the World's Fair of 1904 were saddled with it when Chicago failed to come up with the money and they had to go somewhere. Talk about an afterthought.

Not that the Canadians were put off. Our boys (still only boys) came up with four gold, a silver, and a bronze, putting us sixth overall — though somewhat behind the Americans' 80 gold, 86 silver, and 72 bronze. Few European countries thought enough of the event to send anyone.

George Lyon won in golf (the last time it appeared as an Olympic sport), Winnipeg's Shamrocks won gold in field lacrosse, and Galt, Ontario, sent a club that won in soccer.

Then there was Etienne Desmarteau. Entered in the 56-pound weight throw, Desmarteau first had to get to St. Louis, which meant getting time off from the Montreal Police Department. Nyet, they said. You're not going. Desmarteau decided to go anyway, and the Montreal department promptly fired him.

Off went Etienne, and after tossing the big weight 10.46 metres and earning the gold, Desmarteau became a huge hero in the Montreal press, both French and English. Guess what? When Desmarteau came back home, his job had magically reappeared.

Power of the press, and all that.

Desmarteau only lived another year. He died of typhoid fever at the age of 32. Montreal named a park in his honour.

Canada Gets on a Run

Out of the 1908 games in London were mined a whopping 16 medals (including three gold) for Johnny Canuck and his teammates.

The lacrosse team won again, and Walter Ewing of Montreal took the trap shooting competition. Great achievements, but they didn't rise to the dramatic heights achieved by Hamilton's Bobby Kerr.

Kerr was born in Ireland and raised in the smoky environs of the steel city where he joined a fire brigade that prided itself on speedy members. He made it to the final in what was, and still is, the games' greatest attraction — the 100 metre sprint. Though Kerr had beaten Reggie Walker of South Africa in an earlier meeting, it was the latter that won the race, with the Canadian third in a near dead-heat that three judges called his way, but the chief referee saw in favour of American James Rector.

Apparently, this ref thought the judges were blind — an interesting twist on an old accusation.

Kerr went out that night and got "nicely drunk" and came back the next day to win the 200 metre gold. Amazing what a hangover can do.

Bobby went home a Canadian hero. He would captain the Canadian team in 1928 and was the track and field manager in 1932.

If Only It Wasn't for Jim

It's a shame hardly anyone remembers George Hodgson.

All he did at the 1912 Olympics in Stockholm was win two swimming gold medals and break three world records over the course of seven days. The then-19-year-old should have statues up in front of every pool in the nation.

Hodgson's problem, you see, was one of lousy timing. 1912 happened to be the games of Jim Thorpe, the native competitor from the States who won both the decathlon (10 events)

Quote, Unquote

"It's a coal-heaver's swing."

— Local St. Louis newspaper opinion on George Lyon's golf swing, 1904.

Quote, Unquote

"I went out last night and got nicely drunk, and danced until the early hours of this morning."

— Bobby Kerr's pre-race routine for his 200 metre sprint gold in 1908.

Part 3 ▸ *The Olympic Spirit: A New Kind of Drug*

and the pentathlon (five events) in an incredible performance that made him world famous, despite having the medals stripped by the IOC because he had taken a few dollars for playing baseball (they were returned to the family in 1982).

Back to George Hodgson.

Hodgson had been a pre-race favourite and seemed a good bet to come out of the 1,500 metre final in Stockholm with at least something. And he did. Touching the wall at a nice round 22 minutes, Canada's greatest swimmer of the era broke the world record and took the gold medal. And then kept going.

> **Quote, Unquote**
>
> "Won – George."
>
> — George Goulding's sparse message home to his wife after winning gold in the 10,000 metre walk in 1912.

As Cleve Dheensaw writes, "he told the judges before the final he wasn't going to stop at 1,500 metres, but would keep churning for a full mile." The accommodating officials kept their watches running and Hodgson shattered the world mark in the mile as well.

Self-coached, and obviously self-motivated, Hodgson shattered the 1,500 metre world standard by 48.4 seconds (a record that stood for 11 years), the mile mark by 26.9 seconds. And he added a second gold in 400 metre freestyle.

His was the only Canadian gold in the pool for 72 years.

As Canadian as Mom, Apple Pie, and a Massey Ferguson

How's this for confusing.

Earl Thomson had been born in Prince Albert, Saskatchewan, before being gathered up and moved to California when a young pup. Despite being an all-around American star by the time he grew up, Earl had forgotten to take out U.S. citizenship, so under track rules he had to compete for Canada in 1920 at Antwerp, where he won the gold in 100 metre hurdles.

> **Know-it-alls**
>
> Q. What year was the now-famous Olympic five-ring flag introduced?
>
> A. 1920, Antwerp.

Then there was boxer Bert Schneider. Different sport, different rules. Though he was born in Germany and grew up in Montreal, he was allowed to compete for Canada. Schneider pounded Alex Ireland of Britain, winning the gold in a fight that went one extra round because the judges couldn't make up their minds after three.

The other gold went to the ice hockey team, a subject we'll deal with in more detail in Chapter 13. These three gold would be the last for Canada until the 1928 Games (1924 in Paris produced just three silver and a bronze).

Chapter 11 ➤ *Faster, Higher, Stronger (1900–1936)*

From Triumph to Tragedy

Anyone who knew Percy Williams when he was growing up in Vancouver would have been shocked to learn that he would become one of Canada's greatest Olympians.

Here was a youngster who barely survived rheumatic fever as a child, a malady that damaged his heart, and who never weighed more than 125 pounds when fully grown.

That this young man went on to win both the 100 and 200 metre sprints at Amsterdam in 1928 is astonishing.

In the national Olympic trials, Williams ran the 100 metres in 10.6 seconds, which happened to be the Olympic mark set by Britain's Harold Abrahams in 1924, who also just happened to be one of the guys on whom the movie *Chariots of Fire* was based. Williams went to Amsterdam where he sailed through the heats, overcame a lousy start in the semis, and after two false starts by competitors in the final won that too, going away.

Our young man was the new Olympic star.

In the 200 metre final, Williams blasted out of the pack with 50 metres to go and beat an all-star field, becoming the first man to win the sprint double in 16 years.

Back Home, our Percy was a hero across the land — parties and receptions from coast to coast. Heck, he even got his own chocolate bar.

And if the story had ended there, it would have ended happily. But Williams was fated for worse. His career was ended by a bad injury. Though a successful businessman, he gradually became a recluse, never marrying, never allowing himself to be duly honoured in later life for his accomplishments.

In 1982, Percy Williams took a shotgun and killed himself.

Know-it-alls

Q. What was unusual about Canada's first Olympic ice hockey medal?

A. It was won in the 1920 Summer Games.

Quote, Unquote

"Unrated and unprepossessing...he looked as frail as a frightened fawn."

— Jim Kearney, *Vancouver Sun*, on Percy Williams.

Know-it-alls

Q. What did Percy Williams get from the city of Vancouver for his two golds in 1928?

A. A blue Graham-Paige sports car and $14,500 for his education.

101

Part 3 ➤ *The Olympic Spirit: A New Kind of Drug*

Ethel and the Jets

It was still over the protests of more than one Olympic committee member, but finally, in 1928, women were allowed to compete officially in the games. And it was a group of Canadian women, led by a beautiful 18-year-old from Saskatoon, who would make the first headlines.

Ethel Catherwood, called the Saskatoon Lily, waited until the very last day in Amsterdam to come up with a gold medal in the high jump. In true Canadian style, by the way, she kept warm between jumps by wrapping herself in a Hudson's Bay blanket.

Catherwood had her own hero's welcome in Saskatoon (called, inevitably, a "heroine's welcome"), receiving a nice piano (for those soft parlour nights), paid tuition to a business school (to learn secretarial skills), and $3,500, no doubt for elocution and cooking lessons. But Ethel's performance merely put the capper on a great Canadian showing from the "weaker sex."

Bobbie Rosenfeld, Ethel Smith, Florence Bell, and Myrtle Cook came out of Toronto with a vengeance, looking to take a medal in the 400 metre relay at the Amsterdam track. They went one better — breaking the world record. It was Rosenfeld to Smith to Bell to Cook, and the gold was in the bag.

A rotten judge's ruling stole a gold from Rosenfeld in the 100 metres, handing the "photo finish" (with no photo available to check) to American Elizabeth Robinson, with Ethel Smith third, but that aside, our women came up with a couple of gold, a silver, and a bronze in track and field, which was a notable start toward liberation. Canada would medal in the women's 400 metre relay in the next three Olympics.

Rosenfeld, who like Cook would become a pioneering woman sports writer, would eventually be voted women's athlete of the half century in 1950, and be among the first inducted to Canada's Sports Hall of Fame.

Listen Up!

When Canadian women joined their counterparts in the Olympics in 1928, it was not with total support. Baron Pierre de Coubertin, the Games' founder, was against it. The *Times* of London published a piece by a "learned" doctor who suggested that "Nature made women to bear children and she cannot rid herself of fat to the extent necessary for physical fitness demanded by feats of extreme endurance." Ooh, nasty. Even when the games were over, the men decided that anything longer than 800 metres was too long, and that remained the standard until 1960. Which, if you're counting, would be just about the time most of those old fools had passed away.

Quote, Unquote

"I'd rather gulp poison than try my hand at motion pictures."

— Ethel Catherwood, on rumours of a Hollywood contract.

Chapter 11 ➤ *Faster, Higher, Stronger (1900–1936)*

Gone Hollywood

"Only in L.A." might be a siren call of the modern era, but in at least one case it could also have been applied to Los Angeles in 1932, where the tenth Olympiad got under way on July 30. Canadians came home from Hollywood with 15 medals, of which 2 were gold.

It should have been three.

The women were quick again, especially Hilda Strike, who could really cook when she hit the track, using all 105 pounds of herself to best feminine advantage by blowing the doors off anyone who challenged her in the 100 metres.

Any woman, that is.

At L.A., the final came down to a battle between Strike and Stella Walsh, a Polish-American competing for her mother country as Stanislawa Walasiewicz.

The race was Strike's most of the way, but Walsh found extra strength at the end and nipped out the Canuck sweetheart at the wire for the gold. Both tied the world record of 11.9 seconds. Many pre-race observers had believed that only a man could beat Strike, she was that fast. And how right they were.

Fast forward to January 1981, when an aged Walsh was accidentally shot after stumbling into a robbery in progress in Cleveland. She died. An autopsy was called for, and the first thing the doctors found was that Stella Walsh had male sex organs. She was an anatomically complete man.

The con job that cost Hilda Strike a gold has never been recognized by the IOC, and the medal still belongs to Mr. Walsh.

Sex testing, by the way, only came into the Olympics in 1968.

Also big at Los Angeles was Horace "Lefty" Gwynne, who turned on a boxing-mad country by winning the bantamweight gold medal. He then turned pro.

Whacking Adolf with a Paddle

Canada's contribution to keeping Adolf Hitler away from an all-German glory was a sub-par nine medal performance at Berlin in 1936.

Canoe racing finally made it to the Olympics as a sport in this year, and Francis Amyot of Ottawa, who had already made a name for himself by saving three Ottawa Rough Riders football players

Know-it-alls

Q. What 1936 Canadian pole vaulter went on to an excellent hockey career?

A. Syl Apps.

103

> **Know-it-alls**
>
> Q. What 1936 Canadian hurdler eventually spent 20 years in the top ranks of the IOC?
>
> A. James Worrall.

from drowning in 1933, pulled off an amazing comeback victory in the 1,000 metres at Berlin to win the gold medal.

In the games of America's Black sprinter Jesse Owens, Canada's Dr. Phil Edwards, who had been born in the Caribbean before moving to this country, finished out an amazing three Olympic performance in which he won five bronze medals over 400–1,500 metre distances. It was, and still is, a record haul for a Canadian Olympian.

Many of the Canadian athletes were hoping for another chance at Olympic glory in 1940 at Tokyo.

Adolf Hitler had other plans.

Other Stars of the Era

- George Lyon of Toronto took up golf when he was 38. That didn't stop him from beating 74 other competitors, all Americans, to win the gold medal at the 1904 games. Lyon had a highly unorthodox style. "He wielded the club more like a cricket bat," writes David Wallechinsky. And he won anyway.

- George Goulding (by George, that was a popular name) of Toronto won gold in 1912 for Canada in the 10,000 metre walk, an event so closely judged for improper foot work that the athletes suffered far deeper tension and trauma than the pressure of the race itself would produce.

- Duncan McNaughton won a high jump gold in 1932 at Los Angeles, despite being so unknown that he had to talk his way onto the squad when it arrived in California. Heck, he'd never jumped anywhere near the world record, and at six feet, his winning jump was still more than two inches shy of that mark. But a win's a win.

Canadian Gold Medal Winners of the Era

1900

George Orton
.... 2,500 m Steeplechase

1904

Etienne Desmarteau
.... 56-pound Weight Throw

George Lyon
.... Golf
.... Field Lacrosse
.... Soccer

1908

Bobby Kerr
.... 200 m Sprint

Walter Ewing
.... Trap Shooting
.... Field Lacrosse

1912

George Hodgson
.... 400 m Freestyle Swim
.... 1,500 m Freestyle Swim

George Goulding
.... 10,000 m Walk

1920

Earl Thomson
.... 110 m Hurdles

Bert Schneider
.... Boxing
.... Ice Hockey

1924

None

1928

Percy Williams
.... 100 m Sprint
.... 200 m Sprint

Ethel Catherwood
.... High Jump

Bobbie Rosenfeld,
Ethel Smith,
Florence Bell,
Myrtle Cook
.... 400 m Sprint Relay

1932

Duncan McNaughton
.... High Jump

1936

Francis Amyot
.... 1,000 m Canadian Canoe

The Least You Need to Know

➤ Canada's first gold was won by George Orton, competing for the U.S. in 1900.

➤ Canada did not officially join the Olympic movement until 1904, and didn't send its first "official" team until 1908.

➤ Percy Williams was our greatest Olympian ever, sweeping the sprints in 1928.

➤ Canada's women dominated the track events in 1928.

➤ George Hodgson put in Canada's greatest swim performance of the era in 1912.

Chapter 12

Pure Amateurism (1948–1968)

In This Chapter

- Shaking off the war weariness
- Back to the podium in Helsinki
- Rowing together
- One lone man
- What happened to Elaine?
- Four-legged Olympic glory

In the nine games in which the country took part prior to the Second World War, Canadians won 74 medals. Over the next six after the fighting stopped, Canada would get just 22. Whether it was war weariness, too many good athletes and fathers of athletes left in graves on the world's battlefields, or a simple changing of the guard that saw the United States and the Soviet Union dominate proceedings, the sad fact is that the period from 1948 to 1968 would be mostly dismal for Canadian achievement. In this chapter we'll look at the few Canadian stars of the era, and the development of the Olympic Games from a festival of friendship to a political forum.

Part 3 ➤ *The Olympic Spirit: A New Kind of Drug*

Taking What You Can Get

The story of the 1948 London games, other than the fact they were being held at all, was a slim 30-year-old Dutch housewife named Fanny Blankers-Koen, who would eliminate any leftover doubts about women's talents by sweeping the 100 and 200 metre sprints, the 80 metre hurdles, and, with three teammates, the 400 metre relay.

Four gold medals. Which also happened to be four more than the entire Canadian team earned. There were few highlights.

Patricia Jones of New Westminster, B.C., ran a superb anchor leg in the 400 metre relay to help earn Canada a bronze, but the strong men's basketball team finished ninth despite winning six games. Doug Bennet took silver in the 1,000 metre Canadian Singles canoe race but another medal contender, Eddie Haddad, lost a controversial split decision in the quarterfinals of the lightweight boxing — a result that left the crowd stunned.

All in all, Canada wound up with just one silver and two bronze.

A dismal performance.

Know-it-alls

Q. Name the father-son team that boxed in 1952 (dad), and 1984 (son)?

A. Len and Dale Walters.

Second Class Citizens

"I have observed some athletes wearing the Maple Leaf who would have conferred a favour upon their native land if they had stayed home and gone for a walk with the family dog." So said Canadian writer and long-time Olympic watcher Henry Roxborough. Henry was right on.

Canada won but three medals in 1952, giving the country a whopping six in the two games since the war. Blame what or whom you will, but save a little discredit for the Canadian Olympic Association which was starting to get full of itself — a disease that inflicts most associations today. Among their highlights was telling Jack Burney he couldn't compete for the country in 400 metre hurdles, despite having one of the fastest times in the world, because he hadn't made it to Hamilton for the Olympic trials.

Mr. Burney had been serving in the U.S. Army in Germany at the time and would have been clamped in irons if he'd tried to leave.

Quote, Unquote

"Everybody likes the Canadians at Helsinki. Since we're not beating too many folks, there's no reason why they should be sore at us."

— Milt Dunnell, *Toronto Star*, on the 1952 games.

The country was shut out of track and field medals. Good call, Canadian Olympic Association.

It was left to a trap shooter, George Genereaux of Saskatoon, who learned his craft chasing prairie dogs around, to save face for Canada. The 1952 field was filled with men who just a few years before had been firing guns with their lives on the line, so this was a talented group. And Genereaux was still a teenager.

But Genereaux beat the field by just one clay pigeon and went on to become Canada's athlete of the year, beating out everyone including another Saskatchewan guy name of Gordie Howe (that's the hockey player).

> **Know-it-alls**
>
> Q. What bronze medal winner in 1956 went on to become a well-known diving commentator?
>
> A. Irene MacDonald.

Overall, a gold and two silver proved the point Milt Dunnell of the *Toronto Star* made at the time, that Canada could no longer expect to do well by simply preparing just in the few months prior to an Olympics.

It was a lesson that would take over 25 years to learn.

Row, Row, Row Your Damn Boat!

The 1956 games in Melbourne, Australia, were the first in which politics began to seriously rear its ugly head, but Frank Read wasn't the slightest bit interested. He was interested in one thing — medals — and if the Soviets and Hungarians were mad at each other, too bad.

Read was rich, capable, and driven, demanding everything out of the young men he brought together at the University of British Columbia in the early 1950s to form rowing teams for the 1956 Games.

Those crews, a coxed-eight and a four, worked 12 months a year, twice a day, pounding their way from the boathouse at Stanley Park up and down the waters of Coal Harbour, or up the 10 miles to the Second Narrows Bridge and back.

"If you weren't ready by 5 a.m., he used language like my mother and father never knew. We were scared of him," said team member Lorne Loomer.

But those 13 men also trusted him.

They trusted Read when he said he'd find the money to send everyone to Melbourne (the COA would only pop for the eight-man crew).

They trusted Read when he told the fours crew of Loomer, Don Arnold, Archie McKinnon, and Walter D'Hondt they could win the gold medal. Which they did.

Part 3 ➤ *The Olympic Spirit: A New Kind of Drug*

Listen Up!

Frank Read may have been the Canadian equivalent of Vince Lombardi. The man who coached the country's rowers to four Olympic medals pushed his athletes as hard as anyone has ever done it in this country, and did it with a vocabulary that would make a sailor blush. "I don't pretend to know all the answers," said Read. "But I do know that whatever your goal ... there must be self-discipline, determination and faith. And this sport of rowing does help develop those characteristics." Almost to a man, Read's rowers went on to successful careers after rowing.

Know-it-alls

Q. Why was Gerald Ouellette's perfect score of 600 in prone rifle shooting not a world record in 1956?

A. Because the officials had set the course a half-metre too short.

And they trusted Read when he told them they could do something no one else had done in seven straight Olympics — beat the Americans in the eights. Which they almost did.

In the greatest boat race in Olympic history, Read's eight of Phil Kueber, Richard McClure, Bob Wilson, Wayne Pretty, Bill McKerlich, David Helliwell, Douglas McDonald, Lawrence West, and cox'n Carlton Ogawa, matched the American crew stroke for stroke, losing by just half of a boat length.

Canada's other gold in Melbourne again came from a shooter. Gerry Ouellette of Windsor, Ontario, shared teammate Gilmour Boa's rifle for the small bore event's prone-position final, and coolly came up with a perfect round of 600 to take the gold. Boa won the bronze, making up for his medal miss of four years before.

With six medals from Melbourne, Canada looked forward to 1960 in Rome with optimism.

Silly us.

How Low Can You Go?

If not for Frank Read's UBC eights, the 1960 Games in Rome would have been a total loss for Canada.

One medal. One lousy medal. Thirty-third place. Behind the Ethiopians and the North Koreans. Tied with Ghana, Singapore, and Morocco.

Read came back to the Olympics with a new eight, put together from three members of the fours team of 1956, one from the eights, and four newcomers: Nelson Kuhn, Glen Mervyn, David Anderson, and John Lecky. Again, they came up against the U.S. in the final — a crew from the American Naval Academy. But it was the Germans who took a surprising gold, leading from start to finish, with Canada a close second and the Americans way back in fifth for their first defeat in 11 Olympics.

Bet that played well in the U.S. Navy that night.

And that was it.

Cleve Dheensaw tells a story that says it all for what was wrong in Canada. The rowers — world renowned as they were — had to go with tin cup in hand to B.C. Lions' football games in an attempt to raise enough money to get to Rome.

Humiliating, embarrassing, unnecessary.

It was time for the government to step in with some funding, and for the COA to stop arguing over petty things like which part of the country had more athletes at the games than the other.

Canada's Olympic movement was a total mess. Among the athletes there seemed little hope. Except for one, lonely man...

> **Quote, Unquote**
>
> "The athletes were just pawns in a political chess match."
>
> — Swimmer Bob Wheaton, Rome 1960, on politics in the Canadian Olympic Association.

Not Too Wild About Harry

For those who followed sports in the early 1960s, the name Harry Jerome conjures up images of grace, speed, and dignity. Unfortunately, there are still a few who remember Harry Jerome as a quitter. It was a gross injustice that may have been racially motivated.

Jerome was one of the first Black major athletic figures in this country's history. And he was forced to carry the extra racial baggage that went along with it, while he was trying to rise to the top of the sprinting world.

In 1960 at Rome, the Vancouver resident had gone to the games with a share of the world record at 100 metres of 10.0 seconds. Germany's Armin Hary was the co-holder.

Jerome was expected to win at least a medal and to challenge for the gold, thus becoming the first Canadian man to win the games' most high-profile event since fellow Vancouverite Percy Williams in 1928. In the semi-finals, Jerome was out ahead of the pack when he pulled a hamstring and had to drop out.

Never great with the media, Jerome brushed past them to the dressing room, and it was only an hour later that track officials came out and explained the injury.

Too late. Many had already reported back to Canada that Harry had pulled out for unknown reasons, suggesting he had simply quit. While leading.

Right.

Suffering a major injury in the final of the Commonwealth Games in 1962 didn't help matters either. After all, he should have been able to run right through a completely torn left thigh muscle, shouldn't he?

Fast-forward to Tokyo, where Canada would bounce back from the Rome debacle to win four medals, including one gold (okay, it was a small bounce).

Part 3 ➤ *The Olympic Spirit: A New Kind of Drug*

No one carried as much internal pressure as Jerome, not even distance runner Bill Crothers, a superb athlete who would lose to the greatest distance man of all time — New Zealand's Peter Snell — in the 800 metre final. That was a race in which Crothers set a Canadian record that wouldn't be broken for 29 years.

The Comeback Kid

Crothers hadn't been expected to beat Snell. The Canadian media, and the country itself, was expecting even less from Harry Jerome, whose thigh injury had been so bad the doctor had been able to insert his entire fist into the tear.

Jerome persevered, as he had through his whole difficult life that led his family from Saskatchewan to an all-white neighbourhood in Vancouver.

Making the Tokyo final, Jerome was matched with American Bob Hayes, who had 48 consecutive wins under his belt. Hayes would win the race, while Jerome and Enrique Figuerola of Cuba needed a photo finish to decide silver and bronze, with the nod going to the Cuban.

In 1982, Jerome suffered a brain aneurysm while driving across the Lions Gate Bridge and died in the ambulance on the way to the hospital. He was 42. It was exactly one week since Percy Williams had killed himself.

Listen Up!

Middle distance runners Bill Crothers and Bruce Kidd were two of the most famous Canadian athletes of the 1960s, though neither won Olympic gold. Kidd set a school boy world record in 1961 in a two mile indoor race at Boston when he was only 17, and just a year later won gold in the six mile at the British Empire Games in Australia. Kidd's East York Track Club teammate, under coach Fred Foote, was Crothers, who at one time held all national records from the 440 yards to 1,500 metres. He silvered in the 1964 Olympics, and one year later beat gold medallist Peter Snell in a famous match race at Toronto's Varsity Stadium.

Roger and George Who?

There was so much going on at the track that the entire Canadian press contingent decided to give the rowing finals a pass. Which turned out to be the worst call in the history of Canadian journalism as Roger Jackson and George Hungerford picked that day to win the country's only gold medal for 1964 in a complete media blackout.

Jackson and Hungerford (who had just gotten over a bout of mononucleosis) were coached by Frank Read and put in the coxless pairs to keep them in shape as backups for the eights. Neither had actually been in a pair shell before, and they were still working out how to steer it when they arrived in Tokyo.

But they hung on in the final to beat the strong Dutch team and win the gold.

Media note: When all those Canadian press types heard about the gold medal, they flocked to the athletes' village to get quotes from Hungerford and Jackson. They never got them — the two had gone for a long walk.

Mighty Mouse

If anyone truly understood what Harry Jerome went through in the early 1960s, it would be a high school girl from Vancouver named Elaine Tanner.

She had blasted out of nowhere, all 5 feet, 2 inches of her (hence the name Mighty Mouse) in 1966, by winning in the pool four gold and three silver while shattering two world records at the Commonwealth Games. Against the Americans at the Pan American Games one year later she was equally as dominant.

So, a country that virtually ignored its own amateur athletes, which shed nary a tear at stories of how they had to scrimp for every penny and often pay their own way to meets because the government wouldn't support them, suddenly decided it would climb on a 17-year-old's back and ride her to national glory at Mexico City.

Hypocrites, all of us. The media just egged everyone on, of course. This was for Canada. This was for national pride. People will be devastated if you don't come home with gold.

Tanner should have stuck her tongue out and told everyone to go take a jump off the Capilano suspension bridge.

Mighty Mouse went to Mexico City and turned in the best performance by a Canadian swimmer since George Hodgson in 1912, getting out-touched at the wall in 100 metre backstroke by American Kaye Hall, who never had, and never would again, swim that fast, and finishing just up the pool from Pokey Watson, another American, in the 200 m back.

Two silver. Add a bronze in the women's 400 metre relay, and you have three of just five medals Canadians would win that October (one of the two left came from fellow swimmer Ralph Hutton).

And the country, which wouldn't forgive her, ruined the next 20 years of her life. Tanner couldn't go anywhere without being reminded of what she had done, or rather, not done.

Et tu, Canada.

Quote, Unquote

"My God, this is the Olympics, and we won."

— Roger Jackson, gold medallist, 1964.

Know-it-alls

Q. What year was "O Canada" played for the first time at an Olympics?

A. 1964 in Tokyo.

Quote, Unquote

"I know what a fine line it is to make it or not."

— Elaine Tanner, reminiscing on 1968.

Part 3 ➤ *The Olympic Spirit: A New Kind of Drug*

Know-it-alls

Q. What was the name of musician Terry Jacks' Olympic swimming brother?

A. Ron Jacks, 1968.

Canadian Gold Medal Winners of the Era

1952

George Genereaux
.... Trap Shooting

1956

Gerry Ouellette
.... Small-bore rifle (Prone)

Lorne Loomer,
Don Arnold,
Archie McKinnon,
Walter D'Hondt
.... Rowing Fours

1964

George Hungerford,
Roger Jackson
.... Rowing Pairs

1968

Equestrian Team Trial
(Jim Elder on The Immigrant,
Jim Day on Canadian Club,
Tom Gayford on Big Dee)

Other Stars of the Era

➤ Jim Elder on The Immigrant, Jim Day on Canadian Club, and Tom Gayford on Big Dee came from third place to pull off a big upset and win the gold medal in team equestrian show jumping at the 1968 games. The three were the oldest athletes on the team, and they won the only Canadian gold in Mexico City.

➤ Gilmour Boa of Toronto shot an astonishing 399 of a possible 400 points in the 1952 small-bore rifle competition. Unfortunately, two others went perfect and two others tied him for third (it was the strongest shooting field in Olympic history). He earned a bronze four years later.

➤ George Gratton of Montreal almost turned the gold trick in the 1952 middleweight lifting competition, losing to three-time medallist Peter George of the U.S. Just after the Olympics, Gratton was killed in a car accident.

The Least You Need to Know

➤ Canada struggled for medals in the post-war years.

➤ Elaine Tanner turned in one of the greatest individual performances in Canadian Olympic history.

➤ Harry Jerome rose above racism and injuries to achieve stardom.

➤ Canada was a world power in rowing in the 1950s, thanks to Frank Read.

➤ Canada's only gold in 1968 was won by three horses.

Chapter 13

State-Sponsored T & S (1972–1984)

In This Chapter

- ➤ Misery in Munich
- ➤ Montreal hosts the games
- ➤ Joy in the rain
- ➤ The biggest rip-off in Olympic history
- ➤ Forgotten heroes
- ➤ Conquering the west

The era Baby Boomers remember best is now best remembered for the 1972 Munich massacre, where 11 Israeli athletes were murdered by Palestinian terrorists and the games went on anyway — a slight economic miscalculation, a political mess, and a drug-induced East German Olympic machine. Economics aside, state-sponsored terrorism and steroids were now in vogue. It was the most depressing, disheartening era of Olympic history. That Canadians were able to mine 60 medals in this period is nothing short of amazing. With governments finally kicking in to help Canada's athletes make something of themselves, the results began to show. In this chapter, we'll look at this dark period, and speculate not on what might have been, but on what should have been.

Part 3 ➤ *The Olympic Spirit: A New Kind of Drug*

Know-it-alls

Q. How many of Canada's five medals in 1972 did the swim team earn?

A. Four.

Quote, Unquote

"For me, competing in the Olympics now seemed at the very least incongruous, perhaps tasteless, and certainly irrelevant."

— Debbie Brill, Canadian high jumper, on the aftermath of the Munich massacre, when that games went on.

In the Shadow of Greatness

Finally, something we were really good at.

Canadians, who had shown signs in 1968 that they would be a swim power to be reckoned with, exploded onto the scene in the 1970s, taking their place among the top nations of the world.

First off the blocks was Bruce Robertson, a tough-as-nails Vancouverite who was the best swimmer in Munich. Well, the best from this solar system.

Representing the rest of the Universe was one Mark Spitz, disguised in an American stars and stripes Speedo bathing suit, but obviously from somewhere out past Alpha Centuri. Spitz, who was Jewish (and that would become truly significant before the games were over), would win seven (!) gold medals during the swimming competition, making it kind of hard for anyone else to push into the spotlight.

Including Mr. Robertson, who won the all-human event going on behind Spitz by beating East Germany's Roland Matthes for the silver in the 200 metre butterfly, and adding a bronze as a member of the 400 metre medley relay team.

Leslie Cliff, also of Vancouver, won the silver in the 400 metre individual medley (butterfly, backstroke, breaststroke, and freestyle), while Donna Marie Gurr of Vancouver took bronze in 200 metre backstroke.

Canada won just five medals in 1972, and four of them were in the pool. The other came in soling class yachting.

From Hero to Bum in 1.5 Billion Easy Steps

Jean Drapeau was responsible for one of the most famous quotations in Canadian sports history: "The Montreal Olympics can no more have a deficit than a man can have a baby," quoth the mayor of the city that would host the first Olympic Games ever held on Canadian soil.

Poor, deluded soul.

Drapeau, who had tried for the 1972 games and missed, made sure Montreal got the 1976 version and wound up sending the people of Quebec down an economic slope that took them years to get off of.

Voodoo Economics would be coined in an American election some years later, but it could have been created for the Montreal mayor who figured about $124 million for the games. His advisors thought $310 million. The cost, after construction overruns, delays, some fancy footwork on overtime by a few unions, and Drapeau's incredibly inept management, was $1.5 billion.

And, the main stadium itself, forever after called derisively "The Big Owe," wasn't even completely finished in time. The Quebec government had to take the Olympic project over before things got so far out of hand they'd wind up with a provincial debt that could scare the United States.

Amazingly, the games themselves went off quite smoothly, even if they were held behind high fences, guarded by huge numbers of heavily armed troops and police, partially overshadowed by a political controversy over whether Taiwan could compete as the Republic of China with the Chinese flag (over objections by the Canadian government of Pierre Trudeau), and boycotted by 30 African countries because New Zealand had sent a rugby team to banned South Africa and the IOC wouldn't throw the Kiwis out.

> **Listen Up!**
>
> Canada didn't want Taiwan at the Montreal Games in 1976, but trading with the erstwhile Republic of China was another thing. From *Sports Illustrated*, 1976: "On the underside of the tongue of many of Hanover's Ponies (Pony athletic shoes made in Germany), is a label that reads, 'Official Shoe of the Canadian Olympic Team.' The inside heal is stamped, 'Made in Taiwan.'"

> **Know-it-alls**
>
> Q. How many years did it take Montreal to pay off its debt from the Olympics?
>
> A. 18 years.

A Crown Stolen and Never Returned

Gymnast Nadia Comaneci of Romania was the story of the Montreal Games, winning five medals, including three gold.

It could have easily been Nancy Garapick, star of the incredibly talented Canadian women's swim team that won seven medals, a silver and six bronze, in the garish pool at the main Olympic site.

If not for the state-sponsored steroid program initiated by the East Germans to prove that Communism, especially East German Communism, was a superior system to that of the West, Garapick would have been a double gold medal winner, and would have gone down in history as one of our greatest Olympic champions. In fact, without the tanked-up East Germans, the women would have won 11 medals, including a gold for Cheryl Gibson, five silver and three bronze.

Part 3 ➤ *The Olympic Spirit: A New Kind of Drug*

> **Quote, Unquote**
>
> "We could not conceive of the scale of the cheating. Sports just had not been like that."
>
> — Nick Thierry, editor of *Swim Magazine*, on East German steroid use.

Most observers were certain in 1973 when the East German women exploded onto the scene at the world championships that the whole team was on steroids, but they couldn't prove it. The worlds didn't have drug testing at the time, and the pitifully inadequate testing at Montreal was easy to get around.

But how obvious did it need to be? Led by Kornelia Ender, who was possibly the most muscled 17-year-old to walk the face of the Earth, the East German women were huge compared to swimmers from other countries.

It was only in 1991, after the Berlin Wall fell, that former East German officials admitted what they had done. The medals, including Ender's (she blames "medical men" and refuses to part with her ill-gotten gains), have never been returned. And the IOC, not surprisingly, has turned a blind eye to the issue, claiming that they couldn't overturn the results because who knew who was actually on steroids anyway, and they can't very well rerun the races now, can they?

> **Quote, Unquote**
>
> "It's one of those moments that stays galvanized in the mind for the rest of your life."
>
> — Graham Smith on his silver and sister Becky's two bronzes in 1976 at Montreal.

The East Germans won 9 of the 11 gold medals available in the women's events.

But the real stars were Nancy Garapick and her teammates. And considering the embarrassment Canada went through as a nation for being the only host country not to win a gold, someone owes those young athletes an apology.

Take That, Dwight Stones

American Dwight Stones was a tremendous high jumping talent who also had the knack for opening his mouth wide and shoving one of his spiked shoes deeply inside it. The world record holder came into Montreal as the prohibitive favourite, and proceeded to alienate Quebeckers by accusing organizers of being rude for not finishing the stadium — meaning the roof — completely forgetting that Olympic rules would have required the roof be open for all events anyway.

It didn't take long for the virulent Quebec media to twist that around to an attack on all the people of the province (especially the French).

Okay, so the bad guy has been identified. Now for the good guy.

Out of the late afternoon mists came this skinny fella anyone outside of the track world would have been hard pressed to identify. He was Greg Joy. Stones, knowing the steady rain falling on event day meant he was toast, went out at 2.21 metres, picked up his kit and stormed off, leaving Joy and Poland's Jacek Wszola.

The Canadian and the Pole both cleared 2.23 metres and the crowd went nuts. But Wszola cleared 2.25 metres and Joy couldn't match. It didn't seem to matter, because the crowd at the stadium, which had watched pre-Olympic hopes Debbie Brill (high jump) and Bruce Simpson (pole vault) bomb out, finally had a hero.

A few notes:

Joy would go on to run a food bank in Ottawa by the 1990s.

Wszola would go on to finish second in the boycotted Olympics of 1980.

And Stones? He went to Philadelphia and broke his own world record four days later.

Meet Graham Smith

Graham Smith had a dream for 1980. But because of political considerations, because of the last real battle of the Cold War, because some idiot in the Kremlin decided invading Afghanistan on December 28, 1979 would be a fine idea (Vietnam? What happened in Vietnam?), Smith's dream, and that of thousands of other athletes, was killed.

American President Jimmy Carter and his advisors had three choices: cut off trade (too expensive), or diplomatic relations (out of the question), or the easy way out, threaten to boycott the Moscow games if the Soviets didn't get out of Afghanistan.

To make a long, dreary story short, most governments around the west went along with it, including Canada, and Moscow was given a pass. And that left Graham Smith, a shoo-in for at least two medals and possibly many more, up the pool without a swimsuit.

Lots of other athletes were caught as well. There was gymnast Philip Delesalle, who missed the chance to show he was Canada's best in the gym ever. There was the men's basketball team, under coach Jack Donohue, which could have shocked the world. And many others.

But Smith was special. Of eight family members, seven represented Canada internationally in swimming. Graham, the youngest, was also considered the best. A definite gold possibility. Didn't happen.

Thanks a lot, Jimmy.

Quote, Unquote

"You always grow up thinking politics and sport don't mix. But they do. And it's not a great mixture."

— Jay Triano, now national men's basketball coach, on missing the 1980 Olympics.

Part 3 ▶ *The Olympic Spirit: A New Kind of Drug*

Quote, Unquote

"This is like a dream."

— France Gareau, 17, wins a silver medal in the 400 metre track relay in 1984.

Know-it-alls

Q. Who won a weightlifting medal in 1984, Canada's first in 32 years?

A. Jacques Demers (not the hockey coach).

Spirit of the West

Off to Los Angeles everyone went in 1984, minus the Soviets, East Germans, and their allies (which was hardly unexpected, given that the Americans had organized the Moscow boycott), for the first Nike/Adidas/Coke/Pepsi/McDonald's/Burger King/IBM/Apple/Conceptrol/ Frank's Dry Cleaners Summer Olympics.

Okay, the successful attempt by games chair Peter Ueberroth to make the event turn a profit and not cost taxpayers a dime may have led to an excessive amount of commercialism, but given what happened in Montreal, Canadians were hardly in a position to whine and complain. At least these games were paid for.

Many have written that Canada's outstanding effort at the 1984 Games was artificial, because the Soviets and their satellite countries refused to attend. If you take a look at the world rankings of the time, Canada was in a position to win upwards of 30 medals, communists or no communists.

As it was, Canadian athletes came up with 44. So even with the Eastern Bloc nations, Los Angeles would have been the country's biggest games.

Swimming golds went to Alex Baumann (twice), Victor Davis, and Anne Ottenbrite. Shooter Linda Thom (there's that Canadian marksmanship again) won in pistol. Diver Sylvie Bernier picked up a gold. Lori Fung, in the new sport of rhythmic gymnastics, returned to Vancouver with the big prize. And on the water, canoeist Larry Cain, and kayak pairs crew Hugh Fraser and Alwyn Morris also turned the trick, as did the men's rowing eights.

Victor, to the End

"If there was ever a role model for living with passion, for living life to its fullest, it was Victor. He was rebellious, rough and seemingly undisciplined. He had a wild energy that nobody seemed able to control."

— Olympic champion swimmer Mark Tewksbury, writing on Victor Davis.

When Victor Davis was growing up in Guelph, Ontario, it became obvious to his father, Mel, that the youngster needed something that would corral his energy and hard-driving nature. Dad enrolled him in swimming.

Chapter 13 ▸ *State-Sponsored T & S (1972–1984)*

In 1982, Davis won the 200 metre breaststroke at the worlds, setting himself up as a favourite for a medal in 1984. He had also established a reputation as a bit of a hothead — tossing chairs at the Commonwealth Games in 1982 in front of Queen Elizabeth II having gone a long way towards confirming that.

In L.A., Davis won a silver in the 100 metre breaststroke, and another in the 400 metre medley relay (with Mike West, Tom Ponting, and Sandy Goss). His gold, however, was back in that 200 metre breaststroke, a race in which Davis shattered his own world record.

Davis was aging (by swimming standards) in 1988 at Seoul, and he was unable to pick up an individual medal despite a close finish for bronze in the 100 metre breaststroke. There was a silver, however, in the medley relay with Tewksbury, Ponting, and Goss, which he told the press was the most satisfying result of his career.

Victor Davis retired from swimming. One year later, in November of 1989, Davis got into an argument in a Montreal bar that wound up on the sidewalk. Somehow in the scuffle, Davis was hit by a car driven by one of the young men with whom he was arguing.

Know-it-alls

Q. Who was the first Native Canadian to win an Olympic gold medal?

A. Alwyn Morris, a Mohawk from Kahnawake, near Montreal, in the 1984 kayak pairs with Hugh Fraser.

Know-it-alls

Q. How many rowing medals did Canada win in 1984?

A. Six.

Listen Up!

Alex Baumann's family was out of Czechoslovakia in 1968 visiting New Zealand on a work project when the Soviets rolled into Prague and took over. They never went back, going to Canada instead. Baumann was so proud to be a Canadian that when he made the national team for the first time, he had a red maple leaf tattooed over his left breast. He went on to win two swim golds in 1984 for his country. That maple leaf tattoo has become traditional for all Olympic team swimmers. Easy to pick out a former Olympian at your local health club.

121

Part 3 ▸ *The Olympic Spirit: A New Kind of Drug*

> ### Quote, Unquote
> "The term 'accident prone' was meant for people like Anne Ottenbrite."
>
> — Writer David Wallechinsky.

> ### Quote, Unquote
> "I think Canadians feel good enough about being Canadians today that they will think the investment is worthwhile."
>
> — Abby Hoffman, Sport Canada director, after 1984 Games.

> ### Quote, Unquote
> "I hope a lot of forty-year-old housewives will see what I've done and decide to try something themselves."
>
> — Linda Thom, gold medal pistol shooter, 1984.

An investigation eventually exonerated the driver, but after lingering in a coma for a few days, Davis died on November 13, 1989.

There are two stories on Victor's ashes. One has them scattered at sea, along with a quart of water from lane four of the USC pool where he had won his gold medal. The other has his ashes secretly scattered in the pool itself, with the former story invented as a cover. No matter.

"He hadn't lived life as if he was waiting for it to happen," wrote Tewksbury. "He attacked it, lived every day as if it was the most important."

Anne and Alex

Without the drugged East Germans, Canada was finally able to win a gold medal in women's swimming when Anne Ottenbrite of Whitby, Ontario — a walking advertisement for medical insurance (gashed arm, dislocated kneecap, whiplash from a car accident, strained thigh muscle playing a video game) — brought home the bacon in the 200 metre breaststroke. She wasn't finished, adding a silver in 100 metre breaststroke despite being miles behind at the halfway mark.

Alex Baumann came out of Sudbury to take the swim world by storm, heading to Los Angeles as the favourite for the 400 metre individual medley. He won it. Then there was the 200 medley. He won that. Two world records (beating marks he held himself).

The memory of George Hodgson had been honoured.

Other Stars of the Era

▸ Linda Thom was a normal housewife in every way, except that she was a crack shot in her recreation time. Thom won a shootout with American Ruby Fox to win the 1984 gold medal in pistol.

▸ Dean Crawford, Pat Turner, Paul Steele, Kevin Neufeld, Grant Main, Mark and Mike Evans, Blair Horne, and cox'n Brian McMahon won the 1984 gold in rowing eights. Without the East Germans

Chapter 13 ➤ State-Sponsored T & S (1972–1984)

it was said the gold was tainted, but the same crew had blitzed that team in the prestigious Lucerne Regatta just before the games, proving they were worthy of the Olympic gold.

➤ John Wood was one of the world's top canoeists when he went to Montreal in 1976. After a tough, tight competition, he thrilled the home crowd by coming home with a silver in the 500 metre Canadian singles.

➤ Michel Valliancourt continued a strong tradition in equestran events in 1976 by mounting Branch Country and taking silver in the show jumping competition.

Canadian Gold Medal Winners of the Era

1972–76
None

1980
Did not compete

1984
Alex Baumann .... 200 metre individual medley
.... 400 metre individual medley
Victor Davis.............. 200 metre breaststroke
Anne Ottenbrite ...... 200 metre breaststroke
Linda Thom .... Pistol
Sylvie Bernier........... Diving
Lori Fung .... Rhythmic Gymnastics
Larry Cain................ 500 metre C-1 canoeing
Hugh Fraser and
Alwyn Morris .... 1,000 metre Kayak Pairs
Pat Turner,
Paul Steele,
Dean Crawford,
Kevin Neufeld,
Grant Main,
Mark Evans,
Mike Evans,
Blair Horne,
Brian McMahon
(cox) .... Rowing Eights

The Least You Need to Know

➤ Canadian swimmers came to the forefront in this period.

➤ Nancy Garapick was denied stardom by doped-up East German swimmers.

➤ Montreal hosted the 1976 games, which were a financial travesty, but an artistic success.

➤ Canadian athletes were denied a chance in 1980 when western nations boycotted Moscow.

➤ Los Angeles produced Canada's greatest medal haul.

Chapter 14

Back from the Depths of Despair (1988–1996)

In This Chapter

- ➤ Ben Johnson
- ➤ The Dubin Inquiry
- ➤ Sylvie gets jobbed
- ➤ Recovery on the track
- ➤ Donovan burns Atlanta
- ➤ Other stars of the era

It wasn't so much a defining moment, as it was a deciding moment. Ben Johnson took a hypocritical Canada to the height of chest-thumping pride (sort of like Celine Dion doing the theme from Titanic) and then to the depths of finger-pointing despair in the space of just 24 hours, one day in 1988. The country asked itself What Price Glory? Would we play the dirty game everyone else was in order to win tarnished medals? Or would we play it clean and take our chances? The 1992 games in Barcelona confirmed the ultimate decision, but it was 1996 in Atlanta that proved it correct. In this chapter, we'll look at Ben Johnson's case, the inquiry that followed, and the way the country dug itself out of a hole and restored itself to its rightful place: among the best of the middle packers.

Part 3 ▶ *The Olympic Spirit: A New Kind of Drug*

Ben Johnson, Canadian

In the aftermath of the scandal that swept Seoul in 1988, after Ben Johnson had tested positive for steroids following his crushing victory over the hated Carl Lewis in the 100 metre final, the sprinter's identity as a Canadian suddenly changed.

He was no longer one of us. He was "the Jamaican-born sprinter." He was "Jamaican-Canadian Ben Johnson."

How typically Canadian of us. No excuses for breaking the rules, but Ben Johnson was the culmination of years of Canadian frustration over perceived Olympic failures. The standard bearer for fighting back against the forces of sporting evil, which we believed included the holier-than-thou, but dirtier-than-you-could-imagine Americans. The man who would avenge the dirty tricks of the drugged-up communists who stole medals from our girls and boys.

He was our entry to the world stage. He was the salve to our insecure, easily wounded pride.

He was ours.

It was coach Charlie Francis who took the painfully shy, teenaged Johnson (whose family came to Canada when he was 14) and turned his excellent talent into something more — the fastest man ever. In 1981, Francis believed that most of the world's top sprinters were on muscle building anabolic steroids, and he was hardly alone.

Rather than play it clean anyway, Francis put Johnson and a number of his other sprinters, including Angela Issajenko, on a steroid program that, by Seoul in 1988, had seen Johnson go from a bronze at Los Angeles to the world record holder (9.83 in 1987) and thus to a major international star.

Even better, Johnson was beating the hated Carl Lewis, whom Canadians perceived as arrogant — the true ugly American.

Heading for the Olympics, Johnson injured a hamstring in February that just wasn't healing properly, so his doctor, Jamie Astaphan, gave him a shot of steroids to help with the muscle recovery. It was too close to Seoul. The drug wouldn't flush out of his system fast enough.

Know-it-alls

Q. What Canadian men's gymnast tore knee ligaments during the 1988 Games but kept going?

A. Phillippe Chartrand.

Know-it-alls

Q. What Canadian women's gymnast broke her ankle during the 1988 Games but kept going?

A. Lori Strong.

9.79

The simple facts are these: September 25, 1988 (Seoul time), Ben Johnson settled into the blocks for the 100 metre final. Carl Lewis was three lanes to his left.

The gun goes. Johnson hammers out of the blocks and turns in possibly the greatest single sporting performance of all history to that point — an impossible 9.79 (which wouldn't be equalled for 11 years until American Maurice Greene did it in 1999). Canada goes wild. Our Ben! Our Ben Johnson! Canadian Ben Johnson! "Ben Johnson — a national treasure," trumpets the *Toronto Star*. Even the Prime Minister called.

But, after having his urine tested (twice — A and B samples), Johnson, the thirty-ninth Olympic athlete caught for steroids, is stripped of his gold — chef de mission Carol Anne Letheren goes to his room to get it back — and Lewis is declared the winner.

The country is stunned. The biggest story in Canadian sports history is still just that, but for different reasons. And so it began — the great national questioning of motives and affixing of blame. As does the attempted handing back of Johnson to his Jamaican past.

Ben Johnson, Canadian. As long as he wins.

Fear and Self-Loathing in Toronto

Now, a little soul searching.

The Canadian government immediately ordered an inquiry into the Ben Johnson affair that would be chaired by Charles Dubin, an associate chief justice of the Ontario Supreme Court. Thus, the Dubin Inquiry. Meeting in Toronto, Francis and Astaphan told Dubin that Johnson had been on steroids for seven years, ingesting a menu that included Dianabol, stanozolol, furazabol, testosterone, diuretics, and human growth hormone.

> **Quote, Unquote**
>
> "We are all proud of you."
>
> — Prime Minister Brian Mulroney to Ben Johnson, before his fall.

Yummy.

Johnson took the stand on June 12, 1989, and admitted to the steroid use, and that he had lied to cover it up.

Two things came of the Dubin Inquiry. One, it made recommendations about testing and moral standards that would do no good unless the rest of the world got in line and decided to do something serious about drug use (and it never really has despite pages of testimony about drug use elsewhere). And two, Canadians would be among the cleanest of the world's athletes.

Part 3 ➤ *The Olympic Spirit: A New Kind of Drug*

Historical footnotes: Ben Johnson was caught using steroids again in 1993 and was suspended for life. In April 1999, a judge said the second suspension was badly handled and he applied for reinstatement by the world track body.

Dennis Mitchell, who ran in the 1988 100 metre final and would appear in two more Olympics — during which time he rose to be chair of the athletes' advisory committee in track — was found to have an abnormally-high testosterone ratio in a 1998 drug test. He was suspended.

Kristen Otto Give Them Back

In the week before the storm broke over Ben Johnson stealing a gold medal by being on steroids, Kristen Otto of East Germany was busy stealing six of them.

Otto, who was one of the swim athletes used as steroid guinea pigs by the DDR, also later used the excuse that she didn't know what was happening and thus shouldn't have to return the medals.

The IOC, which practically sprinted towards removing the gold from Ben Johnson, has still done nothing to remove the East German medals.

And on and on the drug story goes.

Carolyn Can-Do

Now for some good news.

Carolyn Waldo of Beaconsfield, Quebec, beat American Tracie Ruiz-Conforto, who had bested her by three points in 1984 when synchronized swimming had made its Olympic debut. And in the duet, with Michelle Cameron of Calgary, Waldo picked up gold number two, thanks in part to a little hometown judging by the Canadian official.

Don't think the Americans didn't notice that, as Sylvie Frechette would discover four years hence.

Quote, Unquote

"It's all hypocrisy. The IOC makes millions of dollars from the Olympics and no one would pay to see a 100 metres run in ten seconds."

— Ben Johnson.

Quote, Unquote

"Otto had more testosterone in her than the entire starting team of the Dallas Cowboys."

— Phillip Whitten, editor in chief, *Swimming World* magazine, on East Germany's Kristen Otto.

Know-it-alls

Q. What Canadian decathlete took bronze in 1988 and then became a Windsor firefighter?

A. Dave Steen.

Chapter 14 ▶ Back from the Depths of Despair (1988–1996)

Ring of Fire

Lennox Lewis was born in England, moved to Canada at the age of 12, grew up to win a superheavyweight boxing gold medal at the Seoul Olympics for his adopted country, moved back to England and won the World Heavyweight Championship as an Englishman.

Not the type of thing that promotes bouts of nationalism in Canada, but it was very honest and human.

"This victory was for my mother, first of all, for the Canadian people and for all the guys on the boxing team," was Lewis' statement afterwards.

Excepting Edgerton Marcus, who lost the gold medal match in middleweight because of a broken right hand, the rest of the boxing competition was a complete scandal.

Ray Downy lost in the questionable welterweight semifinal to Park Si-hun of South Korea, who got five straight dirty decisions from the judges, including one in the final against flamboyant American Roy Jones Jr. that was such a blatant miscarriage of justice that even Park apologized.

Listen Up!

Edmonton's Larry Lemieux became a true hero at the 1988 Olympics in Seoul. Sitting in a solid second place in a sailing event, Lemieux saw Joseph Chan of Singapore tip over and begin to drown in the heavy seas. Lemieux abandoned the course (automatic disqualification) and rescued the injured Chan, trading the medal he had trained half his life for, to save the life of another human being. The IOC gave him a special award, and Lemieux became the only non-medal winner to be inducted in the Canadian Olympic Hall of Fame.

Listen Up!

Toronto had wanted to become the second Canadian city to host the Summer Games when it applied for the 1996 version. Seven cities were in the original running, but out-glossied by big sponsors behind the Atlanta bid, and defeated from within by a lobbying campaign from a local left-wing citizens' group called Bread Not Circuses, the Toronto bid failed and the games went to the Peach State. After an IOC official blew the whistle in 1998 on graft by IOC members when it came to voting on the games' sites, Toronto officials published a report it had sent to the IOC eight years earlier outlining everything dirty that had gone on. Though it didn't get the games, Toronto would wind up having an influence on how future games would be awarded.

Part 3 ➤ *The Olympic Spirit: A New Kind of Drug*

Didn't give the medal back, though.

Halifax's Jamie Pagendam knocked his Mongolian opponent down three times in the second round of his first fight — an automatic win in international boxing — but the referee lost count and thought it had been only two and let the battle continue. Pagendam was knocked down in the third and the Mongolian won. Canada protested and won the decision, but Pagendam had to go home anyway because of an automatic medical suspension for getting knocked down by a blow to the head.

The referee was sent home in disgrace.

The Third Baseman's Wife

If you put yourself in American Kristen Babb-Sprague's mind for a moment, it's easy to see why she followed a path that made her, for a few days, the most despised woman in Canada. She had trained most of her life for the solo synchro final at the Olympics, and when the judges told her she had won the gold, she celebrated.

In anyone else's mind, however, Babb-Sprague's actions were unforgivable — even if she was the wife of Ed Sprague, then a popular young backup third baseman with the World Series bound Toronto Blue Jays.

This is what happened: First day, compulsory figures, Sylvie Frechette of Canada is swimming despite a broken heart caused by the suicide death of her boyfriend Sylvain Lake just days before she had left for Barcelona. The Brazilian judge goes to record a 9.7 in the computer (right in line with all other marks) and mis-hits her keys, putting 8.7 in instead. She immediately calls the head judge (an American) over, who refuses to change it. Canada appeals. The chief referee (also an American — wonder if they remembered the homer judging in the previous Olympics?), refuses the appeal.

So, Babb-Sprague leads by a mile going into the final.

Quote, Unquote

"Whoever said 'Better late than never' must have received an Olympic gold medal a year and a half late, just like me!"

— Sylvie Frechette, in *Gold at Last*.

Frechette, with her swimming alter-ego Karine (a nickname that had been bestowed on her by swim teammates, and a character she used to calm her mind during her exceptionally difficult routines) in control, swims the scum off the scuppers but can't catch the American and finishes with the silver.

After the games, after Babb-Sprague had pranced around the Olympic pool with her medal and flag draped around her neck, Frechette went home to a hero's welcome.

Dick Pound, who was Canada's representative on the IOC executive and a vice-president to boot, went to work behind the scenes.

Chapter 14 ➤ Back from the Depths of Despair (1988–1996)

Despite the craggy nature of the IOC, in December 1993, Sylvie Frechette finally received her gold medal (there would be two officially given — Babb-Sprague wasn't giving her gold back), in a full-blown medal ceremony at the Montreal Forum.

"I was never more proud to be a Canadian than when I watched the Canadian flag being raised and heard our anthem being played in the Forum," said Frechette.

Her country was never more proud to have an athlete like her.

A Troubled Gold

Mark Tewksbury's performance in the 100 metre backstroke in 1992 was superb — right up there with any of those that had gone in the 92 years before him. He had already won a silver for the medley relay in Seoul and was looking to pick up another medal in the pool in Barcelona. Racing American world record holder Jeff Rouse, Tewksbury hit the wall at the halfway mark almost a full body length behind. Rouse had it wrapped up. But the Canadian reeled Rouse in with a thundering final 50 metres, finally touching out the American in 53.98, well below Tewksbury's previous personal best of 55.19 — a huge drop in a 100 metre race.

> **Quote, Unquote**
>
> "It was truly magnificent — big, heavy, solid — and it was mine."
>
> — Mark Tewksbury, quietly studying his gold medal in 1992.

With his excitable, outgoing personality, Tewksbury became a media star in Canada and an excellent inspirational speaker, but all was not well. Attempting to handle his new fame and battling with a secret, he was headed for a fall.

"I had absolutely no self esteem, which was strange because I had to have a lot of it to get to the top," said Tewksbury.

After seeking counselling, the hero of Barcelona began to find himself in Australia, where he lived for two years. Back home in Canada, he was convinced by the summer of 1998 that to be happy he had to be himself. So Mark Tewksbury turned his back on a lot of future endorsement deals and began the process of publicly outing himself as a homosexual — through a touching and hilarious one-man show at a Toronto theatre dedicated to gay and alternative works. He now lives in Toronto, gives his show on occasion, and works as a motivational speaker.

Silken

Silken Laumann had won world championships in single sculls rowing in both 1990 and 1991 and seemed a good bet to win the gold at Barcelona until a terrible accident at a regatta in Germany changed the course of her life.

Part 3 ➤ *The Olympic Spirit: A New Kind of Drug*

Laumann's boat was hit broadside by a German double sculls mens' team going through warm-up. The injury to her right leg was so bad it was thought she might never walk properly again and any recovery might take six to eight months even after five separate surgeries in Victoria.

Laumann had other ideas. She talked friends and teammates into taking her to Elk Lake, B.C., every day so they could physically carry her into the racing shell and send her off to excruciatingly painful workouts.

Somehow, the flesh healed enough to support Laumann's try in the Olympics. On race day, it took a magnificent final effort for her to nip-in to the bronze medal. It was, by the way, her second bronze — having teamed with her sister, Danielle, for third in double sculls at Los Angeles. She would add a silver in 1996 in her swan song.

Silken Laumann became a Canadian hero for having the courage to show up.

Know-it-alls

Q. What Canadian synchro swimming sisters came back from five years' retirement to win silver in 1992?

A. Penny and Vicky Vilagos.

And on the Rest of the Lake...

Under men's coach Mike Spracklen, sort of a second-off from the Frank Read mould of the 1950s, and women's coach Al Morrow, the Canadian rowers dominated the water at Barcelona, winning four gold and Laumann's bronze.

The men's and women's eight crews both took top spot, as did the women's fours and the women's double sculls team of Marnie McBean and Kathleen Heddle.

Rowing in Canada had simply become the best. Best in the world, that is.

The Burning of Atlanta

If Donovan Bailey never heard the name Ben Johnson again, it would be way too soon.

The world's fastest clean sprinter was the definitive favourite to win the gold medal, which was too much for the Americans who simply didn't have anyone who could match Bailey in the 100 metre final. Even worse, it looked like the Canadians had a chance to upset the U.S. in the 400 metre relay final — a race the Americans had never lost.

Time to go to plan B.

Ooh, remember Ben Johnson? There must be something wrong with that Bailey, he's too fast. Remember Ben Johnson? Bailey has to be on something. Remember Ben Johnson?

Geez.

But Canada was the only country with legitimate surprise drug testing and Bailey was the most regularly tested athlete in the world. He was a clean machine.

Bailey not only won the 100 metres, he did it in world record time — 9.84 seconds — the fastest clean 100 in history. And the Americans were shut out. The Canadian (of Jamaican heritage, by the way, something of which the thoroughly Canuck Bailey said he was enormously proud) was the world's fastest man.

Time to go to plan C.

Michael Johnson of the U.S. won the 200 metres in world record time of 19.32 seconds and picked up a second gold in the 400 metres. Ah, said *Sports Illustrated,* he's the world's fastest man. No one bought that.

Time to go to plan D.

There was always the 400 metre relay. But Bailey, Robert Esmie, Glenroy Gilbert, and Bruny Surin combined to blast the silver medallist Americans right off the Atlanta track.

How about Plan E?

A year after the Olympics, Bailey and Johnson met in a 150 metre match race at Toronto's SkyDome. Bailey cruised to the win while Johnson pulled up with an injury — some said he pulled up because he realized he wasn't going to win. Whatever.

Donovan Bailey. World's Fastest Man. No question.

Jobbed Again

Marianne Limpert of New Brunswick can relate to Nancy Garapick, who was cheated out of two gold by East German steroid-women in 1976.

With half the Chinese team kicked out of the 1996 games for drug use, it looked like it might be a clean competition. Wrong.

Michelle Smith of Ireland suddenly went from run-of-the-mill mid-packer to three-time Olympic gold medal winner (with a bronze to boot). This was a different, less naïve world that Ms. Smith was competing in, however, and the drug savvy athletes, media, and television viewers were sure they saw a ringer.

Limpert swam the race of her life to finish second in the 200 metre individual medley behind the suddenly super Smith.

Clean as a whistle, said Smith's drug tests. Well planned drug program, said critics.

In January of 1998, FINA, swimming's world body, administered a drug test to Smith and found, writes *Sports Illustrated*'s Gerry Callahan "a potent concentration of whisky — which acts as a masking agent" had been slipped into her urine.

Caught red handed was the red-headed Smith. Banned for four years. But because she hadn't failed her Atlanta tests, the medals stayed.

The Sunny Summary

All in all, Canadians left Atlanta with 18 medals (led by 6 in rowing and 1 in kayak) which gave the country a grand total of 216, including 48 gold, for the century.

Thanks to the last three games, Canada moved up to sixteenth overall in the standings, not a bad result for a country that went four Olympics with barely a sniff.

Other Stars of the Era

- Marnie McBean and Kathleen Heddle, the Dynamic Duo, did something that no other Canadian Olympic athletes have ever done. After both winning two gold medals in rowing at the 1992 games (together in pairs and as members of the eights crew) they came back in 1996 to win pairs again. They also each had a bronze to their names for a total of eight medals between them. Perfectly matched inside the racing shell, they were complete opposites outside of it—McBean a complete extrovert and Heddle a quiet person who was shy with the media.

- Mark McKoy had walked out of the Seoul Olympics in disgust, feeling teammate Ben Johnson was being unfairly singled out. He came back in 1996 to win the gold in the 100 metre hurdles.

Chapter 14 ➤ Back from the Depths of Despair (1988–1996)

Canadian Gold Medal Winners of the Era

1988

Carolyn Waldo.......... Solo Synchronized Swim

Carolyn Waldo and Michelle Cameron.... Duet Synchronized Swim

Lennox Lewis............ Superheavyweight Boxing

1992

Sylvie Frechette........ Solo Synchronized Swim

Mark Tewksbury....... 100 metre backstroke

Marnie McBean, Kathleen Heddle ..... Women's Pairs Rowing

Kirsten Barnes, Brenda Taylor, Jessica Monroe, Kay Worthington...... Women's Fours Rowing

Barnes, Taylor, Monroe, Worthington, McBean, Heddle, Megan Delahanty, Shannon Crawford, Lesley Thompson (cox)........................ Women's Eights Rowing

John Wallace, Andy Crosby, Mike Forgeron, Bob Marland, Darren Barber, Mike Rasher, Bruce Robertson, Derek Porter, Terry Paul (cox)........ Men's Eights Rowing

1996

Donovan Bailey........ 100 metre sprint

Bailey, Robert Esmie, Glenroy Gilbert, Bruny Surin............... 400 metre relay

Marnie McBean, Kathleen Heddle...... Women's Pairs Rowing

The Least You Need to Know

➤ Ben Johnson won a gold medal in the 100 metres in 1998 and had it taken away 24 hours later when it was found he had used steroids.

➤ Canada shared domination with the Americans in synchronized swimming.

➤ Sylvie Frechette was cheated out of a synchronized gold medal but eventually got it back.

➤ Silken Laumann made a courageous comeback from injury to win a rowing bronze.

➤ Marnie McBean and Kathleen Heddle each won three rowing golds over two Olympics.

➤ Donovan Bailey became the world's fastest man.

135

Chapter 15

The Winter Olympics: In the Arena

In This Chapter

- ➤ Hockey when Canada was king
- ➤ The Soviet invasion
- ➤ Latter day memories and dreams
- ➤ Struggling through the early days of skating
- ➤ From Barbara Anne to Toller
- ➤ The elusive gold
- ➤ Other stars of the era

Canada's Winter Games history began four years before the games themselves actually were instituted. But however you count the medals, wins on the ice, either in ice hockey or figure skating, have been few and far between in the last 50 years. In this chapter, we'll look at how Canada fell from the top of Olympic hockey, and its struggles to make it to the top of Olympic skating after a wonderful 1948. In this chapter we'll look at those sports and the debut of one other, curling.

When Canada Ruled the Ice

When the first official games opened on January 25, 1924 at Chamonix, France, Canada was looking to win the first official gold medal, having won the 1920 crown in the summer games when hockey first appeared.

No problem, thanks to the Toronto Granites who outscored their lousy opposition 104-2 before playing with the Americans, 6-1, in the final.

Canada won again in 1928 and 1932. Each time, interestingly, the difference in scores began to drop as other countries got better.

Yawn. And so it was expected to go.

It all came undone, however, in 1936, when Canadian officials started an ugly fight over the eligibility of a number of ex-Canucks on the British team which got the rest of the Brits so upset they came looking for Canucks to take it out on. The Port Arthur Bear Cats were representing Canada, and they became the target.

Meanwhile, the IOC (perhaps tired of the Canadians dominating) started to mess around with the scoring system, deciding (after the second round was over and they saw Canada wasn't perfect) that earlier games would count in the standings during the third round, which basically eliminated the Canadians.

The Canucks blamed the officials. Of course, if Canada had beaten the British (who won the gold) when they were supposed to, none of this would have happened.

After the Second World War, the youth of the world reconvened in 1948 at St. Moritz, Switzerland, for the fifth Winter Games.

The Royal Canadian Air Force Flyers won that tournament in a close affair and the Edmonton Mercurys pulled the trick in 1952, despite having been shaken up in a bus accident prior to the Oslo games.

There was word around that the Soviet Union would be interested in playing in 1956, but the Canadians didn't take that too seriously. After all, how good could they be?

First Ripples of a Red Tide

When the Kitchener-Waterloo Dutchmen got to Cortina, Italy for the 1956 games, their first question was: Who are those guys in the old, moth-eaten red uniforms and ill-fitting equipment? Those are the Soviets?

Haw, haw.

Everything was going along fine after that until Canada lost to the U.S., 4-1. Then, there was a shocking 2-0 defeat at the hands of those ill-clad Soviets, who passed the puck so much it made everyone's head spin.

Chapter 15 ➤ The Winter Olympics: In the Arena

What was that all about?

The Dutchmen were back again in 1960 at Squaw Valley, California (where the Canadian press was picking on them for their $60–125 a week living allowance as juniors and seniors, and the Soviets were already playing the "our players get absolutely nothing" game that would go on for another 20 years), and despite beating the Big Red Machine, the Canadians lost the gold to the U.S. and red hot goalie Jack McCarten, 2-1.

Clearly, it would no longer do to send a club team — the competition was getting too tough. Something else would have to be done.

Father Bauer's Boys

In 1962, Father David Bauer, by then teaching at the University of British Columbia, came up with the idea that the best senior and college players would stay together for a year preparing for world championships and the Olympics.

The CAHA went for it. So did the players when they were offered free education and living expenses at UBC. (Amateurs? What amateurs?)

The Olympic team, which included future NHLers Rod Seiling, Terry Clancy, Marshall Johnston, and Brian Conacher, played a 33-game schedule in Canada, but not against the pros. The club hit Innsbruck, Austria for the Olympics, posting a 5-2 record after losses to the Czechs (3-1) and the Soviets (3-2).

Three teams tied for second, and under the tiebreak system agreed upon, Canada would get the bronze. But during the third period of the last game, Bunny Ahearne (who some felt despised Canadians, for some reason — maybe he remembered 1936?) and the IIHF directors decided to change the formula. No one told the Canadians, who took to the ice in their blazers expecting to get the bronze, only to be told they wouldn't.

Quote, Unquote

"For every snowball you throw, we will put five pucks in your hockey net tonight."

— Final words from a Canadian before a huge, happy snowball fight at the 1956 Winter Games.

Listen Up!

Father David Bauer became an Olympic hero during Canada's game with Sweden in the 1964 Winter Olympics. Carl Oberg of Sweden threw his broken stick away in disgust and accidentally hit coach Bauer on the head. Bauer had himself bandaged up, kept his players from starting a huge brawl with the Swedes to get revenge, and the next night invited Oberg to sit with him in the stands to watch a game. Bauer was given a special gold medal after the games by the IOC for his actions.

Part 3 ▸ *The Olympic Spirit: A New Kind of Drug*

Quote, Unquote

"Canada has withdrawn from the phony world of international hockey and the vast majority of Canadians will applaud such a decision."

— Jim Coleman, *Toronto Telegram*, January 5, 1970.

Jobbed again.

Historical footnote: As writer Andrew Podnieks points out, the Canadians discovered while touring Czechoslovakia that that country's players, and the Soviets, were getting paid to play, though officially it was for "factory work" that was never done.

Hmm.

Canada came back again for the Olympics at Grenoble, France, hoping to medal. Beating the pros from the Soviet Union seemed out of the question.

With Father Bauer managing, and Jackie McLeod coaching, they finished third, losing to the Soviets 5-0 in front of 15,000 people, almost all of whom were pulling for Canada.

The CAHA had seen all it wanted of the Soviet pros. They sent an ultimatum to the IIHF: Let our pros play too, or we're pulling out of the Olympics and world play.

The IIHF thumbed their noses back across the Atlantic, and it would be two Olympics before Canada reappeared.

Beyond the Summit

The Soviets were anxious to prove their worth against Canada's best pros, so the 1972 Summit Series was created. And though the Soviets lost 4-3-1, they proved their point. They also proved that their players really were pros, in the meantime, but that was another matter.

By 1975, with the 1972 games already held without Canada's hockey team and the 1976 version about to do the same, a major change had come over the IIHF. Ahearne was out, Gunther Sabetski was in. And within two years, Canada was back in the world championships, with NHLers who had been eliminated from the playoffs. For the Olympics, former pros who had been redeclared amateurs (there's a sleight of hand) were okay.

Basing out of Calgary, the Nats looked towards their Olympic return in Lake Placid, 1980. There, the United States pulled off the Miracle on Ice, beating the Soviets. Canada failed to make the medal round, but played well in a 6-4 loss to the Soviets.

By the games of 1984 in then-peaceful Sarajevo, Yugoslavia, Dave King was coaching a squad that was beginning to look a little more like a very young pro unit, with a lot of NHL clubs lending juniors whose rights they owned to the team. Canada really struggled, even with strong graduating juniors such as Russ Courtnall and Kirk Muller on the team. They were shut out by the Soviets and the Swedes and wound up fourth. A consolation: Every member of the Canadian team went on to play in the NHL.

Chapter 15 ➤ The Winter Olympics: In the Arena

Calgary and Onwards

Finally, after years of trying, Calgary was awarded the games for 1988 (and did a superb job, by the way) and Sabetski finally got rid of the ridiculous rules, saying, "Canada can use Wayne Gretzky if it wants to."

The NHL said, uh, no. We're not going to let our best players leave the league for four weeks in the middle of the schedule.

Some NHLers did make it, including goaltender Andy Moog of Edmonton, who was in a contract dispute, and teammate Randy Gregg who basically took a leave of absence. Four other players were loaned by Canadian NHL clubs, and there were all those kids who had given three years of their lives to stick with the program rather than trying for the pros right away.

> **Know-it-alls**
>
> Q. Who scored to end the shootout in 1992 that avoided a German upset of Canada?
>
> A. Eric Lindros.

Canadians loved it. Almost four million tuned in for Canada's first game, a surprisingly tough 1-0 victory over Poland. But Canada needed to beat the Soviets in the preliminary round to have a shot at the gold, and lost 5-0. Despite going 5-3-2, Canada finished out of the medals.

Albertville in 1992 was interesting because of the involvement of one Eric Lindros, sitting out a year rather than sign with the Quebec Nordiques who had drafted The Big E. Again, the team was made up of youngsters out of the national program and recycled NHLers.

And wouldn't you know it. With the Soviets on the verge of breaking up the Dark Empire (they played as the Unified Team), Canada went 4-1 in the preliminary pool (lost to the Unifieds), survived a chilling 4-3 shootout win over Germany in the medal round, beat the Czechs 4-2, and finally lost to the Unifieds 3-1 for the gold.

That silver looked awfully pretty.

Same deal in Lillehammer 1994. The IOC had decided to hold a special two-year Olympics to separate the winter and summer games, thus maximizing TV revenue.

Canada had the old national team rolling, added a few disgruntled NHLers and a former Czech now with Canadian citizenship (Petr Nedved) and wound up with a silver medal to show for it.

The Swedes won the gold in a shootout (a terrible way to decide a hockey game) when Peter Forsberg scored on the thirteenth shot and Paul Kariya missed on the fourteenth.

Gold Was in the Bag

Nagano, Japan. February 1998. The IOC and the NHL had come to an agreement that would see the pro league take a couple of weeks off to let all of the world's best players into the Olympics.

141

Part 3 ➤ *The Olympic Spirit: A New Kind of Drug*

Wayne Gretzky. Trevor Linden. Eric Lindros. Patrick Roy. Everybody would be there for Canada. Despite having lost the inaugural World Cup to the Americans in 1996, Canada was favoured. And why not?

This was our chance. This would be our gold medal. This would be The Great One's opportunity to live his lifetime Olympic dream.

This would be Czech goaltender Dominik Hasek's finest hour.

While the Americans were making idiots of themselves, playing badly and trashing the Olympic Village after they were eliminated, the Canadians began to come together and moved into the semi-final match with the Czechs.

Hasek, known as "The Dominator" with the Buffalo Sabres, was almost unbeatable. A late goal by Linden sent the game to overtime, where nothing was decided. In the shootout (those damn shootouts!), Hasek stoned the Canadians. Gretzky wasn't chosen to even attempt a shot (huge controversy).

Canada lost. Let down, they also lost the bronze medal game to Finland. Doom and gloom.

> **Quote, Unquote**
>
> "I remembered my father, and felt happy, sad and proud, all at the same time."
>
> — Barbara Ann Scott, on receiving her Olympic gold medal.

Figure Skating — The Elusive Gold

After being shut out of the skating medals in the first two Winter Olympics, Canada picked up its first prize, a 1928 bronze from Montgomery Wilson in men's singles (he would be a close fourth in 1936). Over the next 15 Olympics, through the 1998 Games in Nagano, Canadians would win 17 more medals and be shut out just three times.

But only 2 of those 17 would be gold, and both of those were won by 1960. For the last 40 years of the century, a golden jinx would descend on the country's skaters.

Stealing a Country's Heart

The most oft-told story around Barbara Ann Scott involves the canary yellow convertible her fans in Ottawa presented to the newly crowned 1947 world champion upon her return to the nation's capital. Avery Brundage, chairman of the IOC, made her give it back or no Olympics.

Amateurism, and all that.

Scott's nickname was Tinker. She was the daughter of Clyde Scott, who as a lieutenant in the Great War had been severely wounded in both hips, a knee, and an eye. Left for dead on the battlefield he had been taken to a German hospital where he willed himself to live. That will was passed on to his daughter.

Scott would change the world of figure skating for women, adding athletic double loop jumps, and when she went to St. Moritz for the Olympics in 1948 Scott was favoured to win the gold. She didn't disappoint.

Only two inches over five feet, and weighing all of 100 pounds, Scott thrilled a huge crowd and put on a superb performance despite terrible ice conditions caused by two hockey games that had been played just before the free skate final.

After she won, the Canadian hockey team picked her up and carried her around the ice.

Back in Canada, Scott (who would marry Tom King and move to Chicago in 1955) was a national hero, inspiring hundreds to take up figure skating, which would in turn have an important effect on the sport's future in the country.

She even made the cover of *Time* magazine.

> **Know-it-alls**
>
> Q. What future Canadian sports minister joined with his sister Maria to finish fourth in skate pairs at the 1960 Games?
>
> A. Otto Jelinek.

Wow, Can You Believe Their Luck?

Barbara Wagner and Robert Paul were looking a little tight in the early going of their pairs final event in 1960 at Squaw Valley, when an amazing thing happened.

The needle on the record player skipped right across the disk and the music stopped. Oops. It seemed coach Sheldon Galbraith (Canada's most famous coach, who had taught the couple for eight years), had been trying to get a better view with his movie camera when he somehow, inadvertently you understand, knocked the needle off the record.

They had to restart.

Once again, now completely relaxed, they took the ice and when it was all over the judges voted 5-2 in their favour, and the gold medal went to Canada.

Way to go coach! Except that this seemed to use up all the "luck" Canadian Olympic figure skating was going to get.

A Little Bad Timing

Donald Jackson was just 18 when he won a bronze medal in 1960. In 1962, he would turn the figure skating fraternity on their ears by winning the world championship and landing the first triple jump in history. But just before the 1964 Olympics, he realized that after watching his parents practically impoverish themselves supporting his skating, it was time to support himself. He turned pro.

Part 3 ➤ *The Olympic Spirit: A New Kind of Drug*

Quote, Unquote

"(Amateur skating) is an expensive practical joke."

— Toller Cranston, mad at the judges at the 1972 Games.

Know-it-alls

Q. What television skate commentator won a bronze in 1964, with partner Guy Revell?

A. Debbi Wilkes.

Missed that gold medal.

Donald McPherson followed in Jackson's footsteps, winning the worlds in 1963. His dad had to cash in an insurance policy to get him there. There just was no money left to get the young skater through the next season. So, he turned pro in Europe.

Way to go Canadian government!

Missed another gold medal.

Karen Magnussen was so mad at losing to Trixie Shuba of Austria in the 1972 games at Sapporo, Japan (she finished a strong second, and shouldn't have been hard on herself as she was simply a year away) that she dedicated every second of her life the following summer and winter to taking the world championship for 1973. Which she did.

But no Olympic gold medal.

Toller Cranston was years ahead of his time in performance but those darn compulsory figures at the beginning of each competition would just do him in every time.

After scoring as low as 3.3 (out of 6.0) in the figures, he went out in 1976 and won the short program, finishing a close second in the long. That years later, skating would finally drop figures entirely (too easy for judges to skewer their marks) was no help to Cranston during his career.

No gold in 1976, either.

By 1984, Canada was ready to burst back onto the international skating scene in a huge way, but the Olympic Gods just wouldn't co-operate.

Brian and Liz

Brian Orser was not quite ready for prime time himself when he won the silver medal at the 1984 Olympics. But, by 1988, with the '87 world championship gold in his back pocket, Orser was set for one of the most spectacular showdowns in Olympic history. And it would happen right in Calgary, with a huge national television audience watching.

It was the Battle of the Brians: Orser vs. Brian Boitano of the United States.

Skating had never seen anything quite like it.

After figures and the short program, Boitano had a minuscule lead going into the free skate, which was worth 50 percent of the final mark.

Boitano went first and "gave a stunning performance," said writer David Wallechinsky. But the judges left a tiny hole for Orser to skate through, if he, too, could be perfect.

Orser two-footed a triple flip and turned a triple axel into a double (really the killer, right there). Boitano wound up winning 5-4 in the complicated scoring system.

Couldn't have been closer.

But no gold.

The women's competition that year was supposed to be another showdown battle between Katarina Witt of East Germany and Debra Thomas of the U.S. But though Witt wound up winning the title, it was Elizabeth Manley of Canada who came from way outside to take the silver.

Only five feet tall, Manley soaked up the atmosphere of skating in front of a home crowd by putting on the best free skate of her life. It was absolutely brilliant. Manley won the free skate going away, with seven first place marks to just three for Witt.

Unfortunately, the judges hadn't been looking her way during the short and figures section of the program, so Manley didn't have the previous marks necessary to nose out Witt for the gold.

But she left Calgary a true champion.

It's Enough to Make a Hound Dog Cry

Jinxed.

Jinxed, I tell you.

There's no other explanation for what happened in the 1992 and 1998 games.

Kurt Browning won three straight world championships starting the year after the Calgary games, and was going to win that gold in 1992 at Albertville. Absolutely no question. Until a serious back injury ended those hopes, and Browning was sixth.

In 1994, he was healthy again, but had already been talked out of one retirement and admitted afterwards that he wasn't sure "I had that fire, that focus, that killer thing."

Listen Up!

The story behind the story of Liz Manley's surprise silver medal at the Calgary Olympics in 1988 is that the skater was "on the verge of pneumonia" just 20 days before the event. As Manley told writer Steve Milton, she was bedridden for most of the time leading up to the women's event. Among the cures she and coach Peter Dunfield tried was taking Manley to a woman the skater referred to as a "witch doctor" who boiled red radishes by her head to help clear out her sinuses.

Quote, Unquote

"Timing is so important."
— Robert Paul, Canadian Olympic pairs skate gold medallist.

Part 3 ➤ *The Olympic Spirit: A New Kind of Drug*

> **Quote, Unquote**
>
> "The disappointment cut like a knife, ripped through every part of me."
>
> — Brian Orser, 1988 skate silver medallist.

Despite a superb long performance, the twelfth place finish after short just wasn't enough to cut it.

No gold.

But, there was hope. Young Elvis Stojko, who came in ranked fourth, sprang up and took the silver medal. There was, after all, a chance in 1998 at Nagano.

Elvis dominated the world stage over the next three seasons. He and his quads seemed unbeatable (and where have we heard this story before?).

But Elvis tore up his groin in training some months before the Olympics. He kept it quiet and gamely tried to put in a gold medal winning performance at Nagano. It wasn't to be. He finished second. So injured was Stojko, that he had to walk out to the podium for the medal presentation, rather than skate out.

No gold.

The jinx holds.

Schmirler the Curler

Curling made its debut as an official medal event in 1998 and the men's rink from Ontario, skipped by Mike Harris (no, not the Premier), came up with a silver medal after losing to Switzerland in the finals.

It was the women who pulled off the big prize.

Sandra Schmirler was a minor surprise in even winning the right to represent Canada at the games, but she and her rink of Marcia Gudereit, Joan McCusker, Jan Betker, and spare Atina Ford did the country proud in Nagano, beating Denmark's Helena Blach Lavrsen in the gold medal final.

Other Stars of the Era

➤ Isabelle Brasseur of St. Jean sur Richelieu, Quebec, and Lloyd Eisler of Seaforth, Ontario, pulled a rare double in 1992 and 1994, winning the bronze in the pairs competition both times. In 1993, they won the World Championship. Creative and unique, they went on to a strong professional career.

➤ Frances Dafoe and Norris Bowden beat an Austrian couple on points in the 1956 pairs final at Cortina, but lost the gold on a technicality because they had one less second place vote from the judges than the other couple (both pairs had four firsts). The Canadians went into the competition as defending world champions.

Chapter 15 ➤ *The Winter Olympics: In the Arena*

- ➤ Terry O'Malley made his Olympic hockey debut in 1964 with the Canadian hockey team as one of Father David Bauer's boys. His devotion to the national program was such that he would make his last Games appearance on defence 16 years later, at Lake Placid in 1980.
- ➤ Tracy Wilson and Rob McCall went to Calgary in 1988 and won the bronze medal in pairs skating. Wilson went on to a career as a television commentator, McCall sadly passed away in 1991 of AIDS.

Canadian Gold Medals (Arena sports)

1920–1928
Men's Hockey

1932
Men's Hockey

1948
Men's Hockey

Barbara Ann Scott......... Singles skating

1952
Men's Hockey

1960
Barbara Wagner and
Robert Paul .... Pairs skating

The Least You Need to Know

- ➤ Canada dominated the early hockey tournaments at the Olympics.
- ➤ Arguments over the definition of amateurism led to Canada dropping out of international hockey and missing two Olympics.
- ➤ Pros were eventually allowed into Olympic hockey.
- ➤ Barbara Ann Scott won our first Olympic skating gold medal.
- ➤ Barbara Wagner and Robert Paul won Canada's second, and to this date, only other skating gold.
- ➤ Canadian women won the first official curling gold medal.

Chapter 16

The Winter Olympics: The Great Out (and In) Doors

In This Chapter

- Anne Heggtveit breaks Canada's maiden
- A Nancy a day
- The Great Gaetan
- Magnifique Myriam
- Speed skaters rule
- Other stars of the era

When it comes to Olympic skiing in Canada, the women rule. Since the start of the skiing events in 1948, Canadian men have won just six medals, including two gold. The women have won 10, of which 6 have been gold. In speed skating, the name for the ages is Gaetan Boucher, who put on a show in 1984. Canada has had its share of luck in bobsledding as well, picking up a couple of gold. As the era ended, however, it was a new breed of athlete in a new breed of sport that would pick up the flag and snowboard off with it. In this chapter, we'll look at Canada's outdoor, and formerly outdoor, winter Olympic heroes.

Part 3 ▶ *The Olympic Spirit: A New Kind of Drug*

> **Quote, Unquote**
>
> "There you jerks, that'll teach you."
>
> — Steve Podborski's thoughts on hearing that Ken Read had fallen in the 1980 downhill. He was angry at the intense media pressure on the Canadian team.

A Long Row of Empty Necks

Canadian men's alpine (down the hills) and nordic (cross-country and biathlon) ski teams went 32 years without an Olympic medal.

In 1976, at Innsbruck, a breakthrough occurred when Ken Read skied to a strong fifth place in the men's downhill. Read was one of the Crazy Canucks, a group that included Jungle Jim Hunter (the trail blazer), Dave Irwin, Dave Murray, and Steve Podborski, who were finally beginning to make a major splash on the international scene's World Cup.

By 1980, Read and Podborski were tabbed as gold medal contenders at Lake Placid — especially the former, who was now an established star in the ski world. Up at the top of Whiteface Mountain, away from the intense pressure put on the pair by the Canadian press, the race began. Read went first and fell, and Podborski won the bronze. Podborski, who would become the first non-European to win the World Cup downhill championship, finished eighth in the 1984 Olympic downhill, and retired.

Canada would not pick up another men's Olympic downhill ski medal until Edi Podivinski earned a bronze in 1994.

That's downhill. There have been no medals in slalom, giant slalom, or super giant slalom.

Not so much as a sniff.

The Tricksters

Hoping to attract a new breed of fans to the Winter Games, the IOC introduced freestyle skiing as a medal sport in 1992 when the moguls (skiing down a course with big bumps) competition was first held. Aerials were introduced in 1994.

Jean-Luc Brassard had finished seventh in the first moguls event at Albertville, following that up by dominating the World Cup over the next two seasons.

When his next chance came, at Lillehammer in 1994, the Quebecker did not disappoint, beating Sergey Shupletsov of Russia and France's Edgar Grospiron with a spectacular display of tricks and skill.

In the same Olympics, Philippe Laroche and Lloyd Langlois, two other members of the Quebec Air Force (that became the Canadian Air Force), came up with silver and bronze in the aerials competition.

That's three medals in the same games — more than Canadian men's skiers had done in all other games put together.

Raging Ross

Ross Rebagliati went to Nagano in 1998, and won the gold medal in another new sport — giant slalom snowboarding.

After his race, the IOC announced that traces of marijuana had shown up in Rebagliati's post-event testing (the snowboarder said he picked it up at a party just before he left where everyone else was smoking grass and he ingested the fumes), and for a few days the country had another Ben Johnson crisis on its hands. But the COA appealed, and the independent appeal body decided that Olympic rules around marijuana usage were so ambiguous that the medal had to be returned.

Ross went home with his gold. Many suggested his chances of capitalizing on it were now nil, but they were way off the mark. A number of Canadian companies, seeing he was now a hero with Generation X (18–29-year-old) consumers, hired him as a spokesperson.

Rebagliati swore what happened would not cause him to change friends, making him even more of a hero to young people.

> **Quote, Unquote**
>
> "The only people I could see being interested in him would be the Hemp Growers of America."
>
> — New York management consultant on Ross Rebagliati's chances at getting endorsements. He was wrong.

> **Know-it-alls**
>
> Q. Who won Canada's first Olympic ski medal?
>
> A. Lucie Wheeler, a bronze in 1956.

Another Ottawa Girl

Anne Heggtveit was so far back in all three ski events she entered in 1956 it would have taken a search party to find her.

She was, however, merely 17, and there for the experience. Four years later, after working in Europe with coach Pepe Salvenmoser, the Ottawa resident went to Squaw Valley with the U.S. championship in her pocket (there was no World Cup in those days), and a gold on her mind.

The slalom was no contest. Heggtveit finished over three seconds in front of the field to take Canada's first skiing gold. There would be five more women's gold before the century ended.

How Greene Was Chamrousse Valley

When the 1968 Olympic ski events were convened on the hill at Chamrousse, outside Grendale, France, one of the most experienced competitors on the hill was Nancy Greene, of Rossland, B.C. This was her third games, and the year before had become

Part 3 ▶ *The Olympic Spirit: A New Kind of Drug*

Listen Up!

Nancy Greene learned how to ski without fear the hard way. Growing up in Rossland, B.C., she and her siblings took their first ski steps on Red Mountain, which featured incredibly steep slopes. Robert Greene, dad, was an engineer who taught all of his kids by tying a rope around their waists and sending them down the steep slope. If they fell, writer Ron Sudlow reported, dad would reel them back in. It worked. Greene became a fearless skier, which allowed her to push to the limit.

Quote, Unquote

"I had a headache for the next two days."

— Nancy Greene on the giant slalom time clock that kept running even after she crossed the finish line. The gold was still hers.

the first winner of the World Cup of skiing while making only six of the nine races.

In Europe, she was known as The Tiger, for the way she attacked a course and how she loved speed and danger. In fact, Nancy Greene was the original Crazy Canuck. She was also, at times, the original overwound Canuck.

At Chamrousse, Greene had a tenth in downhill and a silver medal in the slalom by the time the final event — the giant slalom — came around. Time for the "Go For It" girl to go for it.

Time for a little sports psychology.

About 45 minutes before the race, Greene's coaches brought her to the top of the hill and sat her down for tea and rolls at a nearby restaurant. Except, they just "happened" to stay a little too long and didn't make it to the start until the race was already on, and only four skiers were in front of the Canadian at the gate.

With no time to think about it, Greene bombed down the course almost three seconds faster than anyone else and won going away, despite a malfunctioning clock.

Race and Wait

Kathy Kreiner was an 18-year-old from Timmins, Ontario, when she travelled to Innsbruck for the 1976 games to compete in the giant slalom. Rosi Mittermaier of West Germany was the heavy favourite in the race (she won gold in downhill and slalom in that Olympics), and Kreiner had drawn the first starting spot which meant after she skied all she could do was wait.

Kreiner was dead on, hitting the gates perfectly and putting up a 1:29.13. Mittermaier went fourth, led at the halfway point, but took too straight a line into a gate and lost just a hair of time.
She was .12 of a second behind Kreiner.

On and on they came — a list of the world's best skiers — but no one was close. Kathy Kreiner, Timmins teenager, was the gold medallist.

Chapter 16 ➤ *The Winter Olympics: The Great Out (and In) Doors*

Golden Dreams

This story is true, so park your disbelief somewhere else.

In 1990, Kerrin Lee-Gartner, who had grown up just down the street from Nancy Greene's parents in Rossland, B.C., found herself in dreamland. An announcer's voice came through her subconscious, saying, "medaille d'or, Kerrin Lee-Gartner."

Now Lee-Gartner barely spoke a word of French, but she knew what medaille d'or meant — gold medal.

Two years later, we find Lee-Gartner at the top of the Meribel hill in Albertville, staring down at what many felt was the toughest women's downhill course ever devised. Like all the Crazy Canucks before her, male and female, she damned the torpedoes and went full steam ahead, crossing the line in 1:52.55.

It was the fastest time by just .06 of a second, ahead of Hilary Lindh of the United States.

Dreams do come true, after all.

The Mighty Myriam

Myriam Bedard had first picked up a biathlon rifle while a member of her local army cadet corps (which is where many biathletes in this country get their start). That marriage of cross country ski skills and superb shooting eye (the sport's motto is "ski fast, shoot straight"), created one of the best Olympic athletes Canada has produced.

In 1994 at Lillehammer, everything came together.

In the 15 kilometre race, Bedard shot beautifully and powered down the final straight to beat Anne Briand of France by 47 seconds — fairly close.

Nothing compared to the 7.5 km, however. With her shooting right on, Bedard came down the final stretch and, not to be indelicate, busted a gut. With Canadian television announcers providing memorable, if not journalistically sound, commentary ("C'mon Myriam. C'mon Myriam…"), Bedard put the pedal to the metal and surged across the line with a 26:08.8.

That was 1.1 seconds in front of Svetlana Paramygina of Belarus.

Two gold for the Mighty Myriam. And three medals overall, when you count the bronze from 1992.

Bedard went home, took a hiatus to have a beautiful baby, and came back to compete and push her sport across Canada. She finally retired for good in 1999.

Know-it-alls

Q. Name the first Canadian man to place in the top eight in an Olympic biathlon event?

A. Steve Cyr, eighth in 1992.

Part 3 ▸ *The Olympic Spirit: A New Kind of Drug*

Know-it-alls

Q. In what year did Canadian men finish third, fourth, and fifth in 500 metre speed skating?

A. 1932. Alexander Hurd, Frank Stack, and William Logan.

Listen Up!

Gaetan Boucher put Canada's allergy to success perfectly when he was invited to speak to the 1984 summer games team at Los Angeles, in the same year he won two speed skating gold medals. "We didn't seem to understand it, but we were always preparing to lose — beaten before we even started," he said. "I was expecting to win in Sarajevo last winter. It wasn't a question of hoping. I was there to win, and I detect the same thing here." Inspired, the Canadian team put on its best ever summer performance, and almost all credited Boucher's talk with helping them get their head straight.

Into the Teeth of the Wind

Back in the bad old days (pre-1988), when Olympic speed skating was held outdoors and skaters had to deal with bitter winds and wildly divergent temperatures in their races, Canada had started quite well out on the frozen oval.

At Lake Placid (1932 version), Alexander Hurd and William Logan both won two medals, and Frank Stack one, for a spectacular five medal performance (silver and four bronze). But for a shared bronze by Gordon Audley in 1952, however, Canada disappeared off the speed skating podium until 1976 at Innsbruck.

Suddenly, Canadians rediscovered the sport.

Cathy Priestner finished second to triple-medallist Sheila Young of the U.S. in the 500 metres, and was sixth in the 1,000 metres, a race in which Canada's Sylvia Burka finished fourth.

One of the athletes inspired by Canada's performance was a young skater from Ste. Foy, Quebec named Gaetan Boucher, who had finished sixth in the 1,000 metres. Eight years hence, he would become Canada's greatest winter Olympian.

Out From the Shadow of Eric

Gaetan Boucher went to the Olympics in 1980 and won a silver medal in the 1,000 metres. Hardly anyone noticed because a young American named Eric Heiden, who obviously hailed from the same far-off planet that created swimmer Mark Spitz, won five gold medals and stole all the headlines.

If Boucher wanted a place of his own in the heavens, he would have to earn it in 1984 at Sarajevo.

Boucher was all wrong for speed skating. He was too short. His stride wasn't long enough. He had a habit, critics said, of choking in the big races. In short, he didn't have what it took to win. It didn't help that Boucher had broken an ankle racing in an indoor (short course) meet a year before Sarajevo (what was the man thinking?), which Boucher would later say was a blessing in disguise because the eight weeks off skates refreshed him.

Chapter 16 ➤ *The Winter Olympics: The Great Out (and In) Doors*

Jump to February 10, 1984. Boucher lines up for the 500 metres — his worst race — and comes up with a surprising bronze. He said sometime afterwards that he knew, right then, that if he could medal in the 500, the later 1,000 and 1,500 were in the bag.

And they were.

February 14, 1984. Boucher against his chief rival Sergei Khlebnikov of the Soviet Union. No contest. Boucher by almost a second.

February 16, 1984. Boucher against Khlebnikov. Again, no contest. The Canadian by half a second.

A new Canadian hero. One who didn't think Canadians cared about speed skating until he got home and discovered he was now the toast of the town, from coast to coast.

> **Quote, Unquote**
>
> "I went to Sarajevo expecting, not hoping, to win."
>
> — Gaetan Boucher, to the *Toronto Star*.

The View from the Inside

Speed skating went inside for the first time at the Olympic Oval in Calgary, for 1988. In front of the home crowd, Boucher said goodbye with a fifth in the 1,000 metres, but no Canadian would be able to break into the medals.

Must have been the bright lights.

When the same thing happened in 1992, it looked as though Canada's speed skating prominence would be just a passing thing. But Susan Auch would come up with a silver in the 500 metres at Lillehammer in 1994, and the Canadians began to show the flag on the world scene over the next four years.

It was left to Catriona LeMay Doan to restore the country's place at the top when the youth of the world met again in 1998 at Nagano. The 500 metres, by this time, had become a two-race event, with best combined time to win. Auch set down a blazing combined total of 1:16.93, and it was going to take a brilliant effort to deny her the gold.

Cue LeMay Doan who did nothing more than set an Olympic record with her second-run time of 38.21, which was good enough to beat Auch by .33 of a second.

Canadians one-two.

LeMay Doan came back to take a bronze in the 1,000 metres.

> **Know-it-alls**
>
> Q. What Canadian athlete has won the most winter games medals?
>
> A. Speed skater Gaetan Boucher, four.

The men were strongly represented by Jeremy Wotherspoon and Kevin Overland in the 500 metres.

Again, Canadians one-two.

Canada was back as a world power on the frozen oval.

In the Land of the Wild and Wooly

Canadian short-track speed skating is based mostly in Quebec, where hockey arenas are turned into small racing courses, with lots of padding around the outside to catch the inevitable falls. Those are often caused by pushes and other dirty business, which is what the Canadians had always especially accused tough American Cathy Turner of pulling.

True or not, the American, who left the sport for eight years to become a lounge singer before getting back into it when short track became official at Albertville in 1992, had a nasty reputation as a dirty piece of work. Sure enough, Canadian world record holder Sylvie Daigle went into the first turn of her first heat at the Olympics, clashed with Turner, and wound up in the wall — eliminated. Turner would win the gold.

Revenge would be the Canadians', however, for the 3,000 metre relay event pitted the top-ranked Canucks vs. Turner and her American teammates. It was no contest, as Angela Cutrone, Nathalie Lambert, Annie Perrault, and a triumphant Daigle took the gold.

On the men's side, Frederic Blackburn of Quebec broke the world record in the 1,000 metres. Unfortunately, so did three others, and it was Kim Ki-hoon of Korea who took the gold to Blackburn's silver.

As one of the world powers in short track, Canada was expected to mine its share of gold in 1994, but while the skaters won two individual medals and women's relay silver, no one made it to the top of the podium. Oh, Turner won a gold, which bugged the Canucks no end.

On to Nagano, and this time it was four medals — including two gold. Annie Perrault won a tough 500 metre event by inching out Chinese and South Korean competitors for her second Olympic victory in three games. And the men's 5,000 metre relay team beat South Korea and China to win gold there.

In all, over 16 events in three Olympics, Canada's short trackers came up with nine medals. No other winter games sport has produced such a medal haul for the country in as short a space of time.

Still Bobbin' Along

When Canadians heard that Vic Emery, his brother John, Peter Kirby, and Douglas Anakin had won the four-man bobsled competition at the 1964 games in Innsbruck, they assumed that the quartet had simply rented a sled, jumped in, and pulled off a miracle. Kind of a Cool Runnings/Jamaican bobsled team sort of thing.

Hardly.

Chapter 16 ➤ *The Winter Olympics: The Great Out (and In) Doors*

If it was a miracle, it was one forged by eight years of hard work and dedication. The four Montreal bachelors had fallen for bobsledding (or bobsleigh, as it's properly called), at the Cortina Games in 1956, and immediately went out and raised as much money as possible to rent sleds and pay for training costs so they could learn what they were doing.

Skipping the 1960 games, they set their sights instead on 1964. By then, Vic Emery had become one of the top bob pilots in the world, and the Canadian times were right with the traditional European powers. Canada's first ever Olympic bob team was ready.

> **Know-it-alls**
>
> Q. How many luge medals have Canadians won in Olympic history?
>
> A. None.

The Canadian foursome set a track record in their first of four runs, and were not headed by anyone after that, beating off a late charge by the Italians with a solid, but not spectacular, final run.

Gold medal, Canada.

Vic Emery and Kirby, by the way, had proven it wasn't a fluke by coming within an eyelash of winning a medal in the two-man.

Nothing Like Kissing Your Sister

That was it for Canadian bobsledding success for 34 years, until, with its international program finally clawing back due to solid commercial sponsorship, the red and white finally got another medal.

And again, it hardly came out of nowhere. Canadian sleds had been among the world's best for four years by the time Nagano 1998 came around.

There, Pierre Leuders and Dave MacEachern found themselves locked in a tooth-and-nail battle with Italians Guenther Huber and Antonio Tartaglia. Someone had to break in the cold of night.

Or did they?

After the last of four runs the scoreboard read: Canada, 3:37.24. Italy, 3:37.24.

A dead-heat tie. Two gold awarded for the first time in bobbin' history.

And nobody's sister in sight.

Other Stars of the Era

➤ Karen Percy broke off a two Olympic drought for Canadian women skiers by doubling in 1988. Percy took third in the downhill event won by Marina Kiehl of West Germany, and then grabbed a second bronze in the super giant slalom behind Sigrid Wolf of Austria.

157

Part 3 ➤ *The Olympic Spirit: A New Kind of Drug*

➤ Lucie Wheeler came home from the 1956 games with Canada's first ever ski medal, a bronze in the downhill behind Madeleine Berthod of Switzerland.

➤ Sylvia Burka speed skated with severely limited vision in one eye. But that didn't prevent her from competing in three Olympics. She missed a bronze medal in the 1976 1,000 metres by just .33 of a second.

Canadian Gold Medal Winners — Skiing, Bobsled, and Speed skating

1960
Anne Heggtveit...... Slalom

1964
Vic Emery, John Emery, Peter Kirby, Douglas Anakin...... Four-man bobsled

1968
Nancy Greene........ Giant slalom

1976
Kathy Kreiner......... Giant slalom

1984
Gaetan Boucher...... 1,000 metre speed skating
.... 1,500 metre speed skating

1992
Angela Cutrone, Nathalie Lambert, Annie Perrault, Sylvie Daigle........... 3,000 metre women's short-track relay

Kerrin Lee-Gartner .... Downhill

1994
Myriam Bedard........ 7.5 km biathlon
.... 15 km biathlon
Jean-Luc Brassard .... Freestyle moguls

1998
Ross Rebagliati.......... Snowboard giant slalom
Catriona LeMay Doan .... 500 metre speed skating
Annie Perrault .... 500 metre short track
Eric Bedard, Derrick Campbell, Francois Drolet, Marc Gagnon .... Men's 5,000 metre short-track relay
Pierre Leuders, Dave MacEachern.... Two-man bobsled

The Least You Need to Know

➤ Anne Heggtveit won Canada's first skiing gold, in 1960.
➤ Nancy Greene won a gold and silver in 1968.
➤ Myriam Bedard won two biathlon gold medals in 1994.
➤ Gaetan Boucher, speed skater, with four medals, is Canada's greatest Winter Games athlete.
➤ Short-track speed skating is one of Canada's best winter sports.
➤ Canada has won two bobsled golds — 34 years apart.

Part 4
Canadian Football: The Heroes of the Game

It may seem strange for today's young sport fans to imagine Canadian football as anything but a second-tier game. But for over 100 years, football was ranked ahead of baseball as this country's second sport, and from the end of the Second World War until the 1970s, the Canadian Football League was considered very much a major league venture, every bit as good as the National Football League. Crowds were huge, the heroes were real, the game was talked about from sea to sea, and the Grey Cup was a truly national week-long event. In this section, we'll look at the origins of the Canadian football, the birth of the Grey Cup, our football heroes, and how the game eventually fell from grace — mostly through the incompetence of its owners and executives.

Chapter 17

The Family of Football (1900–1941)

In This Chapter

- ➤ Club origins
- ➤ Three to make 10
- ➤ Awarding of the Grey Cup
- ➤ The Big Train
- ➤ The West joins in
- ➤ Introducing imports
- ➤ Other stars of the era

By 1900, most of the teams we know today were in place, in one form or another, and already divided between east and west. It took a long while for the rules to become standard across the land, and the real power in football continued to lie with universities, rather than private clubs. Eventually that would change as the "amateur" club players became stronger. All the game really needed to make the big time was a few recognizable stars — and it got them. In this chapter, we'll look at football from the turn of the century to the middle of the Second World War.

Blue, Cerise, and Rouge

During the 39 years from the time the first recognizable game of football was played at the University of Toronto in 1861 (between two faculties) to the turn of the century, clubs were founded in most of the cities that would eventually make up the Canadian Football League.

First out of the gate was the Hamilton rugby football club (1869, first colours were orange and black), a group that can fairly lay claim to being the oldest football team in North America. Montreal had a club team three years later, Toronto (in the form of the Argonaut Rowing Club and wearing dark blue) in 1873, and Ottawa in 1876 (with the interesting colour scheme of cerise and French grey). They would be kicked out for rough play in 1897 and be reformed a year later as the Ottawa Rough Riders, with red and black as the colour scheme.

The name Rough Riders, by the way, was chosen in honour of the Canadian battalion that fought with future U.S. president Teddy Roosevelt and his Rough Riders in the Spanish American War.

Winnipeg, Edmonton (whose team would become the Esquimaux in 1908, and the Eskimos by 1910), Regina, and Calgary all came up with teams between 1879 and 1891, the year Edmonton beat Calgary 6-5 in the Alberta final.

These teams, and many others, needed organizations to look after schedules, decide on rules, and act as arbiters for arguments. And the one thing the game wasn't short of in the early years was arguments.

Especially over rules.

Growing Pains

In 1882, the Quebec Rugby Football Union and the Canadian Rugby Football Union were formed, followed a year later by the Ontario Rugby Football Union. The Canadian Intercollegiate Rugby Football Union came along in 1897 as the organizer of the college game.

That many governing bodies in such a young game virtually guaranteed a confusing array of rules, mainly centred around how much football was going to differ from the game invented by the English on the playing fields of Rugby School. The biggest arguments were over the snapback system, devised by the Americans and involving the passing of the ball back through the legs to the quarterback that we know today, and the method of heeling the ball out of a scrum of bodies into the backfield.

One guaranteed a team on offense would keep possession, while the other left it freeform.

Eventually, the leagues agreed on a relatively set rulebook, and over a 40-year period brought the laws of the game more into line with what we recognize today.

Chapter 17 ➤ *The Family of Football (1900–1941)*

Much of the credit for that goes to a former University of Toronto player named Thrift Burnside, who proposed a number of changes to the rules in 1905, including dropping the number of men from 14 to 12, adopting the snapback system (which the Canadian Rugby Union took over 15 years to agree with), requiring the offensive team to make 10 yards on three downs, and more.

These rules, presented to the Canadian Rugby Union in 1905, were adopted slowly over the following decade, but for a long time to come the game still resembled rugby in the way players would lateral the ball out from the scrimmage to a succession of backs racing down the field.

Any Sport Will Do, as Long as the Trophy Says "Lord Grey"

Sir Albert Henry George, Earl Grey, Viscount of Howick, Baron Grey of Howick, and a passel of titles following that, was Governor General of the land from 1904 to 1911.

> **Know-it-alls**
>
> Q. What year did Canadian football adopt the standard 110-yard by 65-yard field?
>
> A. 1896.

> **Know-it-alls**
>
> Q. Who was the first Canadian player known as The Big Train?
>
> A. Smirlie Lawson.

Having noticed that a number of former governors general had left their name behind by inscribing it into a nice trophy (Lord Stanley started the trend with his cup for hockey), Grey wanted to do the same thing.

His first choice, apparently, was hockey, but that sport was up to its waist in silverware. Soccer had the Connaught Cup, lacrosse the Minto Cup. What was left?

So, football it was. Lord Grey paid about $48 Canadian for a nice little cup from Henry Birks and Sons, appointed three trustees to look after it, and two years later left Ottawa unaware that his trophy would become the second most well-known in the country.

The only trouble with the new Grey Cup was that when the first game was played, on December 4, 1909, it wasn't ready to be presented.

Who Has the Cup?

The Dominion championship had been held for a number of years before the first Grey Cup game, and it had done well, drawing thousands of fans. And what those games had shown was that the best football of the time was being played in the universities.

Part 4 ➤ *Canadian Football: The Heroes of the Game*

Listen Up!

If the Grey Cup was first awarded in 1909, how did the 1908 Hamilton Tiger Seniors get on the old mug? According to Stephen Thiele, when the Tigers won their second cup in 1915, they decided to get even with the University of Toronto for holding onto the mug in 1912 and 1913 because the Varsity Blues felt until someone directly beat them in a Grey Cup game, they could keep it. So, the Tigers sent the cup out and had it engraved with the 1908 winners. In the Canadian Football Hall of Fame, you can still see it, affixed to the original base of the silver mug.

Know-it-alls

Q. From what famous heavyweight boxer did the Winnipeg Blue Bombers adapt their name?

A. Joe Louis, the Brown Bomber.

With Hugh Gall, one of the country's first football stars, and Smirlie Lawson leading the way, the University of Toronto won that first Grey Cup, 26-6 over the Parkdale Canoe Club. Gall, who had eight singles in the game (still a record), was actually a member of the Parkdale club when not studying at the university. But while of college age, he was a Varsity Blue all the way and would help his team to three straight Grey Cup wins.

On this first occasion, however, there was no actual trophy. It wouldn't be ready until February 7, 1910.

More Arguments

In 1907, the best teams in the Ontario and Quebec unions got together to form the Interprovincial Rugby Football Union, known ever after as the Big Four — Toronto Argonauts, Ottawa Rough Riders, Hamilton Tigers, and the Montreal Football Club.

The 1909 league winner was Ottawa, and they challenged the Varsity Blues for the cup. No way, said the trustees, who recognized the ORFU champs as legitimate contenders, and declared that someone, either Ottawa or U of T, had to play Parkdale, or no cup.

Ottawa and U of T went ahead and played anyway in front of 11,000 people in Toronto, and the Rough Riders were pounded 31-7.

Writer Frank Cosentino says that so little was thought of ORFU football, that by the time the cup game was played a week later hardly anyone showed up. Only 3,800 paid to see the game at Rosedale Field.

That wasn't the last game of the season, however. On December 11, the Riders and Tigers gave a demonstration of Canadian football in New York in front of nearly 15,000 people in a game that would help the American college version straighten out some of its own problems with violence and a grinding style.

Chapter 17 ➤ *The Family of Football (1900–1941)*

Football as a Teenager

During 1910–20, football began to grow up in Canada, both as a spectator sport and as a game. By the end of the decade, the rules that would take it through the rest of the century were mostly in place, though arguments continued over specific points, especially "interference," or blocking.

And, the sport survived a four-season hiatus caused by the booming of the big guns over in Europe.

As writer Frank Cosentino points out, the big question of the period was whether the intercollegiate teams (led by U of T and a suddenly strong McGill, under former Notre Dame star Shag Shaughnessy, an American and the first truly professional coach in Canada), would continue as the power in Canadian football, or the city teams such as those in the Big Four would gain prominence.

McGill refused to play for the Grey Cup in 1912 because the game was considered too close to exams. They did it again in 1913. Slowly, a split was opening up between the city leagues and the universities that would eventually lead the colleges to drop out of Grey Cup play altogether.

> **Quote, Unquote**
>
> "Not more than 50 percent of the players really know the rules under which they are playing."
>
> — Retiring player Bill Hoare, 1920, on continuing intra-league arguments over rules.

> **Know-it-alls**
>
> Q. What was the original name of the team we know as the Calgary Stampeders?
>
> A. Calgary Tigers, born 1908.

From Out of the West They Came...and Lost

The game underwent significant changes in a two year period during 1920–21, the most important of which were a complete housecleaning of the Canadian Rugby Union (finally, the snapback system was installed) and the inclusion of Western Canada Rugby Football Union teams in the Grey Cup games.

The cup had become truly a national institution.

Western football had been developing at a slower pace than out east, and the prairie fathers of the game realized one of the key factors for future growth would be matching up with their Ontario and Quebec brethren.

Part 4 ➤ Canadian Football: The Heroes of the Game

Quote, Unquote

"Perhaps the day is not too far distant when many of the important games of football will be played at night."

— *Toronto Globe*, 1930, after the first eastern game under lights.

Quote, Unquote

"Pro football is going ahead by leaps and bounds in the United States, and we intend to have a shot at it."

— Lionel Conacher, 1932.

Know-it-alls

Q. What was the last university team to play in the Grey Cup?
A. University of Toronto, 1926.

Edmonton's Eskimos applied to challenge for the Grey Cup in 1921 and were destroyed 23-0 by the Toronto Argonauts of Lionel Conacher and Harry Batstone. The superb Queen's University club beat the Edmonton Elks 13-1 a year later, and Regina's Roughriders then played patsies to Queen's in 1923, coming out on the losing end of an embarrassing 54-0 score.

Grumbles were heard in the east over letting the west play for the cup.

Dissension in the Winnipeg team kept them out of the 1924 game, and a different team from that city, the Tammany Tigers, were walloped in 1925 by the Ottawa Senators. The CRU had seen enough and changed the system again to ensure the best two teams played, such as in 1927 when Balmy Beach beat Hamilton Tigers 9-6 in the first of a long line of "greatest games ever played."

The Big Train

Lionel Conacher, known as "The Big Train," was voted Canada's best athlete of the first half-century. Though he played in the NHL, his favourite sport was football, at which he was considered the best player of his day.

After playing for the Torontos in the 1920 cup (a loss to the Argos), Conacher moved across town to the champs and starred in the 1921 version of the national championship. The Argonauts went undefeated that season with Conacher leading the way, and beat Edmonton 23-0 in the cup final. The big guy actually left that game early, to be in uniform for the Toronto Granites seniors in an important hockey game that night.

Conacher would go on to form the first fully professional team in Canada — the Cross and Blackwell Chefs, who played against teams from Rochester and Buffalo in 1933, drawing good crowds. That move helped convince the Big Four and Western leagues to move toward professionalism themselves.

Passing the Torch

During 1928–34, the Regina Roughriders made it to six Grey Cup games and lost all of them, including the last one, despite the fact an astrologer in Saskatchewan had predicted the planets would be properly aligned for a win.

But the Roughriders did have a lasting effect on the game by introducing the forward pass in 1929, which confused eastern referees no end. Ever the last to be innovative, the Canadian Rugby Union banned the play in 1930, but it was back in for good in 1931.

The forward pass, more than any other weapon, would go on to define Canadian football over the next 70 years. With the wider and longer field than found in America, and with one less down to make 10 yards, the pass became a staple north of the border. The honour of throwing the first touchdown pass in cup history went to Warren Stevens of the Montreal Winged Wheelers in 1931.

Two major events changed the game in the 1930s. After years of dominance, the universities realized they could no longer compete with the now semi-professional city club teams, and they dropped out of Grey Cup play altogether to concentrate on their own championship.

And, out west, the introduction of the import player began an argument that would continue, off and on, for another 70 years.

Quote, Unquote

"We're just about fed up with efforts to keep pace with the authority flaunted over us by the Canadian Rugby Union."
— Western view of the CRU, 1935.

Know-it-alls

Q. What was the nickname of the Montreal city club in the 1930s?

A. The Montreal Indians.

Importing a Victory

By 1935, eastern football dominance suddenly changed when the Winnipeg Winnipegs (we don't name 'em, just write about 'em), upset the Hamilton Tigers 18-12 to take Lord Grey's mug to the edge of the flatlands for the first time.

The west had taken the lead in football development by inviting a number of American imports to play on their clubs. Winnipeggers had raised $7,500 to bring seven men across the border for the season.

Listen Up!

In 1940, the Grey Cup game was played twice. The Canadian Rugby Union decided to turn the classic into a two-game, total point affair to maximize gate receipts. In game one, at Toronto, a huge blizzard covered the field with snow just before kickoff and the game ended 8-2 for the Ottawa Rough Riders over Balmy Beach. Game two, in much better conditions, saw the Riders win 12-5. Dave Sprague of Ottawa played both games with a seriously infected leg in a heroic effort.

Quote, Unquote

"$100 to keep me in cigarettes, and a teaching job."

— The price of getting Johnny Metras to turn down the Detroit Lions' $4,500 offer and come play in Canada in 1934 for St. Mike's of the Ontario RFU.

Eastern clubs convinced the CRU to place severe restrictions on imports and on two occasions, 1936 and 1940, the western representative was banned from Grey Cup play because of the import argument.

Ironically, the Sarnia (Ontario) Imperials were able to come up with a strong enough football team to win the cup in 1934 and 1936 precisely because they could entice Americans to come and play by offering them jobs in the oil industry. And, according to Cosentino, the Montreal team was paying so much money under the table that the MAAA became known as the Montreal Almost Amateur Athletic Association.

The Winnipeggers, now thankfully renamed the Blue Bombers, would win three Grey Cups between 1937 and 1941, when the game put the regular club teams on hold for the duration of the Second World War.

Weather Report

Football in Canada has often been as much about the weather as the game itself, and the early days were no exception.

After getting away without bad weather for its early years, the Grey Cup ran into Mother Nature in a big way in the mid 1920s. The 1925 game between the Ottawa Senators and Winnipeg Tammany Tigers was won by the Bytown boys 24-1 in a driving rain storm that left the field a virtual mud hole that helped decide the game by causing a key Winnipeg fumble.

One year later, Varsity Stadium in Toronto was a sheet of ice as Ottawa won again, this time 10-7 over U of T. Fans were so cold many rushed the box office demanding their money back.

Nothing in the era, as Steven Thiele reports, could top 1931 however. The Regina Roughriders saw a frozen Montreal Stadium field the day before the Grey Cup and came up with an idea. They sent out for an order of tennis and lacrosse shoes to be delivered before game time. The shoes didn't show up, and both the Roughriders and Montreal Winged Wheelers slid around the field for the first half.

Chapter 17 ➤ *The Family of Football (1900–1941)*

At the start of the second, the Regina players were shocked to see the Montrealers take the field in tennis and lacrosse shoes. Their own shoes! Seems the delivery boy had messed up and taken them to the wrong dressing room.

Montreal ran Regina right out of the park. It was a story that would be repeated almost 50 years later.

Other Stars of the Era

➤ Harry Batstone was a little guy with a big heart. Only 155 pounds, Batstone nonetheless starred as a halfback who could run and kick. Won his first Grey Cup with the Argonauts in 1921, but it was when he entered Queen's University that he hit his stride, leading the Golden Gaels to 26 straight wins and three Grey Cups.

➤ Joe Tubman led Ottawa to cup wins in 1925 and 1926. He turned in a legendary play in the muddy first game when he fielded a punt, realized no Winnipeg players were anywhere in sight, and stopped to carefully wipe the mud and water off the ball before kicking it back.

➤ Jeff Russell starred for the Montreal Winged Wheelers from 1922 to 1925 and seemed on his way to a long career. In 1926, repairing a power line in a rainstorm, he was accidentally killed. The Jeff Russell Trophy was established to honour the top player in the east.

➤ Ted Reeve became known to millions of readers as "The Moaner," for his columns with the *Toronto Telegram* and *Toronto Sun*. Before that he was a fine football player and coach who played for both the Argos and Balmy Beach, specializing in blocking kicks and providing stalwart defence.

➤ Fritz Hanson was the first American to star in Canada. Playing for Winnipeg Blue

Grey Cup Winners of the Era

1909–11	University of Toronto
1912	Hamilton Alerts
1913	Hamilton Tigers
1914	Toronto Argonauts
1915	Hamilton Tigers
1916–19	No game played
1920	U of T
1921	Toronto Argonauts
1922–24	Queen's University
1925–26	Ottawa Senators
1927	Balmy Beach
1928–29	Hamilton Tigers
1930	Balmy Beach
1931	Montreal Winged Wheelers
1932	Hamilton Tigers
1933	Toronto Argonauts
1934	Sarnia Imperials
1935	Winnipeg Winnipegs
1936	Sarnia Imperials
1937–38	Toronto Argonauts
1939	Winnipeg Blue Bombers
1940	Ottawa Rough Riders
1941	Winnipeg Blue Bombers

Part 4 ➤ *Canadian Football: The Heroes of the Game*

Bombers from 1935, he was known as Twinkletoes, the Golden Ghost, and Fritzy. At the Grey Cup that year, Hanson piled up 300 yards on punt returns and added a 78-yard touchdown run. He fought with the Winnipeg Light Infantry in World War II.

➤ Hugh Gall was the best kicker of his time, and he could do it with either foot. A star with the University of Toronto Varsity Blues, he set a record that still stands by kicking eight singles in the first Grey Cup game.

The Least You Need to Know

➤ It took over 50 years, and countless arguments, for the rules of football as we know it to become accepted.

➤ The Earl Grey Cup became emblematic of the Dominion football championship in 1909.

➤ University teams dominated the game in its early days, right up to the mid 1920s.

➤ Western teams did not catch up competitively until the mid 1930s.

➤ The Winnipeg Winnipegs were the first western team to win the cup.

➤ Lionel Conacher was the biggest star of the era.

Chapter 18

Heroes from Coast to Coast (1942–1969)

In This Chapter
➤ From hardly amateur to fully professional
➤ What happened to the Argos
➤ Jackie and Sam
➤ Bud vs. the Tiger-Cats
➤ Russ and Ronny
➤ Weather report

Over the 27 years from the middle of the war until Russ Jackson retired at the end of the 1969 season, football in Canada was every bit as good as the version played south of the border. And we don't just mean the game itself. Because Canadian teams paid as well, and in some cases better than, the National Football League, many of the U.S. colleges' great stars of the period chose to come here, where they had long careers and stayed afterwards to settle down. The influx of Americans was not completely positive, however. In this era, the Canadian head coach would begin to disappear, and by the end of it the Canadian quarterback would be legislated almost out of existence. But one thing was certain — football was Canada's second favourite professional sport, and its championship game, the Grey Cup, became the biggest one-day party in the land. In this chapter, we'll trace the game for the three decades from the middle of the war until the end of the 1960s.

Part 4 ➤ Canadian Football: The Heroes of the Game

Amateur only in Name

Unlike in the First World War, Canadian football did not take a hiatus during World War II. Military teams came to the rescue, providing entertainment for those on the home front, and featuring many of the men fans were already familiar with.

The Toronto Royal Canadian Air Force Hurricanes won in 1942, beating the Winnipeg RCAF Bombers. Hamilton's Flying Wildcats beat the same Winnipeg club again the next year, and the 1944 Cup went to the St. Hyacinthe-Donnacona Navy, representing the Quebec naval base.

Most of the regular teams came back for 1945, with a couple of important exceptions. Montreal AAA, which had dropped out with money problems in 1936, was still gone, leaving the city without professional football (a situation that would solve itself one year later when Lew Hayman and Leo Dandurand formed the Montreal Alouettes), and the Edmonton Eskimos didn't come back from the war until near the end of the decade.

By this time, all the teams had by now given up on the pretense of amateurism and gone fully professional, which left some of the clubs in difficult financial situations.

The biggest brawls of the period revolved around the question of signing Americans. Right after the war, the Canadian Football Union passed a rule allowing five imports a team, with some confusing regulations regarding what, exactly, was an American. The number of non-Canadians on clubs would slowly rise until there were 15 imports by the 1980s.

The other effect of American influence on the Canadian game was the virtual elimination of the Canadian head coach. By the early 1950s, only Anis Stukas was still holding the reigns of a club.

With the death of the All-America Football Conference, many more good U.S. players were available, and both the CFU and National Football League teams went after them full force. Ultimately, the fight for players between the two remaining pro leagues resulted in a cross-border legal and recruiting war that was eventually solved to the satisfaction of both — we wouldn't steal theirs still under contract, and the NFL would do the same.

The Grand National Drunk

The Grey Cup had been a relatively staid affair until 1948, in keeping with our national character. But, when the Calgary Stampeders came to Toronto for

> **Listen Up!**
>
> In 1947, a huge fire broke out in the offices of the Toronto Argonauts, destroying all records, photos, and trophies. Except for one item. As Gordon Currie writes: "Apparently in falling from a shelf during the fire, it hooked on to a nail. The other cups fell into the blaze and were melted or heat-twisted beyond recognition. This one trophy survived intact. It was the Grey Cup." Polished up and restored to its grandeur, the lucky cup was ready for the 1948 season.

Chapter 18 ▶ *Heroes from Coast to Coast (1942–1969)*

what would be a victorious appearance in the cup final that year, they brought trainloads of their fans with them.

And folks, the party was on.

While coach Les Lear kept his Stamps in an Oakville hotel, safely away from the insanity, the Calgary fans turned Toronto the Good (and boring) into one big celebration.

Riding their horses up and down the streets (and, according to one lasting legend, into the lobby of the Royal York Hotel), holding flapjack breakfasts on the steps of the city hall, parading here and there with their bands, big hats, big boots, and even bigger yells, the good times went on almost all week.

While the game was going on (won 12-7 by the Stamps over Ottawa), hotels were removing furniture and other breakables from their lobbies to prepare for the post-game parties.

Grey Cup week would never be quiet again.

Arrrrgooooos!

The Toronto Argonauts had been Canadian football's best franchise, and so often its best team, for such a long time that no one thought it possible that the double blue could fall from grace.

Over the eight years from 1945–52, the Argos won five out of eight Grey Cups, led by such stars as Royal Copeland and Joe "King" Krol (still considered by many the best all around player in Canadian history), and overseen by coaches such as Ted Morris, Lew Hayman, and Frank "The Professor" Clair. Three of those seasons, Toronto played with not a single import in its lineup.

But, from 1953 to 1983, the Argonauts failed to win a single Grey Cup. Not one. And during that time the club became the laughingstock of Canadian sports, at once despised for their free-spending, idiotic ways, and pitied for their long-suffering, ever-loyal fans who packed Varsity Stadium and then the Canadian National Exhibition Stadium for most of that run.

Know-it-alls

Q. What year did the Regina Roughriders become the Saskatchewan Roughriders?

A. 1946.

Quote, Unquote

"I'm mighty proud of Eagle."

— Edmonton coach Pop Ivy on lineman Eagle Keys, who played most of the 1954 cup final on a broken leg.

Know-it-alls

Q. What two teams combined to become the Hamilton Tiger-Cats in 1949?

A. Hamilton Wildcats and Hamilton Tigers.

Listen Up!

Writer Jay Teitel's definition of the "Argo Bounce," which used to be a good thing: "The unluckiest bounce in the world, the one that usually arose from the Argos' uncanny ability to lose critical games in the dying minutes by committing an improbable blunder that resulted in a momentarily free football — more often than not a fumble — which then found its way into the hands of the opposition."

Quote, Unquote

"Joe has no equal as a football player, in my books."

— Royal Copeland on Argonaut teammate Joe Krol, 1946.

What happened?

Writer Jay Teitel, whose book *The Argo Bounce* covered that awful period, has one simple explanation: Harry Sonshine happened.

"You got any notions, Harry?"

That was what a small gathering of Argonaut Rowing Club officials, owners of the football team, said to one Harry Sonshine during a meeting in Winnipeg just before the 1954 season opened.

Which was the start of Sonshine's control over the famous double-blue, a short reign that would have tragic (for fans) ramifications, spreading all through the 1950s and into the 1960s. A former Argonaut who had made it big in manufacturing and become a superfan, Sonshine would alienate coach Frank Clair (and chase him off to Ottawa where he would win three more cups), fire the entire team's imports after 1954, spend fabulous amounts of money on players and get almost nothing in return, set off a range war with the National Football League, and get the Argos so preoccupied with American football that they would forget for almost a quarter-century that you win by building a strong base of non-imports, not by airlifting a half-dozen new faces a week from south of the border.

Harry was gone by the end of the 1955 season when the rowing club unloaded its interest, but his legacy would live for almost three complete decades.

It was the Argonauts, appropriately named for Jason's famous crew on the good ship Argo, as Greek tragedy.

Jackie and Sam

Canadian football by the 1950s, with its wide field and 25-yard end zones, had become what it still is today — a passing league. And that meant the quarterbacks became the big stars.

Nowhere was that more the case than in Edmonton and Montreal, where Jackie Parker and Sam "The Rifle" Etcheverry showed what a quarterback could do out on the wide expanses. The two teams met in three straight cup finals, starting in 1954, and it was the Eskimos who came out on top each time.

Chapter 18 ➤ *Heroes from Coast to Coast (1942–1969)*

Parker carried two nicknames — the Fast Freight from Mississippi State, or Old Spaghetti Legs — and he could play defensive back and running back on top of quarterback. He scored 750 points and lasted 15 seasons with Edmonton, Toronto, and British Columbia.

His most famous score, though, came as a rookie. In the 1954 Grey Cup, with his team trailing 25-20, Parker scooped up a fumble at his own 20 yard line and ran it all the way back for the touchdown.

Parker played halfback in the 1956 game as Don Getty, who would later become premier of Alberta, quarterbacked.

Etcheverry, clearly the better pure passer of the two and among the best tossers of a football to play in Canada, threw for over 25,000 yards and 174 touchdowns in his career, utilizing the talents of receivers such as "Prince" Hal Patterson to do it. Though he didn't win a Grey Cup as a player, Etcheverry did turn the trick as a head coach with Montreal in 1970.

Quote, Unquote

"Don is a great football player. He proved it under pressure..."

— Jackie Parker, on future Alberta premier Don Getty, 1956.

Know-it-alls

Q. What sparkling backfield led the Edmonton Eskimos to three straight Grey Cups in the 1950s?

A. Normie Kwong and John Bright.

Holy Mackinaw!

Let's take a timeout to learn the Hamilton Tiger-Cats' chant.

All together now:

Oski-wee-wee

Oski-wah-wah

Holy Mackinaw!

Tigers. Eat 'em raw!

We now return you to your regularly scheduled chapter.

Nipping the Tigers in the Bud

If you came to sensibility in the later 1950s, your earliest football memories would revolve around two teams — the Winnipeg Blue Bombers and the Hamilton Tiger-Cats.

Six times in the nine seasons from 1957, those two teams locked up in classic Grey Cup battles, which went Winnipeg's way on four occasions.

Listen Up!

The weirdest incident in Grey Cup history happened on November 30, 1957. In a game won easily by Hamilton over Winnipeg, Ray "Bibbles" Bawel of the Cats picked up a fumble and scampered down the sideline to an obvious touchdown. Except, someone stuck a foot out from the crowd on that sideline and tripped him. The perpetrator fled out of the stadium and no one could identify him. Turned out his name was David Humphrey, a young Toronto lawyer, who would go on to become an Ontario judge. Justice apparently lost its head that day.

By now, the cup games were regularly broadcast, coast to coast, on television, and those black and white images produced two stars above all others.

One was a former import player who went on to coach the Bombers — Harry Peter "Bud" Grant. The other was a huge, menacing Hamilton defensive tackle named Angelo Mosca.

Hamilton was an incredible club, especially on defence, and they would dominate the about to be renamed Canadian Football League (for two seasons the Canadian Football Conference, before a quick switch in 1958 to the name it carries today), making it to the Grey Cup 9 times in 11 years.

But the club carried a blue and gold mental block — the Bombers. Especially after easily beating them 32-7 in 1957.

After that, the Bombers beat the Cats four times in the next five years.

Mosca spent two seasons with Hamilton, went to Ottawa for 1960 and 1961 and then came back to the Cats again, where he earned national acrimony for what was considered by many to be a late hit on B.C.'s Willie Fleming — it took the latter out of the '63 final, which Hamilton would win. The Cats lost the following season. In 1965, the Cats beat the Bombers in a driving win.

Whew.

After another victory in 1967, most of the top Cats retired. But Mosca stayed on until 1972 and one final Grey Cup victory before going into pro wrestling.

He later joined teammates John Barrow, Bernie Faloney, Joe Zuger, Garney Henley, Tommy Joe Coffey, Cookie Gilchrist, Don Sutherin, Hal Patterson, Vince Scott, and Tommy Grant in the Hall of Fame.

And coach Grant? He'd go on to the NFL, take the Minnesota Vikings to four Super Bowls, and lose them all.

Russ

Ironic, isn't it? In a league where the Canadian quarterback went the way of the dinosaur by the end of this period because of a silly addition to the "designated import" rule (complicated — basically it meant an import could be designated as a backup pivot and go in and out of the game at will, which meant another "more talented" American on the roster), the best quarterback of the era was a Canuck.

Russ Jackson, a kid out of McMaster University in Hamilton, Ontario, came to the Ottawa Rough Riders in the late 1950s, and proceeded to win three Schenleys as league's best player, four as best Canadian, make six Eastern all-star clubs, and be voted All-Canadian three times.

He led the Black Riders to three Grey Cups, including two straight in 1968–1969. It was the '69 game — Grey Cup in Montreal, Front de Libération du Québec postal box bombs going off at random, and a death threat on Jackson's life to boot — that stands above all others. He played most of it with a separated shoulder and still found a way to throw four touchdown passes in the win over Saskatchewan.

In a career where he mostly played 14-game seasons (as opposed to the 16 contests latter day quarterbacks would get), Jackson threw for 24,592 yards and 185 touchdowns.

Of course, in retirement he lost his head and tried to coach the Argonauts out of their mess, which didn't work. But who cared? Russ Jackson would be a winner for the rest of his life — one that included television commentary and becoming an educator and high school principal in Mississauga, Ontario.

> **Quote, Unquote**
>
> "Nothing can beat us now, except an act of God."
>
> — Leo Cahill, head coach, Toronto Argonauts, 1969. They lost.

> **Know-it-alls**
>
> Q. What distiller sponsored the outstanding player awards for 35 years from 1953?
>
> A. Schenley.

Weather Report

Fog Bowls, Mud Bowls, Ice Bowls, this era had them all.

It snowed hard in the days before the 1950 Grey Cup game at Varsity Stadium in Toronto, and officials thought it would be a great idea to have snowplows and tractors move it off the field. Unfortunately, it left the field a muddy mess — hence the Mud Bowl. Argos won 13-0 over Winnipeg, but the most famous play from the game occurred when Bud Tinsley of Winnipeg was found facedown in a deep puddle. Fearing he was drowning, referee Hec Crighton rolled him over and "saved him." Forty years later,

Part 4 ➤ *Canadian Football: The Heroes of the Game*

> **Know-it-alls**
>
> Q. In what season was the Grey Cup game called before time was up when fans swarmed the field?
>
> A. 1960. Ottawa led Edmonton by 10 points with just seconds left and the Riders with the ball.

Tinsley told writer Stephen Thiele that he wasn't unconscious, just numb and mad from getting a charley horse.

The Battle of the Bog was the result of another pre-game blizzard and subsequent melt at Toronto's CNE Stadium in 1959.

1961 saw the famous Fog Bowl game between Winnipeg and Hamilton, in which a heavy blanket covered the CNE field for most of the game, but became impenetrable by the fourth quarter. Officials called the game off at that point, and it was completed the following day.

It seemed half of the western finals in that era were played in snowstorms. And, in 1969, the Ice Bowl saw Ottawa, wearing broomball shoes, send the Argonauts slip-sliding out of the second game of the Eastern final on a field covered with, well, ice.

Other Stars of the Era

- ➤ George Reed is the greatest running back in Canadian pro history, rushing for over 16,000 yards in 13 seasons with the Saskatchewan Roughriders from 1963–75. He still leads most of the rushing categories in the CFL record book. Had 11 1,000-plus rushing yard years, including six in a row and then another five straight. Appeared in four Grey Cup games.
- ➤ Bernie Faloney quarterbacked Hamilton to seven Grey Cup finals. Started with Edmonton in 1954, retired from B.C. in 1967. Famous for a 111-yard run back of a Toronto punt in 1961 that, though called back on a penalty, broke the Argos' spirit for the overtime and gave the Cats the win.
- ➤ When Dick Shatto retired from the Argos in 1965, he had more pass receptions, more touchdowns scored, and had piled up the most offensive yardage of anyone in Canadian history. As a 12-year Argo, however, he also never won a Grey Cup.
- ➤ Normie Kwong, known as the China Clipper, had a 13-year career as a running back, teaming with John Bright in the Edmonton backfield. Kwong ran for over 9,000 yards in his career, scoring 78 touchdowns. Bright played the same 13 seasons, also split with Calgary and the Eskimos, and piled up almost 11,000 yards and 69 touchdowns.
- ➤ Royal Copeland, the only player to score a major in three straight Grey Cup games, was one half of the Gold Dust Twins, with Joe Krol, on the Toronto Argonauts.

Chapter 18 ➤ *Heroes from Coast to Coast (1942–1969)*

➤ Jake Gaudaur spent 50 years in Canadian football as a player, coach, general manager, team president, and finally, commissioner of the CFL. In the latter job, he brought the league into the modern era and was instrumental in gaining major television contracts for the loop.

The Least You Need to Know

➤ Canadian football went from amateur to fully professional in the 1950s.
➤ The Canadian game became dominated by American coaches and import players.
➤ The Canadian Football League was founded by the amalgamation of East and West leagues, in 1958.
➤ Russ Jackson was the game's greatest quarterback, and its last regular Canadian at that position.
➤ Fights over the number of imports allowed on a roster became regular occurrences in this era.

Grey Cup Winners of the Era

1942	Toronto RCAF Hurricanes
1943	Hamilton Flying Wildcats
1944	St. Hyacinthe-Donnacona Navy
1945–47	Toronto Argonauts
1948	Calgary Stampeders
1949	Montreal Alouettes
1950	Toronto Argonauts
1951	Ottawa Rough Riders
1952	Toronto Argonauts
1953	Hamilton Tiger-Cats
1954–56	Edmonton Eskimos
1957	Hamilton Tiger-Cats
1958–59	Winnipeg Blue Bombers
1960	Ottawa Rough Riders
1961–62	Winnipeg Blue Bombers
1963	Hamilton Tiger-Cats
1964	B.C. Lions
1965	Hamilton Tiger-Cats
1966	Saskatchewan Roughriders
1967	Hamilton Tiger-Cats
1968–69	Ottawa Rough Riders

Chapter 19

From the Penthouse to the Outhouse (1970–1989)

> **In This Chapter**
> - Politics and economics
> - Black and Canadian quarterbacks
> - Edmonton's dynasty
> - Nelson's NFL heroes
> - Virtual parity
> - Dropping crowds
> - Weather report

In the 20 seasons from 1970 through 1989, the Canadian Football League went from a healthy, nationally respected institution to a financially strapped organization viewed by many as a second-class minor league. Much of that had to do with television, or the lack of it — the National Football League on the tube all the time, and the blackout rules in Canada keeping a generation of fans from seeing their own team in home games. A succession of financially and competitively insane owners didn't help matters in many cities either. And yet, the game on the field was as good, and as exciting, as it had ever been. Especially with Canadian colleges turning out more skilled players to fill non-import quotas. In this chapter, we'll look at what happened in those 20 seasons.

Part 4 ▶ Canadian Football: The Heroes of the Game

Kiicking the Political Football

Jim Kiick. Paul Warfield. Larry Csonka.

For the first four years of the 1970s, the Canadian Football League seemed like a national treasure that would last forever.

Yes, there had been some murmurs about possible expansion to the United States. Yes, the Montreal Alouettes had struggled for a while, but with new owner Sam Berger, things were straightening out. And yes, it was early in 1970 that the hated quarterback exception to the designated import rule came in.

But, everything seemed hunky dory. Heck, even the Argonauts played well for a time.

All this changed with Jim Kiick, Paul Warfield, and Larry Csonka.

When the World Football League was formed in 1974 as a challenge to the National Football League, a Canadian franchise, owned by Johnny F. Bassett, son of Argonaut owner John Bassett (who was all for Bassett the younger sharing his stadium at the CNE), was awarded to Toronto. They would be called the Northmen, and their first hiring was Leo Cahill, ex-Argo coach, as general manager.

He, in turn, threw a million dollars of Bassett money at three famous Miami Dolphins — Jim Kiick, Paul Warfield, and Larry Csonka.

The CFL was furious, and they had a political ace up their sleeves. Federal Health Minister Marc Lalonde announced that no American team in an American league would be allowed to expand to Canada, because "Football…Canadian football…matters."

After a legal brawl, the Northmen went to Memphis and became the Southmen in a league that lasted just a few years.

Ironically, as Frank Cosentino points out, it was this move that began the slow process of creating a mind set among Canadians that if their game needed the government to protect it, then it must be second class.

Listen Up!

Just days before this era got underway, the Grey Cup was kidnapped from a display case in the offices of the Ottawa Rough Riders. Police were baffled, but realizing it was probably a prank told CFL officials to give it a little time and the mug would show up. On February 16, 1970, Toronto police got a call sending them to a pay phone where they found a key and the number to a locker in Union Station rail terminal. Inside the locker was Earl Grey's Cup, which now sits permanently in the Hall of Fame. A $550 replica makes the rounds.

Quote, Unquote

"…I traded three Super Bowls for a ferris wheel."

— Quarterback Joe Theismann passes up the Miami Dolphins to spend '71 and '72 with the Argos at the Canadian National Exhibition grounds.

Chapter 19 ➤ *From the Penthouse to the Outhouse (1970–1989)*

Oh, it was also at this point that Bassett senior decided he'd had enough of the CFL, and enough of the gate equalization plan that saw him pay other clubs for having weaker attendance, and bailed out of the Argos. His flagship television station, CFTO in Toronto, became very much a negative influence on the CFL, and eventually the entire CTV network would pull out of broadcasting the league.

No one could see all of that coming in 1974, but the seeds were sown.

The Underground Railroad

Leaving aside for a moment the idea that Canadian quarterbacks weren't welcome in their own country, one of the CFL's greatest legacies is the opportunity it gave to Black American quarterbacks who weren't welcome in their own.

Let's not mess around here. Quarterback was the one position in the National Football League that was reserved for whites only, because white, dinosaur-like general managers and coaches thought Blacks weren't smart enough, or imbued with the leadership abilities, to handle it.

That was not the case in the CFL.

After John Henry Jackson and Sandy Stephens had short runs at quarterbacking the Argos in the early 1960s, it was left to Chuck Ealey to be the first Black to make a real impact at the pivot. As a rookie in 1972, Ealey led the Hamilton Tiger-Cats to a Grey Cup championship, which opened a door that many would enter: Condredge Holloway (signed at the same time by Ottawa in 1975 with Tom Clements, a white quarterback from Notre Dame, to share the duties), Warren Moon, J. C. Watts, Damon Allen, Joe Paopao, Roy Dewalt, Tracy Ham, and many more.

> **Know-it-alls**
>
> Q. Who was the first Black quarterback in the CFL?
>
> A. John Henry Jackson, Toronto, 1961.

Black American quarterbacks generally played a different game than white Americans, who tended to be drop-back, stay in the pocket passers. American Blacks were creative scramblers, combining the constant threat of taking off on a run with a strong arm and sharp playcalling — very much like Jackie Parker or Russ Jackson had done in the CFL.

They were perfect for the Canadian game. And, if the NFL was going to be stupid about not allowing Blacks the chance to be quarterbacks, well then Canadian clubs were going to give them that opportunity.

But while emancipation was the rule for American Blacks, it became, after the altered designated import rules came in, hardly an exception for Canadians.

Part 4 ▶ Canadian Football: The Heroes of the Game

Listen Up!

Canadian college football began to make a strong comeback in this era with the broadcasting nationally of the College Bowl game (the Vanier Cup). Conference winners in Ontario, Quebec, the Maritimes, and the West would play off to make the final game, which was transferred full time to Toronto — first in old Varsity Stadium, and then eventually to the SkyDome when it opened in 1989. Though interest was up, however, a number of schools ended their football programs. And there was a lot of pressure on all university athletics to go to the scholarship system used in the U.S. That pressure is still being resisted today.

Quote, Unquote

"The non-important."

— Writer Frank Cosentino's name for what non-imports, Canadians, became in the 1960s and 1970s.

A Bone to Pick with the CFL

Jamie Bone was a good enough quarterback with the University of Western Ontario when he graduated in 1977 that the Dallas Cowboys of the vaunted NFL were willing to give him a serious look.

The CFL, embodied in this case by the Hamilton Tiger-Cats who drafted him, could not have been less interested — giving him just a cursory look. Bone took his case to the Ontario Human Rights Commission, where he was awarded $10,000 in damages and ordered to be given a proper five-day tryout. Tired of it all, Bone went to Dallas, where he impressed a lot of people but didn't make the club.

Rather than pay attention to the spirit of the rights commission's ruling, CFL teams just stopped drafting Canuck pivots completely. Frank Cosentino compiled a list of the forgotten: Dan Feraday, Paul Paddon, Andy Parichi, Dave Pickett, Bob Cameron (who became a punter for Winnipeg), Bone, Scott Mallender, Rich Zmich, Greg Vavra (short career), Phil Scarfone, and Jordan Gagner. All won most outstanding player honours in their college careers.

About the only Canadian to hang around awhile was Gerry Datillio, with Montreal in the late 1970s, and that was because he was a strong special teams player.

Though the designated import rule was eventually dropped, the situation is not much better today. Non-import quarterbacks, trained in the Canadian style of game, are still considered "non-important."

Simply the Best

Lest you think there wasn't any football actually played in this era, let's introduce the Edmonton Eskimos of 1977–82.

Coached by Hugh Campbell, the Eskimos made the Grey Cup final in 1977 and were pummelled 41-6 by the Montreal Alouettes in the famous Staple Game (more to come). But for the following five seasons, the Eskimos were practically unbeatable.

Chapter 19 ➤ *From the Penthouse to the Outhouse (1970–1989)*

Led by veteran quarterback Tom Wilkinson, and by a Black rookie pivot out of the University of Washington named Warren Moon, Edmonton downed the tough Alouettes (twice), Hamilton, Ottawa, and Toronto, in cup finals over that stretch. As a matter of fact, in the 10 cup games from 1973 to 1982, the Eskies were in 9 of them.

They were the perfect combination of talented Americans and Canadians, and Campbell had a knack of knowing exactly the right spot for each of his players.

Receiver Tom Scott, linebacker Dan Kepley, runner Jim Germany, defensive back Larry Highbaugh, defensive lineman Dave Fennell, vertically challenged receiver Brian Kelly, linebacker Dale Potter — the list of classy, courageous, talented players was virtually endless.

But the keys were Wilkinson and Moon. They were an unstoppable duo.

The only team that really scared the Eskies in a final during that string was the young Ottawa Rough Riders, in 1981. Led by J. C. Watts, the huge underdogs (Eastern teams really stunk at this point in the era), the Riders put up a 20-0 lead in the first half.

> **Quote, Unquote**
>
> "I'm just an ordinary superstar."
>
> — Johnny Rodgers, flamboyant Montreal receiver, 1974.

> **Know-it-alls**
>
> Q. Who dropped the Grey Cup, and broke it, when overwhelmed with fans after a win?
>
> A. Edmonton's Tom Wilkinson and Dan Kepley, 1978.

With Moon off-form, Wilkinson came in for awhile and had his own troubles. Moon came back and he led the Eskimos to a huge comeback win.

Moon was on his own in 1982 after Wilkinson retired, and he took the green and gold to a 32-16 victory.

After that, Hugh Campbell went off to a short stint in the shorter-lived United States Football League, while Moon moved to the National Football League's Houston Oilers (where he was still just one of a small handful of Black quarterbacks). He would still be playing, at the age of 41, in 1998 with Seattle.

And Wilkinson? Wilkie led a slew of teammates into the Hall of Fame.

Lord Nelson Loses Trafalgar

Because most of the clubs in the west had been owned by community groups for most of their existence, those cities can't "boast" any of the colourful owners found in the east. At least not yet.

Part 4 ➤ *Canadian Football: The Heroes of the Game*

> **Quote, Unquote**
>
> "He's got to be the number one quarterback in football, tied with Terry Bradshaw or Joe Montana."
>
> — Edmonton coach Hugh Campbell on pivot Warren Moon, 1982.

> **Know-it-alls**
>
> Q. What two-time Grey Cup winning coach with Montreal went on to take the Buffalo Bills to four straight Super Bowl appearances?
>
> A. Marv Levy.

The Eastern owner merry-go-round, however, produced some fascinating characters in this era, but none more so than one Nelson Skalbania (the man who sold Wayne Gretzky from his WHA Indianapolis Racers to the Edmonton Oilers).

The CFL had long struggled with how to make Montreal more of a community team for both the French and English, rather than one only the Anglos showed any interest in. It didn't help at this time that Montreal mayor Jean Drapeau was nosing around for an NFL team, either, and the French press could have cared less about the Als.

It wasn't as though the Alouettes weren't trying — they had a superb team in the late 1970s and tossed a lot of money at good American imports that might raise the profile of the club including Tom Cousineau, a linebacker out of Ohio State, and fine runner David Green.

But Sam Berger had had enough and he sold the Als in 1981 to Skalbania, a Vancouver entrepreneur.

Some worried that Skalbania would try to take the Alouettes into the NFL. But he fooled them. Nelson Skalbania tried to bring the National Football League to the Montreal Alouettes instead.

With Admiral Nelson calling the shots, the Als sent excellent running back David Green to Hamilton for the rights to Los Angeles Rams' quarterback Vince Ferragamo, who had played in the Super Bowl that January. Skalbania gave him $400,000 for the season. Then Montreal got receivers James Scott from the Chicago Bears and Billy "White Shoes" Johnson from Houston, and stole top draft pick David Overstreet, a running back, out from under the noses of the Miami Dolphins.

To satisfied smiles across the rest of the league the Als started 1-8, and only made the Eastern playoffs at 3-13 because the Argonauts were even worse. Ferragamo, who could not adapt to the Canadian style of game, threw interceptions left and right and wound up benched for Canuck Gerry Dattilio before the season was done.

How's that for irony?

The Grey Cup in Montreal failed to sell out, the Alouettes were the subject of ridicule, and the league itself was starting to be seen as a bit of a joke. Unfortunately, that joke would run for the rest of the 1980s no matter what the CFL did to prevent it.

As for Montreal, the Alouettes would go broke and be replaced by the Concordes, disappearing entirely by 1987 (when they folded just three days before the start of the regular season). The city would be without football for 10 seasons, with the exception of a short experiment in the World League of American Football in the 1990s.

A Lot to Be Said for Parity?

The strange thing about the 1980s was that even with all the financial troubles in the league (Calgary, Ottawa, Hamilton, and B.C. especially struggled at times), some of the best football in the annals of the Canadian game was played on the field.

Especially in the Grey Cup.

Between 1983, when the Argos finally broke the 30-year jinx and won the mug for the first time since 1952, and 1989, six different teams won the old silverware, Winnipeg being the only double victor (1984 and 1988).

Almost every season the Grey Cup game would be declared "the greatest ever" (including 1989, when Saskatchewan beat Hamilton 43-40 in what might actually have been the real thing).

> **Know-it-alls**
>
> Q. What do Jake Gaudaur, Doug Mitchell, and Larry Smith have in common?
>
> A. They all ran the Canadian Football League.

> **Know-it-alls**
>
> Q. What brilliant Eskimos receiver was nicknamed Howdy Doody?
>
> A. Brian Kelly.

But the national television contract disappeared. The league had to create its own network to sell the regular season games. The CFL became something of a cable television league. Fans started staying away in droves.

Fuelled by a starkly negative press (much of that negativity, of course, the CFL seemed to bring down on itself), fans became convinced the Canadian pro game was second class, and not worth the time of day.

The question became: Where had all the people gone?

Self-Inflicted Wounds

Where had all the people gone? It's a complicated question revolving around a change in perception of the league itself, helped along by the CFL's own bungling; the rapid growth of the National Football League; the introduction of big league baseball into Montreal (1969) and Toronto (1977); and the availability of so many more things for people to spend their money on other than just tickets to sports events.

Part 4 ➤ *Canadian Football: The Heroes of the Game*

> **Know-it-alls**
>
> Q. What controversial Toronto Maple Leafs' hockey owner bought the Hamilton Tiger-Cats in 1978?
>
> A. Harold Ballard.

If there was a self-inflicted wound that journalists and writers jumped on as much as any other, it was the short-sighted blackout policy of the CFL owners who required broadcasters and cable companies to keep viewers within a certain radius of a stadium from seeing that team.

In Toronto, for example, tickets were so hard to come by in the 1970s that it was hard for younger fans to get into the park to see the Argos, so the obvious second choice was watching on television. But they were prevented from doing that, so young football fans turned to the National Football League.

While the blackout policy may have kept gate receipts higher for a time, those youngsters would eventually grow up to represent the ticket buying, and product purchasing, public. Turned off the CFL by the blackout regulations, many turned away permanently.

Short term gain for long term mega-pain.

Whatever the causes, the CFL headed for the 1990s with a herd of economic problems, all stampeding in its direction.

Weather Report

In 1971, Leo Cahill took his resurgent Toronto Argonauts to Empire Stadium in Vancouver for the Grey Cup game. The powerful offence was led by the passing of Joe Theismann, signed out of Notre Dame, and Greg Barton, who between them had spent much of the season switching off each series of plays. Talented running back Leon McQuay had also been a major spur.

But, Mother Nature was not ready for the Argos' long drought to end. She sent a rainstorm of epic proportions to earth, giving the Calgary Stampeders and quarterback Peter Liske what they needed to stay in the game. Still, Toronto seemed to have a chance to win it after an interception put the ball on the Calgary 11 with the Argos trailing by three points and less than two minutes to go.

Then, Theismann handed off to McQuay on second down and he slipped. Falling to the ground the ball popped loose on the horribly wet turf and the Stamps recovered and won thanks to the most famous fumble in league history.

In 1977, the Olympic Stadium turf was a slimy mess after the ground crew used salt to melt a field full of ice just before the Grey Cup game. In warm-up, Montreal's Tony Proudfoot (or it could have been slotback Larry Smith, depending on who tells the story) grabbed a staple gun off the sidelines and shot staples directly into his cleats — totally illegal. When the rest of the boys saw how well it worked they all did it and wound up pounding Edmonton 41-6 in the now infamous Staple Game.

Chapter 19 ➤ *From the Penthouse to the Outhouse (1970–1989)*

Though it had nothing to do with the weather, the Toilet Bowl of 1982 was interesting because the huge crowd at Toronto's CNE Stadium put such a pressure on the washroom facilities when the skies opened up that many of the toilets backed up, causing an unholy mess.

And at the Tundra Bowl, 1984, in Edmonton where the temperature was –11°C at game time and the field frozen solid, Winnipeg blasted Hamilton 47-17.

> **Quote, Unquote**
>
> "When Leon McQuay slipped, I fell."
>
> — Argos' coach Leo Cahill, later fired, on the 1971 cup final.

Thanks to the building of B.C. Place in Vancouver, three games in the 1980s were played under the western dome, and the 1989 classic was played under the brand new SkyDome roof in Toronto.

Mother Nature would get her revenge for that trick.

Other Stars of the Era

- Ron Lancaster started his 19-year career as a backup to Russ Jackson in Ottawa. Traded to Regina, he led the Saskatchewan Roughriders to five Grey Cup appearances, winning one. His 50,535 yards passing and 333 touchdowns thrown both top the all-time list. Went on to a long coaching career.

- Tony Gabriel played 11 seasons and was chosen All-Canadian eight times as a receiver. In the top five all-time in pass receptions and pass yardage, he caught the most famous pass in Grey Cup history when Tom Clements hit him with a touchdown toss at the end of the 1975 game, giving Ottawa a shocking win over Saskatchewan.

- Gene Gaines played 217 games with Montreal and Ottawa, mostly as a defensive back, including 161 in a row. Won four Grey Cups and spent the last seven seasons of his career as a player-coach with the Alouettes, responsible for the defensive backfield.

- Jim Young of the B.C. Lions was known as Dirty 30 for his enthusiastic style and ferocious blocking and hitting. Played two seasons in the NFL before coming north to play for the Lions where he remained for 197 games as a receiver, running back, and occasional defender.

- Bill Baker, known as The Undertaker, played with Saskatchewan and B.C. and was a perennial all-star. Became CFL president and chief operating officer in 1988 for one year.

- Dieter Brock led the CFL in passing four times and was twice named the league's best player. Played with Winnipeg and Hamilton before going to the National Football League with the Los Angeles Rams.

Part 4 ➤ *Canadian Football: The Heroes of the Game*

Grey Cup Winners of the Era

1970	Montreal Alouettes
1971	Calgary Stampeders
1972	Hamilton Tiger-Cats
1973	Ottawa Rough Riders
1974	Montreal Alouettes
1975	Edmonton Eskimos
1976	Ottawa Rough Riders
1977	Montreal Alouettes
1978–82	Edmonton Eskimos
1983	Toronto Argonauts
1984	Winnipeg Blue Bombers
1985	B.C. Lions
1986	Hamilton Tiger-Cats
1987	Edmonton Eskimos
1988	Winnipeg Blue Bombers
1989	Saskatchewan Roughriders

➤ Jim Corrigall, known as Country, or Cartwheels (for his habit of turning cartwheels after a sack) was a star on some awful Toronto Argonauts teams in the 1970s. In 1975 was chosen the best lineman in the league. Went on to coach in U.S. college football.

➤ Rocky DiPietro played 14 seasons with the Hamilton Tiger-Cats at slotback and receiver. Set the CFL record for most catches in a career in 1989 and wound up with 706 total for 9,762 yards.

➤ Tom Clements came out of Notre Dame in 1975 and signed with the Ottawa Rough Riders where he shared duties with Condredge Holloway. Threw for almost 40,000 yards in his career with the Riders, Saskatchewan, and Winnipeg. Won two Grey Cups.

The Least You Need to Know

➤ The CFL in this era went from a strong league to one hanging on by its fingernails.

➤ Some of the best football ever was played in the latter part of this era.

➤ Montreal lost its football team.

➤ The Edmonton Eskimos won five straight Grey Cups.

➤ The designated import rule practically killed off the Canadian quarterback.

Chapter 20

E Pluribus Unum, Eh! (1990–1999)

In This Chapter

- The Three Amigos
- The American experiment
- Back to being all-Canadian
- Doug Flutie
- Goodbye, Ottawa; hello, Montreal
- Getting down to business

Going to a salary cap had seemed like a good idea in the 1980s, but many teams (did someone say the Toronto Argonauts?) had simply ignored it. Welcoming Hollywood into the league also looked to be a no brainer, but that only lasted a few years.

And, creating a U.S. division must have seemed wonderful to many people too but like a lot of other good ideas, this one also came crashing down.

Despite it all, by the end of the century the CFL was still around, having survived numerous attempts by media, supporters of NFL expansion (also often the media), and disinterested public to put it in the ground. In this chapter, we'll look at Canadian football on the verge of a new century.

Part 4 ➤ *Canadian Football: The Heroes of the Game*

The Great One, the Funny One, and the Crooked One

It was astounding. The good old CFL attracting flocks of media from across Canada, and (gasp!) the United States, to the training camp of the Toronto Argonauts in the summer of 1991.

Heck, *Sports Illustrated* was there, and if the great *SI* thought something in Canada was important enough, then gosh, we must have really made it.

What a balm for our rampant Canadian inferiority complex that season was.

First, Harry Ornest sold the Toronto Argonauts to a group headed by Los Angeles Kings' owner Bruce McNall, hockey legend Wayne Gretzky, and movie star John Candy, the latter a local boy who played football at Neil McNeil High School and grew up loving the Double Blue.

The media went crazy at the announcement, and things were just warming up.

Shortly thereafter the Argos signed Raghib "Rocket" Ismail, a receiving star from Notre Dame, to a contract reputed to be $26.2 million for four years, with an $18.2 million signing bonus. There was, of course, a two-year out clause, but who worried about that?

> **Quote, Unquote**
>
> "Every time he's hit hard, it seems there's a flag."
>
> — Calgary's Pee Wee Smith on the hands-off policy towards Toronto's Rocket Ismail, 1991.

> **Quote, Unquote**
>
> "That dude is awesome."
>
> — Winnipeg's James "Wild" West on Winnipeg linebacker Greg Battle, 1990.

Truly, the American saviour theory that had brought quarterback Joe Theismann (pretty good signing), runner Anthony Davis (total bust), runner Terry Metcalfe (so-so results), and so many more to the Argonauts had reached its ultimate peak.

So what if Ismail's guaranteed $4 million for 1991 was itself a mill over the salary cap for the entire team. McNall made the deal a "personal services" contract, and listed $100,000 with the league.

That season was like no other ever seen in Toronto. Crowds flocked to the SkyDome. Opening night featured Dan Ackroyd and the Blues Brothers in a post-game concert. Cars were given away (your author won one of those), and the team went all the way to the Grey Cup game and won it. McNall flew a jet load of freezing Hollywood celebs to the event.

Chapter 20 ▶ E Pluribus Unum, Eh! (1990–1999)

The Hollywood Influence

The league itself was coming under McNall's influence, and he did have some good effects, such as helping to convince his friend Larry Ryckman to buy the financially strapped Calgary Stampeders. And he forced the lifting of the television blackout for games in Toronto which begat a solid TV contract.

But things started to go sour. Ismail turned out to be a difficult media celebrity — showing up late for events, refusing to go to others. He missed most of a mandatory Meet the Players event on Grey Cup week. And he had a fragile body.

> **Quote, Unquote**
>
> "My arm feels like a rag, but coach, I'm finishing it."
>
> — Quarterback Matt Dunigan plays the 1981 cup final with a broken left collarbone.

Unhappy, Ismail would be released to go to the NFL by the end of the following season.

McNall also brought Detroit's Glieberman family into the fold as owners of the Ottawa Rough Riders (which turned out badly — more to come).

The Three Amigos wouldn't be far behind Ismail. By the spring of 1994, Gretzky and McNall declared they were getting out, and the club was ultimately sold to Labatt Breweries through its holding The Sports Network. Candy, ever the CFL fan and a man who had worked seriously behind the scenes to make U.S. expansion work, hoped to put together a group to buy the club.

But, on March 4, 1994, filming *Wagons East!* in Mexico, Candy died of a heart attack.

Gretzky would continue being The Great One, despite taking a bath with the Argos. And McNall? Within a few years he would be in a California jail, guilty of income tax evasion. It would turn out that most of his riches were on paper only.

Larry Smith Takes the Fall

First: Expanding to the United States was not Larry Smith's idea. It had first come up as far back as the late 1960s, and when the Three Amigos bought the Argos in 1991, they brought along dreams of American expansion as a way of boosting TV money.

Second: Though the idea was heavily panned in some areas of the media, and by a lot of fans, not everyone thought it was dumb. There was wide-ranging support of expansion, if it were handled properly.

Larry Smith, a hero as a player with the Montreal Alouettes, had become commissioner of the CFL in 1992 and suffered through a tough year, what with arguments within the league over television rights and equalization payments, and with shaky franchises in Ottawa, Hamilton, and B.C.

Part 4 ➤ *Canadian Football: The Heroes of the Game*

> **Listen Up!**
>
> Desperate to keep franchises alive, the CFL challenged cities in the 1990s to meet certain ticket and corporate sponsorship goals in order to retain their franchises. Under that pressure, communities in Hamilton (12,000 tickets, $1 million in sponsorships), Ottawa (15,000 and $1 million), and Calgary (16,000 tickets) pulled together to reach the totals. Hamilton and Calgary stayed alive. Ottawa's franchise eventually died.

Pushed by the Argos' owners, and supported by many others, Smith became the front man for U.S. expansion, and like any good employee he went at it with enthusiasm.

The first site looked at was Portland, Oregon, and the league even played an exhibition game there in 1992, which did fairly well, but ownership was never straightened out. Other suckers did appear.

In a nutshell, here's how the American experiment worked out team by team:

➤ The Sacramento Gold Miners were supposed to come in with San Antonio in 1993, but the latter's finances didn't work out (highly embarrassing). The Miners played two seasons at Hornet Field, moved to San Antonio themselves for one year and folded when the American experiment failed.

➤ The Baltimore Colts/CFL Colts/CFLers/Stallions appeared in 1994, did exceptionally well in old Memorial Stadium, played in two Grey Cup games, winning one, had to give up the classic "Colts" name because the NFL went to court, and wound up going to Montreal as the reborn Alouettes after the NFL allowed the Cleveland Browns to move to Baltimore and become the Ravens.

➤ Las Vegas unveiled the Posse in 1994, and that club went on to become the biggest embarrassment in CFL history, drawing flies to the desert heat and at one point playing two home games to a total of 5,000 people. Their last home date was switched to Edmonton and the team eventually folded.

➤ Shreveport, Louisiana, became home to the Pirates, owned by Lonie and Bernie Glieberman, who exercised an option gained when they bought the Ottawa Rough Riders in 1991. Shreveport drew fairly well but lost tons of money, hung on for two years and folded when Baltimore went down and the rest of the owners didn't feel strong enough to continue.

➤ The Memphis Mad Dogs also drew reasonably well, but still lost a bundle and went down with the rest of the American ship, as did the Birmingham Barracudas.

Thus, it was over. Smith left as commissioner and went to Montreal to help run the new Alouettes, the league was taken over by John Tory and Jeff Giles, and a new promotional campaign was started: Radically Canadian.

Here's the real irony for all those who thought the American experiment almost killed the CFL: The league realized over $14 million in expansion fees from gullible owners willing to try the Canadian game south of the border.

Chapter 20 ➤ *E Pluribus Unum, Eh! (1990–1999)*

Without that money, the cash-strapped clubs in Hamilton, Ottawa, B.C., and Calgary wouldn't have survived. Those rich Americans bailed out the all-Canadian game.

A Death in the Family

At the end of the 1996 season, after 121 years of football and more than five years in intensive care, the Ottawa Rough Riders died.

The team named after Teddy Roosevelt's famous Rough Riders, who rode up a hill into heavy fire and on into glory, wound up suffering the fate of the Light Brigade, riding down into the valley of death with the six hundred.

That would be the six hundred or so people who hadn't been totally turned off by what had happened to the team in the 1990s.

In 1991, Bernie and Lonie Glieberman came out of Detroit and poured a lot of money into the struggling team. Unfortunately, they also decided to take a hands-on approach to the club, to the point of changing the famous 'R' logo on the helmet; altering the team colours; and ordering that the football management sign troubled defensive lineman Dexter Manley to a contract, hoping that bringing in a famous American would spur ticket sales.

> **Quote, Unquote**
>
> "(Larry) Smith and the owners are apparently getting what they want; one wonders if they can handle it."
>
> — Doug Smith, Canadian Press, on expansion.

> **Know-it-alls**
>
> Q. What name did American team owners want to change the CFL to?
>
> A. The North American Football League.

Tore a page out of the old Argo book, they did.

The team continued to stink on the field, and in 1994, the Gliebermans stopped flushing money down the toilet and took off for Shreveport to found the short-lived Pirates, leaving the league to find another owner. Bruce Firestone, a local businessman who had been behind the birth of the Ottawa Senators in the NHL, took over for a year, but he bailed out, and a quiet, arms-length business guy named Horn Chen was convinced to toss more money into the pot.

It was interesting, really. Ottawa fans and media complained the Gliebermans had been far too hands on, and they complained Chen was too much the absentee owner.

Chen gave it up in the 1996 season, and the league shut down the Rough Riders for good.

By the end of the century, a couple of groups were sniffing around with the idea of restoring the team, but nothing was thought to be possible before 2000 or 2001.

Part 4 ➤ Canadian Football: The Heroes of the Game

The Diminutive One

Who is the best player in the history of Canadian football?

Ask anyone of a certain age and they will say Joe Krol, who played with the Toronto Argonauts in the 1940s and early 1950s.

Ask anyone of recent vintage and there is but one answer: Doug Flutie.

Doug Flutie was listed at 5' 10", but probably was two inches shorter than that. At Boston College he won the 1984 Heisman Trophy as the most outstanding player in U.S. college football, but with Chicago and New England of the NFL, he couldn't make an impact, in large part because coaches felt he was too small and they wouldn't build an offence around him.

But Doug Flutie was perfect for the Canadian game. Fast, smart, creative, courageous, he was everything a CFL coach could wish for.

Flutie signed with B.C. in 1990 and had a reasonable season as he learned the game. In 1991, the little one exploded, setting 23 league and team passing records and winning most valuable player for the first of four times in a row, and what would be six times in his eight seasons.

Signing with the Calgary Stampeders, Flutie played four years there and teamed with outstanding offensive players such as receivers David Sapunjis and Allen Pitts, and running back Andy McVey. Again records fell like bowling pins, but the Stamps were able to win just one Grey Cup. It was said Flutie couldn't play in bad weather.

In 1996, he signed with Toronto and led the Argos to two consecutive cup victories, one in a blinding snowstorm in Hamilton and the other in freezing temperatures at Edmonton, putting the bad-weather rap to rest.

In just eight years, Doug Flutie threw for over 41,000 yards, putting him third on the all-time list behind Ron Lancaster (19 years) and Matt Dunigan (14 seasons). His 61.3 completion percentage was the best all-time, and his 270 touchdowns were third in league history.

Wanting one more try at the NFL, Flutie signed with the Buffalo Bills in 1998, a team that expected to use him merely as a backup. That idea lasted only a few games, and by the end of the season Flutie had led the team to a playoff spot and been chosen both an All-Pro and league most valuable player.

So much for being too small.

> **Quote, Unquote**
>
> "Today, he was a surgeon."
>
> — Wally Buono, Calgary coach, on quarterback Doug Flutie, 1992.

Chapter 20 ➤ *E Pluribus Unum, Eh! (1990–1999)*

A Blast from the Past

When the Montreal Alouettes were the scourge of the East in the 1950s, they played out of Percival Molson Stadium, on the grounds of McGill University. When they left there in the 1960s for a temporary home at the Autostade, the ghosts must have felt they'd seen the last of the club. But at the end of 1997, tired of lousy crowds (under 10,000 average) in the equally lousy, cavernous Olympic Stadium, the Als moved back to the crumbling old Molson field.

And the fans loved it. Outdoor football. A little beer and poutine in the natural elements, and football was suddenly fun again in Montreal. After some heavy scrambling to fix up the wooden and concrete seats, over 16,000 people showed up to see the Als beat B.C. in the first round of the 1997 playoffs.

The club moved full-time into Stade Molson for 1998 and instantly doubled their attendance. Okay, the dressing rooms were awful, and the clock didn't show nifty replays and endless commercials, but no one cared.

Canadian football was back.

You Can't Keep a Good Game Down

Perhaps it was part of the CFL's karma that off-field pandemonium would forever be tempered by on-field brilliance. As the century came to an end, the league — now down to eight teams in two divisions — continued to present excellent entertainment on the field.

With teams finally following the salary cap, and the "marquee player" (one guy you could pay anything to, whatever the cap) pretty much history, sensible economics was becoming the order of the day.

Know-it-alls

Q. What was the name of Montreal's short-lived franchise in the World League?

A. The Montreal Machine.

Listen Up!

The University of Saskatchewan Huskies dominated Canadian college football in the 1990s. Under coach Brian Towriss, and drawing extensively from the Saskatoon Hilltops and Regina Rams junior programs, the Huskies made five trips to the Vanier Cup final at Toronto's SkyDome, starting in 1989, winning three of them including 1998's matchup with the Concordia Stingers. That run was threatened by the turn of the century however, as the University of Regina entered play in 1999, expecting to draw many of the junior Rams to their school.

Part 4 ➤ *Canadian Football: The Heroes of the Game*

> **Know-it-alls**
>
> Q. What 1997 national college championship head coach passed away of liver cancer in 1998?
>
> A. Casey Smith, University of British Columbia Thunderbirds.

Weather Report

You want weather? How about 1991 in Winnipeg where the temperature at game time was –17°C, with a nice wind blowing to boot? Players and fans were tempting frostbite as Toronto beat Calgary on Rocket Ismail's 87 yard kick-off return for a touchdown.

Told you Mother Nature was looking for revenge.

The CFL had decided the Grey Cup was best played in its smaller cities, which meant outdoors. Only twice was the classic played in domes, once each in Toronto and Vancouver.

Calgary and Baltimore played the Wind Bowl in 1995 at Regina, as a nice gentle 85 kilometre per hour wind blasted down the field.

And at Hamilton in 1995, the Snowdown in Steeltown went to the Argonauts in a snowstorm that packed 40 kilometre per hour winds.

> **Know-it-alls**
>
> Q. What Winnipeg quarterback threw for 286 yards in a Grey Cup win in 1990?
>
> A. Tom Burgess.

Other Stars of the Era

➤ David Sapunjis, known as Spunj (or Sponge) was as sure-handed a receiver as the league had seen. A native of north Toronto and graduate of the University of Western Ontario, he joined the Calgary Stampeders and was chosen the Grey Cup's top Canadian in 1991, 1992, and 1995.

➤ Donald Narcisse went to the Saskatchewan Roughriders in 1987 and was still playing in 1999. The receiver broke the pro record for most consecutive games with a pass reception, and came into the final year of the century with 196. He also led in most seasons with a pass caught at 10.

➤ Matt Dunigan played 14 seasons in the league for Edmonton, B.C., Toronto, Winnipeg, Birmingham, and Hamilton, and finished his career second on the all-time passing list. The quarterback played the entire 1991 Grey Cup game (a win for Toronto) with a broken left clavicle (collar bone).

➤ Michael Clemons, reputed to be the nicest man ever to play any sport, joined the Toronto Argonauts in 1989 after a year in the NFL. Nicknamed "Pinball" by then coach Bob O'Billovich because of the way he bounced off tacklers, Clemons shattered the record for most combined yards in a season (1990) with 3,300 and smashed his own mark in 1997 with 3,840. Could do it all: run, catch passes, run back punts, and catch kick offs.

Chapter 20 ➤ E Pluribus Unum, Eh! (1990–1999)

- Allen Pitts was among the best receivers in CFL history. With over 100 touchdowns caught, Pitts, who came to Calgary in 1990, set the record for touchdown catches in one season in 1994 with 21.
- Running back Mike Pringle became the first in CFL history to rush for more than 2,000 yards in a season, with Montreal in 1998. He also broke the record for most consecutive 100-plus rushing games. In just seven years, Pringle moved into fourth place overall in all-time regular season yards playing for Edmonton, Sacramento, Baltimore, and the Alouettes.
- Ray Elgaard played 14 seasons as a receiver with Saskatchewan, and holds the record for most games with at least one pass catch, 217. A superb possession receiver, Elgaard retired with the most receptions all-time, at 830.

The Least You Need to Know

- The CFL launched an ill-fated expansion to the United States.
- The Ottawa Rough Riders died after 121 years of football.
- Doug Flutie became arguably the best player in league history.
- Rocket Ismail's signing with Toronto in 1991 created the biggest media explosion the league had seen.
- The CFL ended the century still hanging on.

Know-it-alls

Q. What Canadian kicker hit for five field goals for Toronto in the 1996 final, and two years later went to the Indianapolis Colts of the NFL?

A. Mike Vanderjagt.

Grey Cup Winners of the Era

1990	Winnipeg Blue Bombers
1991	Toronto Argonauts
1992	Calgary Stampeders
1993	Edmonton Eskimos
1994	B.C. Lions
1995	Baltimore Stallions
1996	Toronto Argonauts
1997	Toronto Argonauts
1998	Calgary Stampeders

Part 5

Baseball: Diamonds of the Great White North

Ask most Americans and they'll tell you baseball is probably a relatively recent addition to the Canadian sporting scene. After all, the country only entered the Major Leagues in 1969. But as we learned in Part One, the first recorded game of Base in Canadian history was in 1838. And since then, the game has been as much a part of the National scene as any other sport. There have been almost 200 Canadians who have played at the Major League level, representing every province except Newfoundland. But baseball in this country has been so much more than just making the big leagues. Minor leagues and independent associations have flourished, died, and flourished again in this century.

Chapter 21

A Tip O' the Cap, and Other Stories (1880–1935)

In This Chapter

- Tip O'Neill
- A Canadian invention
- Baseball across the nation
- The birth of the Asahis
- A Babe and a Brother
- Other stars of the era

When professional baseball leagues began to form in the latter part of the nineteenth century, Canadian teams battled, often unsuccessfully, to be a part of it. Players didn't have nearly the same problems, as many either born and raised in Canada, or born here and raised in the United States, found jobs in pro ball. At the same time, amateur ball flourished in this country, and everywhere you looked in the spring and summer you could most always find a town or country diamond on which to catch a game. And it wasn't only the white majority playing. On the west coast, in Ontario, and out east, minority players would present some of the best ball seen from coast to coast. In this chapter, we'll look at how baseball in Canada developed to the middle of the Depression.

A Line of Greek Goddesses

How famous was James "Tip" O'Neill?

Every time the pride of Woodstock, Ontario, came to the plate as a member of the St. Louis Browns, Lou Cauz writes, he was greeted by "a dozen maidens in flowing robes who sounded a fanfare on silver trumpets."

Writer Brian Kendall says Speaker of the United States House of Representatives Tip O'Neill was named after him.

> **Know-it-alls**
>
> Q. From where did Tip O'Neill get his nickname?
>
> A. From his ability to foul-tip balls whenever he needed to.

His biggest season was 1887, when O'Neill hit .492 at a time when walks were counted as base hits. Even with the walks taken out, his .438 was the highest of the era.

In today's lingo, O'Neill was "hot" — an absolute heartthrob. And that brought the women fans out in droves, thrilling Browns' owner Chris Von der Ahe, described by Cauz as "a short, fat, uninhibited saloonkeeper."

His team won four straight American Association championships, but like most owners then, and for the next 100 years, he had to have absolute control over his players. O'Neill and the performers for Von der Ahe's travelling circus wanted more money and the end to the new reserve clause, which could tie a player to the same team for life.

So, in 1889, they went on strike against the American Association and the National League. The players formed their own league, which lasted a year, and then crawled back to the established owners.

Von der Ahe got his revenge on O'Neill by trading him to the Cincinnati Red Legs, for whom he played one more season before retiring.

O'Neill made a token few appearances for the Toronto Maple Leafs in the International League, moved to Montreal to operate a bar, and died in 1915.

Foxy's Glove

Any player who sticks a glove out to pick off a ball heading straight for the head can thank Arthur Irwin for the protection. Arthur, you see, invented the modern baseball glove.

Foxy, as he was known, was born and raised in Toronto, before moving to Boston for his teenaged years. He played 13 seasons as a shortstop in the young big leagues, starting in 1880 for Worcester of the National League, then Providence, Philadelphia, Washington, and Boston.

Chapter 21 ▸ A Tip O' the Cap, and Other Stories (1880–1935)

At Providence, Irwin broke two fingers on his left hand, and, according to the Canadian Baseball Hall of Fame, he had an idea. Taking a driving glove, he added padding, put a button on the back to hold it to his hand, and sewed together the third and fourth fingers to create one of the earliest baseball gloves.

The Irwin glove was quickly adopted by many other players and was the forerunner of all the gloves we use today.

Thanks Foxy.

At the Turn of the Century

From 1900 to the Depression, baseball in Canada seemed to fit a standard pattern: Amateur ball flourished, and various promoters in cities across the land would make forays into the professional ranks, only to have to drop out again mostly due to changing economic times or personal finances.

The New Brunswick–Maine pro league hung around two years before the start of World War I did it in. The Western Canada League got together in Alberta in 1906, and did well as a semi-pro loop for a while, but found itself drifting in and out of existence for years.

Out on the prairies, the real strength (distance and travelling costs being what they were) was in weekend tournaments and invitationals, sponsored by local businesses and organizations that would attract the best teams from across the west. Exhibition games were often big money makers as well.

In Toronto, the Maple Leafs of the International League continued to draw well despite bad luck with their stadiums. The club lost two parks on Toronto Islands to fire before building Hanlan's Point stadium there. During the 1910s, the Leafs won three pennants and survived the loss of many players to the outlaw Federal League.

At the same time, however, financial trouble did in the Montreal Royals, and they would not reappear until 1928 when Syracuse's team was moved in.

> **Know-it-alls**
>
> Q. Who was the last Canadian born manager in the big leagues?
>
> A. George "Moonie" Gibson, Pittsburgh Pirates, 1924.

> **Listen Up!**
>
> George Gibson was a Pittsburgh Pirates catcher who grew up in London, Ontario. In the 1909 World Series against Ty Cobb and the Detroit Tigers: Cobb was expected to make mincemeat of Gibson and his less than cannon-like throwing arm, but the Canadian held the hot-headed Tiger to just two steals. It made him even more of a hero in London than he had already been. Over 5,000 people gathered in a local park to welcome him home.

Part 5 ➤ Baseball: Diamonds of the Great White North

Black Balled

With so many American players coming north of the border to play professional or semi-professional ball, it was inevitable that they often brought their racial views with them. Which isn't to say that all Canadians thought Blacks should have an equal chance to play with whites, either.

As Bill Humber points out, Tip O'Neill presented a petition to the St. Louis Browns, signed by eight players, saying they would refuse to play the all-Black Cuban Giants in a game. Not O'Neill's finest hour.

When George Stovey and Moses "Fleet" Walker came to town with Newark in 1887 for a game, a writer in the *Hamilton Spectator* referred to them as a "Coon Battery." Not the *Spectator*'s finest hour, either.

And when the Buffalo club brought Frank Grant to Toronto with them for a game in 1887, many in the crowd yelled, "Kill the Nigger."

Not Toronto's finest hour, for that matter.

Blacks played ball right across the country at the amateur level, sometimes on integrated teams but more often on all-Black squads. By 1900, Black teams had grown down east to the extent that an annual Maritime championship was held.

> **Know-it-alls**
>
> Q. What was the first professional ball team in Edmonton?
>
> A. Edmonton Legislators, 1907.

> **Know-it-alls**
>
> Q. What famous "Hit 'em where they ain't" man played for Toronto in 1911?
>
> A. Wee Willie Keeler.

If you were to get a chance in Organized Baseball (that which was operated under the umbrella of the big leagues), you had to be of mixed blood. Jimmy Claxton did well in the Pacific Coast League as a pitcher in the 1910s, coming out of B.C. with Irish, English, Black, French, and Native heritage.

A few, like Ollie Johnson of Oakville, Ontario, and Bill Galloway of Hamilton, found their way to all-Black teams in the U.S.

Two of the strongest settlements for Black culture and baseball were in the Amber Valley of Alberta, and around the Chatham area of Ontario. Allowed to play against white teams, as was the case in the Maritimes, those clubs did well. Especially in Chatham, where a provincial senior championship club in the 1930s included one Ferguson Jenkins.

His son would go on to make a mark in Major League baseball that would lead to the Hall of Fame.

Chapter 21 ➤ *A Tip O' the Cap, and Other Stories (1880–1935)*

The Asahis

As the Asian community grew in British Columbia, Japanese Canadians wanted a way to integrate themselves into North American culture, without giving up the culture they already possessed. A group of young Japanese athletes in Vancouver found a way — baseball.

Senior ball was huge in Vancouver and Victoria, and one of its best entrants was the Asahis, of the mainland's Terminal League. Out of a population of around 10,000, centred on Vancouver's Powell Street, the Asahis came to life in 1914 thanks to the money and guidance of Matsujiro Miyasaki.

In 1921, half the Asahis, joined by four local occidental players, toured Japan. The club also won the tough Terminal League title in 1926. By the mid 1930s, the club was taking on all comers, including the Tokyo Giants, Japan's best team, who toured North America and made stops in Vancouver and even Saskatoon.

A few of the Asahis disappeared into the Japanese Army in the 1930s, conscripted while visiting the country. And, with the coming of World War II, the bombing of Pearl Harbor, and the internment of all Japanese on the west coast in interior internment (read Concentration) camps for the duration, the Asahi club came to an end.

> **Quote, Unquote**
>
> "Hit another homer Nig, and I'll give you $50."
>
> — Texas cattleman to Nig Clarke during his eight home-run day, 1902.

> **Quote, Unquote**
>
> "It was the applause of the Occidental fans that would make us so proud."
>
> — Iwaichi Kawashiri, former Vancouver Asahis player.

Oh, Brother!

Thanks to the work of writer Colin Howell (somebody give this man a medal), it has only recently come to light that the man who taught Babe Ruth how to play baseball was actually a Canadian.

Think about it. America's most revered athlete and icon was the result of a Canadian's coaching! It's enough to make an insecure Canadian nationalist weep.

Martin Leo Boutlier was born in Lingan, Cape Breton Island, on July 11, 1872. He grew up to be a 6-foot, 4-inch, 240-plus pound muscular monster of a man who entered the Xaverian brotherhood in 1892 (taking the name Brother Matthias) and found himself assigned to St. Mary's Industrial School in Baltimore, Maryland, where he eventually became head of physical activity.

Listen Up!

Jay Justin (Nig) Clarke played nine hard-working but unspectacular seasons in the Majors for Cleveland, Detroit, St. Louis Browns, Philadelphia Phillies, and Pittsburgh, hitting .254. But it was a feat recorded in the Texas League in 1902 for which he is most famous. The Amherstburg, Ontario native hit eight home runs in eight plate appearances during one game. After the fourth hit, a cattleman offered him $50 if he hit another. By the eighth trip, half the Corsicana fans in the stands were waving money. He wound up with 16 RBI in a 51-3 win, and over $500 in cash.

Quote, Unquote

"He was the greatest man I've ever known."

— Babe Ruth, on Brother Matthias, the Canadian who taught him to play baseball.

St. Mary's was a tough place, filled with boys who had run afoul of the law, been orphaned, or simply abandoned by their families.

Into this school, in 1904 at the age of 10, came George Herman Ruth, son of a Baltimore bartender who beat the tar out of him for most of little George's early years.

Ruth grew up in St. Mary's, and it was there that Brother Matthias took a major interest in the youngster and began to teach him as much about baseball, and life, as he could. Remember, he was working with as raw a human as you might find.

When Ruth signed a minor league contract with the Baltimore Orioles of the International League at the age of 19, the last thing Brother Matthias said to him was "You'll make it, George."

And, of course, the big fella did.

Canadian footnote: On September 5, 1914, Ruth came to Toronto with the Providence Grays as a 19-year-old rookie and hit his first and only minor league home run in Hanlan's Point Stadium, off the Leafs' Ellis Johnson.

On to the Dirty Thirties

If you visited a prairie ballpark in the 1920s, you'd be amazed at who you might see in the lineup.

Exhibition games and tournaments were drawing great teams, and the Western League was up and running again. Promoters and owners would often invite touring Black teams (which often brought the great pitcher Satchel Paige and his All Stars to their games) and former Major Leaguers to play.

In the 1920s, for example, many of the eight Black Sox, who had been barred for life from baseball after the 1919 World Series fixing scandal, appeared in the west, especially Swede Risberg and Hap Flesch.

It was the same deal in the Maritimes, where senior ball and semi-pro continued to operate well.

Trouble in Toronto

Difficult times had hit Hogtown, however. In 1926, Maple Leaf Stadium, one of the most beautiful parks of its time, opened on Fleet Street with a seating capacity of 17,500 and a cost of $300,000. Over 220,000 people came to the first year's Maple Leaf season.

But, by the early 1930s, when the Depression hit, crowds began to drop off (it didn't help that the stadium was hard to get to) and the team itself began to drop off in talent.

In Montreal, the Royals franchise, bought by Althanase David and Ernest Savard, came over from Syracuse in 1928 to play in the new Delormier Downs stadium (22,000 seats). By 1931, they were back in financial trouble again until bailed out by three new investors. The team would continue until 1960, when it folded for good.

The most remarkable thing about baseball in the Depression years following 1929 was that it hung on in the west, where much of the arable farm land was turned into a dustbowl by high winds and poor conservation practices. Thousands of farmers were ruined. But, as one Westerner said, "baseball was the only thing many people had left."

Other Stars of the Era

- Bob Brown was an American who became known as Mr. Baseball in Vancouver, managing 10 seasons in the minors before heading to the west coast in 1908. Over the next 50 years, he would form the Vancouver Athletic Club team, help build Capilano Stadium, and organize the first night game in the country.
- Jack Graney was a left-handed pitcher with the Cleveland Spiders (later Indians) in 1908, who was sent back to the minors and changed to an

> **Know-it-alls**
>
> Q. What future prime minister's father Charles-Emile was co-owner of the Montreal Royals in the 1930s?
>
> A. Pierre Elliott Trudeau.

> **Know-it-alls**
>
> Q. Who was the first Canadian to pinch hit in a World Series game?
>
> A. Jack Graney, Cleveland Indians, 1920.

> **Quote, Unquote**
>
> "A lost date in Canada meant a large gate gone forever."
>
> — A barnstorming Black team owner on a rained-out Canadian date.

Quote, Unquote

"You may not be any good as a player, but you can at least try and look like one."

— Edmonton's Deacon White, founder of modern sport in the city, to his players, 1920.

outfielder. He played 1,402 games for Cleveland from 1910–22. Led the American League in walks twice. Later became a long-time Indians' broadcaster. Born in St. Thomas, Ontario.

➤ Blackie O'Rourke (born Francis James in Hamilton, Ontario) was just 17 years old when he took the field in 1912 as a shortstop for the Boston Braves, for whom he played 61 games. He got back to the big leagues with Brooklyn in 1917, and lasted 13 more seasons (he spent 1923 in the minors) for the Dodgers, Washington, Boston, Detroit, and the St. Louis Browns. Hit .254 for his career.

➤ Jimmy Archer was born in Dublin, Ireland, but grew up in Toronto. He caught 736 games over 12 years in the big leagues, mostly for the Chicago Cubs, appearing in two World Series (with the Tigers in 1907 and the Cubbies in 1910). His best year was 1912 when Archer hit .283 with 58 RBI.

The Least You Need to Know

➤ Canadian Tip O'Neill was a star in the early Major Leagues.

➤ Amateur baseball was as popular as hockey in Canada up to the 1920s.

➤ A Canadian, Brother Matthias, taught Babe Ruth to play the game.

➤ Pro teams came in and out of the Canadian scene during this era.

➤ Blacks had more chances to play integrated ball in Canada, but were still shut out of Canadian pro teams.

➤ Babe Ruth hit his first professional home run in Canada.

Chapter 22

Minor only in Name (1936–1959)

In This Chapter
- Canadian baseball survives the Depression
- Minor league ball struggles along
- Western baseball
- Goody, Phil, Dick, and Reno
- The northern girls of summer
- Jackie Robinson
- Other stars of the era

As the Depression finally ground to a halt (nothing like a good war to straighten out that economy), professional baseball struggled in Canada. But sandlot and amateur ball still survived, and with vigour. Through the 1940s and 1950s, Canada continued to produce Major League players, but at a slower pace, as much of the country's youth were left buried on battlefields across the world. During the war, a flock of talented women players found work in a new league south of the border. And after the conflict, the most significant event in twentieth century baseball history occurred in Montreal. In this chapter, we'll look at all those issues.

Part 5 ➤ Baseball: Diamonds of the Great White North

Down but Not Out

The history of pro ball in this country during the era just before, and for 15 years after the war, was one that saw teams arrive, flourish for a short time, and then check back out again. Here's a partial roster:

- ➤ Calgary got the Purity 99s and Buffalos of the Big Four League from 1947–52, then the Stampeders of the Western International League for two years, then nothing until 1977.
- ➤ Edmonton had the Eskimos and Motor Cubs of the Big Four from 1947–52, then moved to the Western International League for two seasons, then nothing until 1981.
- ➤ Vancouver had the Maple Leafs (Western International) for 1937–38, the Capilanos from 1939–42, then the Caps again after the war until 1954, then the Mounties of the Pacific Coast League (Triple-A) from 1956–62, then again from 1965–69 and then nothing until 1978.
- ➤ Winnipeg was in and out. Halifax had the Shipyards in the 1940s and Cardinals in the 1950s, Cornwall had pro for three seasons, Hamilton was in the Pennsylvania, Ontario, New York League during the war, and then again for 11 seasons to 1956.
- ➤ Ottawa popped in and out of low-minor ball, and even had Triple-A from 1951 to 1954.

Listen Up!

Edmonton's John Ducey was Mr. Baseball in Alberta from the 1920s until he died in 1984. Starting out as a bat boy and diamond rat for Edmonton's Western League team, Ducey did it all in baseball — umpiring professionally in the 1930s, and handling the administration of all ball in Edmonton from 1946–59. A key to keeping minor league ball in the city in the fifties, upon his death Edmonton renamed their main stadium in his honour. Ducey was known as the Rajah of Renfrew.

And on and on it went.

Toronto and Montreal were able to hang on to their International League teams through the 1950s, but the Royals would be gone after 1960. The Maple Leafs, helped by good money from Jack Kent Cooke, would experience a renaissance after tough war years through the '50s that would see the sport do well at the stadium on Fleet Street.

Cooke left for the U.S. west coast by 1961, however, and the Leafs themselves would have but six years left.

No Goody, Goody Two Shoes

Goody Rosen was one tough ballplayer for a little guy.

Born and raised in Toronto, when he got to the Brooklyn Dodgers on September 14, 1937, he was a 5' 9", (5' 10" in the official guides), 155-pound, cigar smoking, wisecracking, tough talking dynamo.

Chapter 22 ➤ Minor only in Name (1936–1959)

Sounds like the perfect guy for Leo Durocher, the equally pugnacious manager of Dem Bums. Rosen did well in his first full season of 1938, winning the award as best defensive outfielder in the National League, hitting .281 in 473 at bats and making 113 appearances in the outfield.

But he got hurt the next year, Durocher forced him to keep playing, he got hurt some more and wound up in the minors for the next five years as a bitter man.

With Branch Rickey in charge, but Durocher still the manager, Rosen was called up in 1945 to help fill in — war shortage and all that. That season he hit a massive .325 with a .460 slugging percentage (don't ask for a mathematical explanation for slugging percentage, it will only give you a headache), and would have played in the all-star game if war travel restrictions hadn't cancelled it.

The next season, with Dodger stars back from the war, Rosen was traded to the New York Giants. Far into the year, he ran into an outfield wall at Forbes Field in Pittsburgh, and his career was, for the most part, over.

> **Know-it-alls**
>
> Q. What was Goody Rosen's nickname with Brooklyn Dodgers' fans?
>
> A. Babydoll.

Babe

No, not that Babe. The other Babe.

Phil "Babe" Marchildon, right-handed pitcher, had every right to come back from a German prison camp after the Second World War and pack up his baseball career for the quiet of Penetanguishene (Penetang to all its friends), Ontario.

Marchildon had already been 25 before the war when he brought some of the rawest talent ever seen down for two seasons with Toronto in Triple-A before signing with the pathetic Philadelphia Athletics and their octogenarian manager/owner Connie Mack. He played three years, winning 17 games in 1942 before joining the Royal Canadian Air Force as a tail gunner on a bomber.

Shot down in mid 1944, this Babe spent a year as a guest of Adolf Hitler in a prison camp before coming back, half-starved, nerves nearly shattered, to Canada.

Mack brought him back to the A's, where he formed a one-two pitching tandem with another Canadian, Dick Fowler, on a still-awful team. But Marchildon won 13 in 1946 and 19 in 1947 (could have had the magic 20, but Mack, a notorious tightwad, sat him down in the last days of the season to avoid having to pay a bigger new contract).

> **Know-it-alls**
>
> Q. What was the name of Phil Marchildon's fastball?
>
> A. Johnny Jumpup.

213

Know-it-alls

Q. How many home runs did pitcher Dick Fowler have in his 10-year career?

A. One. (Pre-designated hitter era).

In 1948, as Dan Turner writes, "his nerves caught up with him," and Marchildon had to shut it down for a while to get them back under control. The next season, shoulder problems began to plague the man from Penetang, and he was out of baseball in 1950.

Oh, and About Dick...

Dick Fowler, who pitched 10 seasons in the bigs, made his own mark on the Majors on September 9, 1945, when he threw a no-hitter against the St. Louis Browns. Himself just back from the war, Fowler went to the mound for the first time since 1942 at Shibe Park in Philly and left the Brownies (who would win the World Series that year) stunned.

Fowler, from Toronto, told writer Brian Kendall years later that "I can honestly say I was never in worse shape in my life."

The Browns would surely have disagreed.

The Girls from the Great White North

Philip K. Wrigley had an idea. It was 1943, and the owner of the famous chewing gum company, and even more famous Chicago Cubs, saw the Majors were faced with a huge manpower shortage as more and more players went off to war. What to do?

To make a lengthy story fit a short space, he started the All-American Girls Professional Baseball League (which actually played a modified game of softball for its first three seasons before switching to full baseball), and went looking for enough talented women to fill four teams that would represent small cities in the northern midwest.

Quote, Unquote

"Their actions in throwing and batting do not have the tinge of masculine play like the United States girls."

— Scouting report on Canadian women for the All-American league, 1943.

The league lasted until 1954, and over that time 10 percent of its players, a total of 53, came from Canada. And of that number, 24 came from Saskatchewan, where women's softball was queen.

Many of the stars, however, were from Manitoba. Audrey Haines played five seasons and 174 games, putting together a 72–70 mark as a pitcher. Evie Wawryshen starred for six seasons and had a career batting average of .266 in 544 games. From B.C. came Margaret Callaghan, who in seven years played 672 games at third base, and Helen Nicol of Edmonton would go south and win the league's pitching title in 1943 and 1944.

Chapter 22 ➤ Minor only in Name (1936–1959)

Then there was Dorothy Hunter of Winnipeg, with 82 games under her belt followed by 11 seasons as a chaperone for the Milwaukee/Grand Rapids Chicks.

Chaperone?

Oh yes. The "girls" of the All-American had to be "ladies" first, and good ballplayers second. They were sent to charm school, taught how to hold their forks, how to cross their legs properly, and how to come into a room correctly. And, their uniforms were hilarious — skirted one piece tunics in pastel colours that meant sliding into a base would be a painful experience.

Two Canadian women rose above those petty things and became legends in the AAGPBL. Their names were Bonnie and Ollie.

Bonnie and Ollie

With Bonnie Baker's husband away in the air force, the Regina, Saskatchewan native's mother-in-law talked her into trying out for the All-American, and telling her husband about it later. That worked. By the time he found out about it, Baker was already a star with South Bend. She played nine seasons, appeared in 921 games, hit .235, and was the league's first female manager.

It was Baker, as attractive and stylish off the field as she was tough as nails on it, who was the model for Geena Davis' composite character in the film *A League of Their Own*.

But Baker was also the best poker player in the league. And, she admitted to writer Lois Browne, she would knock off 24 Cokes in a day. Obviously never slept.

Olive Bend Little was pitching for the Moose Jaw Royals in Saskatchewan when scouts from the All-American discovered her. She was, writes Browne, considered "one of the fastest pitchers in the game."

Quote, Unquote

"There was nothing else to do there, except play ball and chase grasshoppers."

— Bonnie Baker on why so many good women players came out of Saskatchewan.

She tossed for just three years, in 1943, and 1945–46, but in that time compiled a 57–43 mark and threw the league's first no-hitter. Little took time out to have a baby in 1944, and when little Roberta was born the league sent the baby a contract for the 1960 season.

The All-American folded after 1954 (sorry Roberta), and the women dropped into obscurity until the Baseball Hall of Fame in Cooperstown, New York, finally honoured them as a group. The Canadian women players were inducted, also as a group, into the Canadian Baseball Hall of Fame in the late 1990s.

A Love for Jackie Robinson

It may be the most oft-quoted sentence written about baseball in Canada. And, it was written by an American, about an American.

"It was probably the only day in history that a black man ran from a white mob with love, instead of lynching, on its mind," wrote Sam Maltin of the *Pittsburgh Courier*.

The Black man was Jack Roosevelt Robinson. The white mob was made up of Montreal Royals' fans, who were trying to catch up with their hero and thank him for leading their club to the Triple-A Little World Series championship for 1946.

Jackie Robinson was the first Black man in the twentieth century to break baseball's "unofficial" but hard and fast colour barrier. Signed by Branch Rickey of the Brooklyn Dodgers, Robinson was told that for three years he had to turn the other cheek when confronted with the virulent racism of the time — and Rickey wasn't kidding. When Robinson went to the Dodgers in 1947, he was subjected to unconscionable abuse from fans and opposing players.

> **Quote, Unquote**
>
> "The tears poured down my cheeks, and you choked up looking at it."
>
> — Dink Carroll, *Montreal Gazette*, on the love shown by the Montreal crowd for Jackie Robinson, final day, 1946.

To make his debut in professional baseball easier, Rickey first sent Robinson to Montreal of the International League, knowing that racism in Canada — while still an issue — would not be nearly as important as in the States.

Montreal actually carried two Black players at the start of the season, the other being pitcher John Wright, whose career would flare out quickly. But Robinson blasted out of the gate, tearing up the league, and changing a lot of minds about him and his race, including that of his manager, Clay Hopper.

"Mr. Rickey," the dyed-in-the-wool southerner had asked his boss before the season, "do you really think a [Black] is a human being?"

By season's end, Hopper had changed his outlook on both Robinson and Blacks.

Robinson hit .349 that season, winning the hitting title, running the bases with abandon, and playing excellent defence at second base.

"He could count on a uniformly warm reception only at home, in De Lorimer (Delorimier) Downs," writes Robinson's biographer, Arnold Rampersad.

Robinson was grateful for that.

"I owe more to Canadians than they'll ever know," he said. "In my baseball career they were the first to make me feel my natural self."

Chapter 22 ▶ Minor only in Name (1936–1959)

After the championship winning game at Montreal, they stormed around Robinson and said, *"Il a gagné ses épaulettes"* — He has earned his stripes.

One Lousy Little Pill

Reno Bertoia was a quiet, studious young man from Windsor, Ontario, who turned the baseball world on its ear for half a season in 1957.

Signed as a "bonus baby" by the Detroit Tigers in 1953, the rules of the time meant the American League club had to keep the young third baseman on the roster for two years. Travelling across the bridge from Windsor to Tiger Stadium every day, Bertoia got into just one game as a rookie and 102 over the next three seasons, never hitting better than .206. But, for a few months in 1957, he was the hottest batter in baseball.

As Dan Turner writes, by late May he was hitting .398 and leading even Ted Williams at the top of the charts.

Then, the media struck. Associated Press reported that Bertoia was taking "happiness pills" — actually, they were tranquilizers (athletes would regularly take them in later years) that helped keep his frayed nerves in check. And Bertoia was completely honest about it, but the press was all over him. So he stopped taking them.

Whether it was the pills, the pressure, or the fact his luck had run out, Bertoia's average began to slip, dropping to .275 by the end of the season. Traded to

> **Know-it-alls**
>
> Q. What Canadian gave up a homer to his first Major League batter (Canuck Sherry Robertson) in 1946?
>
> A. Ralph "Mack" McCabe. His career with Cleveland lasted one start.

> **Listen Up!**
>
> Father Ronald Cullen was raised in Toronto but learned his baseball in Detroit under a Father Martin, a Michigan legend in the sport who himself was actually from Amherstburg, Nova Scotia. Cullen moved to Windsor, Ontario, and took up residence at Assumption High School in the 1950s. Cullen turned out numerous ballplayers, including Reno Bertoia (Tigers), John Upham (pitcher, Chicago Cubs, 1967–68) and Joe Siddall (catcher, Montreal, Florida Marlins, Detroit, 1993–present), and dozens of others who played in the low minors. He also founded the Windsor MicMac amateur organization. Father Cullen is a member of the Canadian Baseball Hall of Fame.

Part 5 ➤ Baseball: Diamonds of the Great White North

Quote, Unquote

He always said "Baseball is a game...a game of life."

— Actor Sean McCann, a former player, on Windsor's Father Ronald Cullen.

Quote, Unquote

"Rocky was our Ted Williams."

— Former Toronto mayor David Crombie, on Rocky Nelson of the Maple Leafs.

Know-it-alls

Q. What Canadian pro set a world record on August 1, 1957, tossing a ball 445 feet, three inches, in Omaha, Nebraska?

A. Glen Gorbous.

Washington, he had one more good year — 1960 with a .265 — but his career was over by 1962.

Bertoia went on to a fine career as a teacher at his old high school, Assumption, in Windsor.

Doing the Maple Leaf Rock

Rocky Nelson was the most beloved player in the history of the Toronto Maple Leafs. He was small, but strong, and his unusual batting stance (both feet pointed towards the pitcher) was as well known to Toronto fans as Mickey Mantle's was to New Yorkers.

Already an experienced back-up first baseman on six Major League clubs (starting in 1949 with the St. Louis Cardinals), Nelson owned Toronto in 1957 and 1958. During the latter year he hit a team record .326 with 43 homers and 120 RBI, winning the International League MVP.

He would finish his career with three seasons at Pittsburgh, playing in the seventh and deciding game of a victorious 1960 World Series against the New York Yankees.

Other Stars of the Era

➤ Oscar Judd was a left-handed pitcher born in Rebecca, Ontario, in 1908, who made the bigs with the Boston Red Sox in 1941 at the advanced age of 33 when so many regulars had gone off to war. He made just seven appearances, but was invited back and won 19 games over the next two seasons. Traded to the Phillies in 1945, Judd pitched there for parts of four more years, winning 20 more times. He had a career earned run average of 3.90.

➤ Sherry Robertson of Montreal played 10 seasons in the bigs from 1940–52, almost entirely with the Washington Senators. Had a career batting average of .230. The brother of Washington, later Minnesota, owner Calvin Griffith, Robertson worked 15 seasons as farm director of the Senators.

Chapter 22 ➤ *Minor only in Name (1936–1959)*

- Aldon "Lefty" Wilkie pitched three years with the Pirates in 1941, 1942, and 1946. Career record of 8–11. Elected to Saskatchewan Baseball Hall of Fame.
- Tom Burgess, known as Tim, played two seasons in the Majors: 1954 with the Cardinals, and 1962 with the expansion Los Angeles Angels. Hit .177 as a first baseman and outfielder.
- Pitcher Bob Hooper of Leamington, Ontario, had a huge rookie year with the Philadelphia A's in 1950, going 15–10. He was 12–10 the following year before injuries cut his effectiveness. Played six seasons with the A's, Indians, and Reds, earning 40 victories.

The Least You Need to Know
- Canada gained and lost many pro teams from the Depression to the 1960s.
- Phil Marchildon came back from a German prison camp to pitch again for the Philadelphia Athletics.
- Dick Fowler became the first Canadian to pitch a no hitter, in 1945.
- 53 Canadian women played in the All American Girls Professional Baseball League.
- Jackie Robinson broke baseball's colour barrier when he joined the Montreal Royals in 1946.

Chapter 23

Developing Some Reputations (1960–Present)

In This Chapter

- Death and rebirth of minor league ball
- Ron Taylor's world
- Fergie
- Two prides of Saskatchewan
- John Hiller
- Larry Walker
- Other stars of the era

There was a lot more to Canadian baseball in this era than simply the birth of the Montreal Expos and Toronto Blue Jays. The best pitcher the country has turned out starred during this time, and so did a man who went from baseball to medicine. But it's fair to say that finally getting in the Major Leagues inspired a lot of youngsters to try for the brass ring themselves. And many of them made it. One went right to the top of the heap. In this chapter, we'll look at those players, and how pro ball continued to fade in and out in Canada.

Part 5 ➤ Baseball: Diamonds of the Great White North

> **Listen Up!**
>
> Canada had won the world men's softball championship before 1972, but it had been a long time. The Richmond Hill Dynes, named for local jeweller and team sponsor Vern Dynes, and managed by Casey Cripps, went to the Phillipines in '72 and helped by a strong pitching staff headed by Bob Dominic, advanced all the way to the final against the heavily favoured United States. Enter Dick Hames, one of three allowed pickups from other teams (he was from London, Ontario), who not only threw a 1-0 shutout but also drove in the winning run. It was considered a huge upset, and made national news across the country.

The Yo-Yo Effect

Pro franchises have had a symbiotically up and down existence in Canada — every time a few teams popped up, others have followed. When one fell, it seemed to take a few others with it.

The Montreal Royals died in 1960, and just seven years later the Toronto Maple Leafs were sold to Louisville and moved out as well. For a while there, only Vancouver had a professional team. With the birth of the Expos and Blue Jays, interest in owning clubs began to rise again, and, in the 1970s and 1980s, pro sides appeared in such far-flung places as Medicine Hat, Alberta, Welland, Ontario, and Quebec City.

In 1990, the Pacific Coast League (Triple-A) had the Calgary Cannons, Edmonton Trappers, and Vancouver Canadians. The Pioneer League (Single A-rookie) had the Medicine Hat Blue Jays and two seasons later would add the Lethbridge Mounties. The New York/Pennsylvania League (Single-A) would have the Hamilton Redbirds, the St. Catharines Blue Jays (later the Stompers), and the Welland Pirates; the Eastern League (Double-A) featured the London Tigers; and the International League (Triple-A) the Ottawa Lynx. In 1994, Regina Cyclones and Saskatoon Riot would join the independent North Central League.

But by 1999, Vancouver was going, and Welland, Hamilton, and London were history. Winnipeg Goldeyes and Quebec City Les Capitales were in the independent Northern League, but Thunder Bay had just lost its Whiskey Jacks in that loop.

Other towns, however, were hanging on, keeping the pro tradition alive.

Dr. Ron

Ronald Wesley Taylor played his sandlot ball in Leaside, Ontario (now part of Toronto), and wound up in the Majors with the Cleveland Indians in 1962 as a right-handed starter and middle reliever. His future was out of the pen, however.

Traded to St. Louis in 1963, by the following season he was a reliever full-time, and that's where he would become a star. He threw four no-hit innings at the New York Yankees in a tough seven game World Series of 1965, getting his first victor's ring, and five years later, as a New York Met, would earn another.

Taylor was a major part of the 1969 Miracle Mets, saving 13 games and winning 9 as the Mets ran down and passed the front-running Chicago Cubs.

In the World Series against the heavily favoured Baltimore Orioles, Taylor came in to face the famous Brooks Robinson with two men on, two out and up 2-1. He got Robinson to ground out to third, and the game was won.

Taylor pitched a total of 11 seasons in the big leagues, and when he was done turned full-time to medical studies. He would earn two more World Series rings as team doctor of the Toronto Blue Jays in 1992 and 1993.

Fergie

Let's give it to you straight about Ferguson Jenkins so there's no mistake. Born in Chatham, Ontario. Entered the Majors in 1965 with the Philadelphia Phillies. Traded to the Chicago Cubs the following year. Right-handed, hard throwing pitcher. Played 19 seasons and won 284 games against 226 losses. Won 20 games or more in a season seven times, including six in a row. Won the Cy Young as best pitcher in the National League in 1971. Voted to the Hall of Fame.

The best Canadian baseball player of all time.

Ferguson Arthur Jenkins Jr. had a 90-mile-per-hour fastball, a Major League curve, devastating slider, and amazing accuracy. His big league career was sparkling, especially with the Cubs and later the Texas Rangers, for whom he won 18 games in 1978. In 1982, after an injury-riddled season the year before, he went back to Chicago and won 14 more times.

After leaving the majors, Jenkins had fun for a year pitching for the London Majors in the semi-pro Inter-County League in Ontario, then went back to his farm in Blenheim to grow corn and have a good life.

Bad luck, some of it created by himself, had a habit of following Ferguson Jenkins. In 1980, he was found with cocaine and marijuana in his baggage on a team flight to

> **Quote, Unquote**
>
> "Doubleheader tomorrow. Barring nuclear holocaust."
>
> — Ron Taylor, New York Mets, 1969.

> **Quote, Unquote**
>
> "I just found out what's driving me crazy. It's baseball."
>
> — Ron Taylor, New York Mets.

> **Quote, Unquote**
>
> "I wanted to be Doug Harvey. Doug Harvey was my idol."
>
> — Ferguson Jenkins on his childhood, and favourite hockey player.

Know-it-alls

Q. Who was the first Canadian to make it to the Hall of Fame, in 1991?

A. Ferguson Jenkins.

Quote, Unquote

"I've always hit wherever I've been, so I can't see any reason why I shouldn't hit here."

— Pete Ward, lacking no confidence, Chicago White Sox, 1963.

Quote, Unquote

"That guy has more guts than anybody else in the clubhouse."

— Watson Spoelstra, Detroit writer, on reliever and heart attack survivor John Hiller.

Toronto. He claimed it wasn't his but refused to say which of his teammates it belonged to, was convicted, and given a discharge. He donated $10,000 to anti-drug campaigns and began to speak to young people about staying away from them.

After he retired, Jenkins faced a lot of tragedy, with the deaths of two children and his ex-wife. He moved to Oklahoma to buy a farm and start a new life as a pro pitching coach, but in the spring of 1999, the farm was devastated by a tornado.

And still, he soldiered on.

A Pitchin' Medical Miracle

People often said that John Hiller's lifestyle would catch up with him one day. He smoked like a chimney. He ate like a horse. Heck, he practically outweighed a horse.

Another Toronto kid, Hiller had just finished his sixth season as a reliever and spot starter for the Detroit Tigers in 1970 when his heart finally sent word that it was checking out for good and not leaving a forwarding address. Cardiac surgeons saved his life, but told him his playing days were done.

Nah, said Hiller. Just 18 months later — July 8, 1972 — he was back on the mound at Chicago's Comiskey Park for a three inning middle relief appearance in which he gave up four hits and a home run. As Brian Kendall writes, not only was he slim and healthy, he was also suddenly superb, going 10-5 with a 1.44 ERA the following season, winning Comeback Player of the Year and Fireman (reliever) of the Year awards, and then picking up 17 wins out of the bullpen in 1974.

John Hiller, medical miracle, lasted 15 campaigns in the Majors and was inducted into Canada's Sports Hall of Fame in 1999.

Just a Big, Easy-Going Guy

Now here's a trivia question: Name the only Canadian to start a World Series game on the mound? Reggie Cleveland of Swift Current, Saskatchewan, you say?

Chapter 23 ➤ *Developing Some Reputations (1960–Present)*

Aw, you peeked.

Yep. Ol' Reg strode out to the mound on October 16, 1975 and proceeded to get the tar beaten out of him, 6-2, by the Cincinnati Reds in game five of what would be a seven game victory over Cleveland's Boston Red Sox.

Okay, it wasn't Reg's finest hour, but if he hadn't gone 13-9 in the regular season, the Sox might not have gotten to the playoffs. And, he got another chance. Coming in at the top of the ninth in game seven, with the bases loaded, two out and the Reds up 4-3, he got Tony Perez to fly out. Boston couldn't score, however, and the series ended.

> **Know-it-alls**
>
> Q. When was baseball's all-star game first played in Canada?
>
> A. July 13, 1982, in Montreal.

"I guess that World Series start was life's big highlight," said Cleveland, to writer Larry Wood, years after finishing a 13-year career that included stops in St. Louis, Boston, Texas, and Milwaukee.

Aw, maybe not. But it was right up there. Not bad for an air force brat.

Another Son of Saskatchewan

Terry Puhl. Played ball and chased grasshoppers while growing up. Played 15 seasons in the big leagues. Hit .280. Other than Tip O'Neill who doesn't count (different era), he was the best non-pitcher Canada ever turned out until Larry Walker came along. But, Puhl was better defensively.

Terry Puhl, the kid from Melville, may be the most forgotten star in our history. Ask anyone on the street to name five Canadian baseball heroes, and you'll be lucky to come up with his name. But, T. Puhl, outfield, was the real deal, playing 14 of 15 seasons with the Houston Astros (finishing with Kansas City in 1991), including two that were something special.

In 1978, in just his second season and first as a regular, Puhl hit .289 and was named to the National League all-star team. In 1980, he hit .282 and then went berserk in the NL championship series against Philadelphia, batting .526 (a record). The Astros lost the famous series, unfortunately.

> **Know-it-alls**
>
> Q. Three Canadians, the most ever, started a Major League game for Montreal in 1993. Who were they?
>
> A. Outfielder Larry Walker, catcher Joe Siddall, and pitcher Denis Boucher.

Over his career, Puhl hit a nice, steady .280 in almost 5,000 at bats. And in six of his seasons he did not make a single error.

Do You Believe in Miracles? (Junior Division)

Forget Lake Placid in 1980, where the Americans won the Olympic hockey gold medal in the Miracle on Ice.

Let's go to August 4, 1991. Brandon, Manitoba. World Youth Baseball Championships for 16- to 18-year-olds.

Canada had won the bronze in this event exactly twice, and despite being the home team nobody thought much of our chances this time.

Nobody, however, counted on Daniel Brabant. The right hander from Longueuil, Québec, had already won three games in a tourney that included the United States, Cuba, and Taiwan. The Canadians themselves, with Todd Betts (now in the Cleveland organization) booming shots all over the field and the rest of the team following suit, made it to the final against Taiwan where Brabant gave it his all for a four-hit six innings before blowing out his right arm.

Canada held on to win 5-2, and the gold medal belonged to us.

Brian Kendall wrote that it was a coming of age for Canadian baseball.

Not Bad for an Ex-Goaltender

When Larry Walker was a young guy in Maple Ridge, B.C., he dreamed of a professional sports career.

That would be as a goaltender, not a ballplayer. But as he told Dan Turner, hockey left him a bundle of nerves. Baseball, however, made him feel relaxed. Cool.

Not that he played a lot of it — a couple of dozen games every summer. Jim Fanning, chief scout, former manager, former general manager of the Montreal Expos only needed a couple of tournament games to know he had a good one in front of him, and he made sure the youngster was signed, sealed, and delivered to the organization.

Know-it-alls

Q. Two Canadians are among just eight American League pitchers to get a hit since the designated hitter was introduced. Who are they?

A. Ferguson Jenkins and Matt Maysey.

Listen Up!

Rob and Rich Butler grew up and played their minor ball in East York, a suburb of Toronto, going on to achieve something no other Canadian brother combination has ever done — they both made the Major Leagues as outfielders. Rob broke in with the Toronto Blue Jays in 1993, playing 17 games and earning a World Series ring. After playing one more season he went to the Philadelphia Phillies organization, getting back to the big leagues for 1998, batting .292 in 43 games. In 1999, he rejoined the Jays farm system. Rich also broke in with Toronto for seven games in 1997, then went to the expansion Tampa Bay Devil Rays in 1998, hitting .229 in 79 games.

Chapter 23 ➤ *Developing Some Reputations (1960–Present)*

Too bad money woes meant they weren't able to keep him. Walker already knew about the value of money. The son of working class parents (mom toiled in a bowling alley and dad managed a building supply company), sports was his ticket to an overwhelming income.

Walker, who battled for years to control occasional outbursts of temper on the field, made it to Montreal in 1989, and became a key member of the team that by 1994 was the best in baseball. Twice he hit over .300, including .322 in that '94 year. But free agency arrived for him, and Walker signed with the Colorado Rockies, moving to Coors Field where in 1997 he hit 49 homers with a .366 average, leading the league in on base percentage and slugging percentage.

> **Quote, Unquote**
>
> "He is not just a Canadian, or the finest prospect on our baseball club. He is a thoroughbred."
>
> — Peter Bragan Sr., owner of the Jacksonville Expos, on a young Larry Walker.

He could have been Canada's Athlete of the Year, an award that was very important to Walker, but instead it went to racecar driver Jacques Villeneuve. Walker grumbled about drivers not really being athletes, but set out to win it the next year.

And what a season that was. 1998. Hit .363 to lead the National League. Won the MVP. Got the Athlete of the Year nod, as well.

Heading into 1999, Walker had a career batting average of .305. And that, folks, is a Hall of Fame number.

Stay tuned.

Other Stars of the Era

➤ Pete Ward, the son of former Montreal Maroon hockey player Jim Ward, broke into baseball in 1962 with Baltimore. Traded to the Chicago White Sox, his second season, still officially a rookie year, saw him hit .295 with 22 homers and 84 RBI. Was the *Sporting News'* top rookie. His injury plagued career lasted nine seasons, mostly with Chicago, and was ended because of neck problems.

➤ Tim Harkness, of Lachine, Québec, played four seasons in the big leagues, two with the Dodgers and two with the New York Mets, all as a first baseman. Holds two claims to fame. In 1963, he tied the NL record for latest grand slam in a game (14th inning) for the Mets, and in April of 1964, he bagged the first base hit in the history of Shea Stadium. Went on to become a long-time Major League scout.

➤ Dave McKay was the first Canadian on the Toronto Blue Jays. Born in Vancouver, the second baseman played eight seasons with Minnesota, Toronto, and Oakland from 1975–82, and then went on to a long career as a coach under Tony LaRussa with the A's and the St. Louis Cardinals. Hit .229 overall.

Part 5 ➤ *Baseball: Diamonds of the Great White North*

> **Know-it-alls**
>
> Q. What Canadian was the first player selected by the expansion Florida Marlins?
>
> A. Nigel Wilson.

➤ Toronto's Rob Ducey spent parts of six seasons as an outfield backup with the Toronto Blue Jays from 1987–92, before heading to California and Texas. Played in Japan before coming back to the Seattle Mariners for 1997 and 1998. Career .247 hitter.

➤ Pitcher Rheal Cormier of Moncton, New Brunswick, broke in with the St. Louis Cardinals in 1991, where he spent four years before going to Boston for a season and then to Montreal for two more. A left hander, he had a career 38–39 mark.

➤ Paul Quantrill of London, Ontario, broke in as a pitcher with the Boston Red Sox in 1992. Used mostly as a middle reliever and spot starter (64 starts in 341 games), he won 36 games through 1998, for the Sox, Philadelphia Phillies, and Toronto Blue Jays. Missed a third of the 1999 season after suffering a broken leg in a snowmobile accident.

➤ Outfielder Matt Stairs came out of Saint John, New Brunswick, to the Montreal Expos in 1992 where during two seasons he appeared in 19 games. After a year in Boston (where he made the playoffs), Stairs went to the Oakland A's and became a regular as an outfielder and designated hitter, playing in 282 games for 1997 and 1998, hitting .298 and .294 respectively, with a total of 53 homers and 179 RBI.

The Least You Need to Know

➤ In this era, minor ball flourished and increasing numbers of Canadian players were signed or drafted by pro teams.

➤ Ferguson Jenkins established himself as the best player Canada has turned out.

➤ Minor-pro clubs arose and died with great regularity.

➤ Terry Puhl came out of Saskatchewan to star in the Major Leagues.

➤ Larry Walker became the best non-pitcher the country has produced.

➤ Canada's youth team (juniors) won the World Championship.

Chapter 24

Triumphs and Tragedies: The Montreal Expos

In This Chapter

- ➤ Birth of the Expos
- ➤ A love affair between team and city
- ➤ First signs of talent
- ➤ An awful Monday afternoon
- ➤ Unrealized potential
- ➤ The season that almost was
- ➤ Struggles in the 1990s
- ➤ Other stars of the era

Anyone sitting in the Olympic Stadium during the latter part of the 1990s might find it hard to believe that the Montreal Expos were once Canada's team — packing them in at tiny Jarry Park and drawing huge television audiences across the land. Long after the birth of the Toronto Blue Jays, the Expos were still number one. Eventually, however, the crowds began to dwindle as they came to realize that the Big Owe wasn't a great baseball park, and the team became less competitive. And luck was never with this franchise, even when it put together the best team in baseball in 1994. By 1999, the Expos were hanging on in Montreal by their fingernails. In this chapter, we'll look at the team's history and its chances of staying for the immediate future.

Part 5 ➤ *Baseball: Diamonds of the Great White North*

> **Know-it-alls**
>
> Q. The first homer hit by an Expo was by a pitcher, off Tom Seaver of the New York Mets. Who hit it?
>
> A. Dan McGinn, 1969.

> **Know-it-alls**
>
> Q. What hall of fame shortstop had the Expos' first hit, period?
>
> A. Maury Wills, 1969.

Preventing a Still Birth

Nothing has ever come easy for the Montreal Expos. Not even the team's birth.

Most general history tends to credit Montreal mayor Jean Drapeau with bringing Major League baseball to Canada, but it was really Gerry Snyder, a city councillor, who had the idea and saw it through to the end.

After baseball expanded in 1962 by adding franchises in New York and Houston, Snyder approached Commissioner Ford Frick about a team for Montreal. He was told to get a stadium first, which put the councillor in a tough spot since the city had already said no new park without a franchise.

He didn't give up, however, and with the help of a number of other councillors, convinced the National League owners to accept Montreal on May 27, 1968. San Diego was added at the same time.

Great.

Just a month later, however, it looked like this flight was going to be cancelled before it took off as investors started to back out. It was left to Charles Bronfman of Seagram's Distillers to guarantee the money, and he got the other investors — Paul and Charlemagne Beaudry, Lorne Webster, Hugh Hallward, and Sydney Maislin lined up.

Now they needed a place for the $10 million franchise to play. And another seemingly insurmountable hurdle faced the club.

A couple of sportswriters (imagine that), Russ Taylor and Marcel Desjardins, sold the investors on Jarry Park, a little field with a swimming pool over the right field fence that could hold just under 30,000 fans if they were skinny and didn't mind being a little jammed in.

As for the name, that seemed to be between Voyageurs and Nationals, but team president John McHale announced Expos, after Expo 67, the world's fair that had attracted global attention.

And the dream was alive.

Fun? Wow!

The city of Montreal, indeed all of Canada, loved the Expos right from the time they debuted on April 8, 1969 with a win at New York against a Mets team that would win the World Series that season.

Over 150,000 people jammed the streets for a parade introducing the team before the home opener, which was another victory, this time 8-7 over St. Louis. It took about three minutes for the fans to latch onto the red-headed veteran Rusty Staub (Le Grand Orange) as their first hero. And when the flamboyant Mack Jones clouted one into the bleachers during the first home game, the stands were instantly renamed Jonesville.

No one cared the team went just 52–110 behind manager Gene Mauch. It was all so much fun. Twenty game losing streak included.

It only took 10 days for the first no-hitter to arrive, courtesy of Bill Stoneman (who would toss two as an Expo), and a spectacular catch by Don Bosch in centre field to preserve the 7-0 no-no against Philadelphia.

The Canadian Broadcasting Company checked in with great animated commercials explaining French baseball words (the pitcher — *le lanceur* — throws the ball — *la balle* — to the catcher — *le receveur*, etc.).

Everything was fun. Even the public address announcements (John Boccabelllllllaaaaaaa!!!) were memorable.

Baseball was here to stay in Montreal. And, boy, were they jealous in Toronto, which made it even better.

Listen Up!

Montreal fans have always had a special place in their hearts for French Canadian players on the Expos. Pitcher Claude Raymond was the first Canadian on a Canadian team in 1969, spending the last three years of his 12-season career with the Expos. Denis Boucher pitched for Toronto and Cleveland for two years before coming to Montreal in 1993, staying through 1994. Rheal Cormier had thrown four seasons for St. Louis and one for Boston when he came to Montreal for 1996 and 1997.

Quote, Unquote

"You don't need a lawyer to tell the club you had a lousy year."

— Expos pitcher Bill Stoneman negotiates his own contract, 1971.

Riding the Roller Coaster

Gene Mauch guaranteed at least 70 wins in 1970, and the Expos pulled it off, winning an amazing 79 games, thanks to Staub, Stoneman, and pitcher Carl Morton, who would take the National League top rookie award that season by winning 18 games. The team stayed competitive and were in the division race in 1973 until the final weekend.

But from 1974–76, the club went into the toilet, finishing '76 at 55–107, with the lowest ever attendance at Jarry Park.

Dick Williams was hired as manager for 1977 with a hot young outfield of Andre Dawson (The Hawk — 21 seasons in the bigs, 438 homers, 2,774 hits), Ellis Valentine, and Warren Cromartie; star catcher Gary Carter (known as The Kid, he would play

11 seasons with the club and, during his career, play in eight all-star games, and win three gold gloves); and great pitchers Steve Rogers (158 wins in almost 3,000 innings, with a high of 19 wins in 1982 and won four huge games in the 1981 pennant drive), Bill Gullickson, and Scott Sanderson. The team was set to make some noise.

And they had their new Olympic Stadium to play in.

Over the next five seasons, the Expos would finish fifth, fourth, second twice (95 and 90 wins), and take the Eastern Division in 1981.

And they did it with some of the most interesting characters in baseball. Especially one in particular.

Quote, Unquote

"The first guy who lays a hand on this blind old man is fined fifty bucks!"

— Expos manager Gene Mauch breaking up an argument between his players and the umpire.

Quote, Unquote

"Some people give their bodies to science. I gave mine to baseball."

— Expos Ron Hunt sets a season record for getting hit by a pitch, 1971.

Life, the Universe, and Everything

His name wasn't really William Francis Lee, left-handed pitcher for Boston Red Sox and Montreal Expos. His name was really "Spaceman," because that's what he was. And because that's what most everyone came to call him.

Bill Lee reputedly admitted that he had, on occasion, sprinkled marijuana on his breakfast pancakes. He also said, in 1981 near the end of his career while fighting to make the starting rotation, that "One of our starters would have to drop dead, and they are all younger than I am." He also said, "The more self-centred and egotistical a guy is, the better ballplayer he's going to be."

The Spaceman pitched 14 seasons in the big leagues, starting with the Sox in 1969, and finished with a 119–90 record, including three straight 17-win marks for Boston from 1973–75. He came to Montreal in 1979 and won 16 games in his first year north of the border.

Along the way Lee was able to drive every one of his managers and general managers to distraction with his wild antics and forthright opinions (and remember, baseball wasn't big on forthright opinions). Commissioner Bowie Kuhn despised him, and the feeling was mostly mutual.

Lee left the game halfway through 1982 after throwing just 12 innings in seven appearances, moving to an area he had fallen in love with — Moncton, New Brunswick, where he would live a happy life playing pick-up ball, teaching kids the fundamentals of the game, and just being Bill Lee.

Chapter 24 ➤ *Triumphs and Tragedies: The Montreal Expos*

Whatever else The Spaceman may have said, remember he also said this:

"Kids don't learn the fundamentals of baseball at the games anymore. You should enter a ballpark the way you enter a church."

There was a lot to be said for Bill Lee.

Black Monday

For as long as the franchise lasts in people's memories, no Montreal Expos' fan who was alive at the time will ever forget October 19, 1981 — Black Monday.

The Expos survived a players' strike and the sudden exit of manager Dick Williams to win the Eastern Division and face the Los Angeles Dodgers for the pennant and a trip to the World Series.

With the final game tied 1-1 through eight innings, Expo manager Jim Fanning went to the bullpen where he could have chosen between the heavy heat of Jeff Reardon or the veteran savvy of Woodie Fryman. Instead, he chose Steve Rogers, his star starter but a man with no relief experience to speak of. Rogers had won game three on a sparkling five-hitter four days previously.

Talk about flying in the face of Lady Luck.

Rogers got two outs, and then two strikes on the Dodgers' Rick Monday, who had struck out four times in five tries earlier in the series. Monday hit a Rogers' fastball over the right centre field wall in Olympic Stadium, and the Expos went on to lose the game and the series.

It was the only trip to the post season the Expos made in the 30 seasons from 1969 to 1998.

> **Quote, Unquote**
>
> "He sounds a lot funnier when he's winning."
>
> — Expos manager Dick Williams on pitcher Bill "Spaceman" Lee.

The Lost Eighties

The 1980s looked like they would belong to the Expos, but they turned out to be one disappointment after another as a talented team kept falling short.

Under Jim Fanning, then Bill Virdon, then Fanning again, and finally Buck Rodgers for six and a half seasons, Montreal couldn't get over the hump, despite stars such as first baseman Andres Galarraga (The Big Cat), third baseman Tim Wallach, and outfielder Tim Raines.

At the same time attendance began to fall from a high of 2.3 million in both '82 and '83, to 1.4 million in 1990.

Part 5 ➤ Baseball: Diamonds of the Great White North

Know-it-alls

Q. Three Expos have been elected to the Major League all-star team (end of season). Who are they?

A. Gary Carter, 1982; Andre Dawson, 1983; Jeff Reardon, 1985.

Listen Up!

The strangest game in Montreal history was also the longest. On August 23, 1989, the Expos lost 1-0 to the Dodgers in 22 innings. During the game, Montreal had a triple play ruled only a double; shortstop Spike Owen took a relay throw in the butt and couldn't sit down the rest of the night; mascot Youppi was ejected for bugging the Dodgers too much; Larry Walker scored what he thought was the winning run on a tag-up from third in the 16th, but L.A. appealed he left early and Walker was ruled out; and Walker made a phantom catch of a ball hit to the wall by Eddie Murray (he trapped it against the padding). Rick Dempsey won it with a home run in the 22nd.

One crucial man who finally decided he'd had enough disappointment and debt was Charles Bronfman. In 1990, he announced it was time to get out, selling to team president Claude Brochu and 13 other investors on June 14, 1991.

Bad luck seemed to continue, including one incident where a big chunk of concrete fell off the stadium and onto the ground outside (the stadium was empty at the time), forcing the team to play the entire last month of 1991 on the road.

New manager Tom Runnels (in for Rodgers during 1991) couldn't get the club on track in 1992, leaving the Expos looking for a replacement. They came up with Felipe Alou.

Turned out to be the best decision the team ever made.

El Presidente is El Perfecto

Dennis Martinez, known as El Presidente in his native Nicaragua, spent eight years as a Montreal Expo, but his most memorable single outing came on July 28, 1991 in Los Angeles. In 2 hours and 14 minutes at Dodger Stadium he became the fifteenth pitcher in Major League history, and the first Expo ever, to toss a perfect game — 27 up, 27 down.

It took him just 95 pitches, and as always with perfect games, he relied on a couple of great defensive plays to pull it off including a great stab by Larry Walker at first base and his own excellent play on a bunt attempt. The last out came when Chris Gwynn sent a long fly ball to Marquis Grissom in centre field, and the perfect game was won.

Here's a footnote: Ron Hassey became the only catcher in Major League history to handle two perfect games when Martinez pulled the trick. He had been behind the plate for Len Barker's perfect game with Cleveland in 1981, when the Indians beat the Toronto Blue Jays.

Father Felipe

Forget all that "If you can't play, teach," stuff. Felipe Alou could flat out play. In his 17 years of big league ball starting at San Francisco in 1958, he was always near the top of the league hitting charts, finished with a career average of .286, and became the thirty-first player to gain 2,000 hits and 200 homers.

And, on September 15, 1963, he was in on history as Felipe and his brothers Jesus and Matty started in the Giants outfield.

Alou joined the Montreal organization in 1976 as a minor league instructor and worked his way up through the levels, winning two championships along the way.

He took over the Expos full-time in 1992 and finished second in the division, doing it again, with 94 wins, in 1993, and had his team first in the Majors in 1994 when the strike hit.

But Alou's greatest work has come since then.

Understand, the Expos were caught in a mad circle — crowds kept falling, which meant there was less money for the budget, which meant the team couldn't hang on to its stars (heck, even the manager's son Moises bailed on the club), which meant even fewer fans in the park.

Felipe Alou hung in there. Trilingual (Spanish, English, and French), superb with the media, excellent on the nuts and bolts of the game, and a fabulous teacher, after a 66-win year in 1995 he somehow came up with 88 in 1996, and 78 in 1997. With the budget down to $9 million for 1998, while some other clubs were up over $70 million, that season was a trial.

But other teams were lined up to toss huge sums at Alou to leave Montreal and go with them. He refused.

Quote, Unquote

"I didn't know what to think, what to say. I thought I was dreaming."

— Dennis Martinez to reporters after his perfect game, 1991.

Know-it-alls

Q. Only one Expo was named National League player of the month twice. Who was it?

A. Hubie Brooks, May 1986 and September 1989.

Know-it-alls

Q. Seven Expos have won at least one Gold Glove as top defensive player at their position. Who has won the most?

A. Andre Dawson, six times.

Felipe Alou decided he would be loyal to the Expos, and the city of Montreal, right to the end, if need be. Outside of hockey, he may be the most beloved figure in the city's long sports history.

The Darkest Hour

Coulda, shoulda, woulda. Toss that at an Expos' fan, and the first response would be "1994, right?"

Right.

The Expos broke camp that year with a possible players' strike hanging over the Major League season. Union officials and team owners had put their heels in and refused to budge either way, and disaster loomed.

But the team was a dream. Manager Felipe Alou had an exceptional outfield in Larry Walker, Marquis Grissom, and star of the future Moises Alou. Ken Hill, Pedro Martinez, and Jeff Fassero were superb as starting pitchers, and with Mel Rojas the setup man and John Wetteland the closer, the bullpen was excellent.

> **Quote, Unquote**
>
> "I feel like the fisherman who has made a record catch, but has to throw the fish back."
>
> — Manager Felipe Alou after the strike-shortened 1994 season.

Wil Cordero and Mike Lansing were a strong double-play combination up the middle, and catcher Darrin Fletcher was solid.

There had never been a Montreal team like it, not even in the early 1980s.

By the middle of August, the Expos were 74–40, which was by far the best record in baseball. A first trip to the World Series was a definite possibility, and even the fans had started coming back to the Big Owe.

On August 12, 1994, a date that will live in infamy with Montreal fans, the Major League Players' Association walked out. The players threatened. The owners threatened back. Both sides thought the threat of losing the season and the World Series would force the other to give in. But, stupidity was the order of the day, and on September 14, the commissioner's office cancelled the rest of the year.

Baseball, especially in Montreal, has never recovered.

Only the Good, and the Ignored, Die Young

As the 1990s went on, it became increasingly obvious that something was very wrong in Montreal. Too many crowds dipped below 10,000. Fans expressed a serious hatred for the Big Owe. A succession of general managers left town. A succession of stars went with them.

Chapter 24 ➤ *Triumphs and Tragedies: The Montreal Expos*

Ironically, the Expos showed they had one of the best minor league systems in baseball, turning out scads of solid players. But, with no income to speak of, they couldn't keep them.

Not even spectacular pitcher Pedro Martinez, who won the Cy Young Award as NL top pitcher in 1997 with 305 strikeouts, could seemingly turn the tide. Martinez left for the Boston Red Sox after that year.

> **Know-it-alls**
>
> Q. What is the name of the Expos' orange mascot?
>
> A. Youppi.

While management battled to fund a new baseball-only stadium in the downtown area (still up in the air at this writing), rumours began to circulate that the Expos were on their way to Northern Virginia or Washington, D.C. But the club was hanging on.

By its fingernails, again.

Other Stars of the Era

➤ Jose Alberto "Coco" Laboy was one of the early heroes of the Expos. As a rookie third baseman in 1969, he hit .258 in 157 games. Lasted five seasons with the team, playing 397 games at third and a handful at other infield positions, with a .233 career average.

➤ Ron Hunt had eight seasons in, including two all-star seasons with the New York Mets, by the time he joined the Expos in 1971. Played three and a half seasons at second and third base. Known for his ability to get hit by a pitch.

➤ Right hander Bryn Smith broke in with Montreal in 1981 and was worked in slowly as a starter. Spent nine seasons with the Expos before moving to St. Louis and finally Colorado for 1993. His best year was 1985, when he went 18–5 with a sparkling 2.91 ERA for Montreal. Won 108 games in his career.

➤ Ron Fairly played 21 years in the Major Leagues as a first baseman/outfielder. He joined Montreal halfway through 1969, after 11 and a half years with Los Angeles. Stayed just over five seasons. Is the only man who played in both Montreal's and Toronto's first year.

➤ Larry Parrish played the first eight of his 15-year career with Montreal, holding down third base on some of the Expos' best teams. Hit .263 overall, with 256 homers and 992 RBI. Played in two all-star games.

➤ Hubie Brooks made two consecutive all-star teams in 1986 and 1987, while holding down shortstop for the Expos. He played 15 years, including 5 with the Mets and 5 in Montreal. Hit .269 overall.

Part 5 ➤ *Baseball: Diamonds of the Great White North*

> ### The Least You Need to Know
> ➤ The Expos played their first season in 1969.
> ➤ Rusty Staub, Mack Jones, and Bill Stoneman were the first heroes.
> ➤ The club struggled through an up and down 1970s.
> ➤ Expos won their first division title in 1981 but lost the championship on Black Monday.
> ➤ The 1980s were a time of unrealized potential.
> ➤ The Expos were the best team in baseball in 1994 before a strike called it off.
> ➤ Attendance and money woes make survival in Montreal questionable.

Lord Dufferin and his party enjoy an end in an obviously freezing club at Rideau Hall in Ottawa. Although the women in this image from the 1800s are sitting on the sidelines, by the turn of the century, curling would be one of the first sports to welcome female participation.

Ned Hanlan, the Boy in Blue, was the most famous Canadian athlete of the 19th century. He retired from rowing with a record of 344 wins and only six losses.

Howie Morenz, the National Hockey League's first superstar, tries his hand against New York Ranger goalie Andy Aikenhead at Madison Square Garden in the early 1930s. The inspiration of Morenz's sparkling play for Montreal resulted in New York's decision to join the National Hockey League.

Maurice 'Rocket' Richard (left) poses with rookie Jean Beliveau at the Montreal Canadiens' training camp in 1953. Richard scored 544 goals in his career, while Beliveau, the next Habs superstar after the Rocket, scored 507.

Wayne Gretzky, now considered the best all-around hockey player ever, puts his signature to a twenty-one year contract with the Edmonton Oilers back in 1979 as his father, Walter (left), looks on. The Great One's stay in Alberta would last less then 10 years.

Two brilliant Canadian sprinters. On the left is Bobby Kerr, 200 metre gold medallist at the 1908 Olympic Games. On the right is Percy Williams, who took the 100 and 200 metre golds in 1928. This shot was taken in 1929. Williams would go on to lead a quiet life that ended tragically.

The grace and elegance of Barbara Ann Scott. Raised in Ottawa, Scott won Canada's first Olympic skating gold medal in 1948 at St. Moritz, Switzerland.

Nancy Greene, shown here racing the downhill, came home from the 1968 Winter Games in Grenoble, France, with the giant slalom gold medal and a silver in slalom. She became a long-time spokesperson for a famous chocolate bar.

Gaetan Boucher speed skating at the 1984 Winter Olympics in Sarajevo. The young man thought to lack the heart to win big races won two golds and a bronze at those games, the greatest one-games haul by a Canadian Olympic athlete.

The Fastest Man in the World, 1996 version, was Canadian Donovan Bailey, here winning the Olympic 100 metre men's final at Atlanta. Bailey's win helped erase the bitter memory of Ben Johnson's steroid-supported victory eight years previously.

Lionel Conacher, Canada's male athlete of the half-century, practices his punting in the summer, wearing a Chicago Black Hawks sweater borrowed from his winter employer, the National Hockey League. Conacher, amazingly, played both pro football and hockey.

It snowed hard before the Grey Cup game in 1950, so officials brought in tractors and snowplows to move the white stuff off the Varsity Stadium field in Toronto. The result was the famous Mud Bowl game, played between Toronto and Winnipeg. Bud Tinsley of the Blue Bombers reputedly almost drowned when he lost consciousness face down in a puddle after a heavy hit.

Canadian Press freelancer Shaun Best snapped this famous shot of Joe Carter hitting his series-winning homer in game six of the 1993 World Series. The Toronto Blue Jays won baseball's big prize twice in successive years.

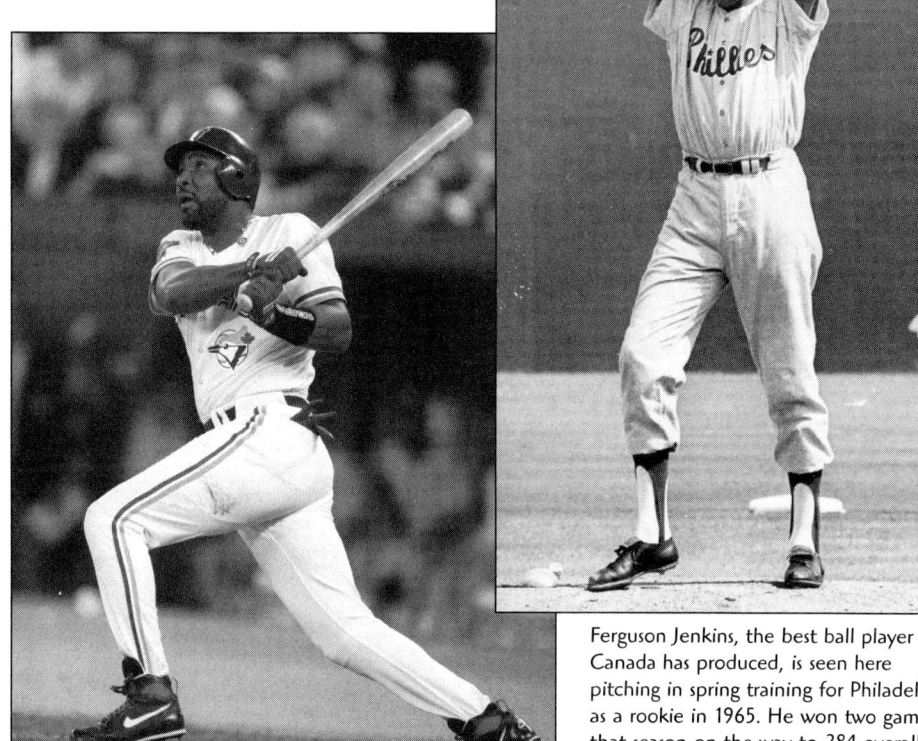

Ferguson Jenkins, the best ball player Canada has produced, is seen here pitching in spring training for Philadelphia as a rookie in 1965. He won two games that season on the way to 284 overall, and became the only Canadian elected to the hall of fame in Cooperstown, New York.

In 1891, at Springfield, Mass., James Naismith of Almonte, Ontario, took a soccer ball and two peach baskets and turned them into the game of basketball. Ironically, the new game would become far more popular in the United States than in Canada.

One of the great teams turned out by the Edmonton Grads women's program from 1915-1940. During those 25 years, the Grads went 502-20, won 147 straight games during one stretch and were gold medallists at the world championships 17 consecutive times. The basketball team of 1924 is pictured here.

Northern Dancer smiles for the camera after winning the Kentucky Derby, the famous Run for the Roses, in 1964. In the saddle is jockey Bill Hartack, while holding the bridle is owner E.P. Taylor, the most influential figure in Canadian racing. The Dancer may have been smiling because he knew what his future would bring — the opportunity to become the best sire in modern history.

When Marilyn Bell touched the breakwater at the Canadian National Exhibition in Toronto on Sept. 9, 1954, she became the first person to swim across Lake Ontario. Her 40-hour ordeal crossed 32 miles of water. A crowd of over 250,000 people met her in Toronto.

The most famous photo in Canadian sports history was taken by Frank Lennon of the *Toronto Star*, seconds after Paul Henderson (centre) beat Vladislav Tretiak with less than a minute to go in game eight of the Summit Series in 1972. Canada won, but hockey would never be the same as the Soviet style of play began to exert a deep influence on the sport in North America.

Chapter 25

Climbing the Tallest Mountain: The Toronto Blue Jays

In This Chapter

➤ The birth of the Blue Jays
➤ Early struggles
➤ First taste of success
➤ Cito takes over
➤ World Series One
➤ World Series Two
➤ Late '90s struggles
➤ Other stars of the era

The Toronto Blue Jays debuted as Canada's second Major League team in a snowstorm in 1977, and for the first few years things were competitively dismal. It didn't take long for the bloom to come off the rose. But led by president Paul Beeston and general manager Pat Gillick, the team took off in the early 1980s and became annually one of baseball's best, and most respected, clubs. After getting close a number of times, the Jays came up with back-to-back World Series championships in the early 1990s. Hurt by the 1994 players' strike and the cancellation of the season, and struggling with a mediocre team, however, the Jays began to run into troubles. In this chapter we'll look at the Jays' history.

Part 5 ➤ *Baseball: Diamonds of the Great White North*

Who *Is* This Guy?

Writer Stephen Brunt tells this great story: In 1969, Paul Godfrey was a young, unknown borough councillor in North York (a suburb of Toronto) who paid his own way down to the winter meetings, and, after getting a little advice, stood at the bottom of the stairs in the hotel and waited for commissioner Bowie Kuhn to come down.

When the big guy did show, Godfrey told him he was representing the city of Toronto (okay, he lied, so what?), and that he wanted a franchise (the young guy had guts). Kuhn put a hand on Godfrey's shoulder and told him to get a stadium and baseball would consider the franchise.

Great. Except no stadium.

Godfrey had become Metro Toronto chairman by 1973, and he made an agreement with Ontario premier Bill Davis to spend $15 million to turn Exhibition Stadium from a football field to a baseball/football facility. A lousy one, to be sure (it came to be known as the Mistake by the Lake), but it was something. And besides, hadn't the Expos started in tiny Jarry Park?

Okay, got the stadium. Now for the franchise. And that meant finding someone to sign the cheque.

Show Us the Money

Enter Don McDougall, 36, president of Labatt Breweries of Canada. First, the company, with partners R. Howard Webster and the Canadian Imperial Bank of Commerce, decided to go after the San Francisco Giants of the National League. The deal was done for the 1976 season. Cheque sent. But mayor George Moscone of 'Frisco stepped in, went to court to stop the sale, found a local investor, and kept the team in the Bay Area.

Quote, Unquote

"I see the 1980s in Canada as being beer, baseball and the Conservative party."

— Don McDougall, president of Labatt Breweries, soon to be owners of the Blue Jays, 1976.

Now what?

The National League said hang on, we'll find a way to get you an expansion team. But they hemmed and hawed and left American League President Lee McPhail Jr. an opening to solve his own problem. Seattle, which lost its team after just a year in 1970, had sued and were going to win. Therefore, they had to have a franchise, and you couldn't just bring one in. Had to be two.

And there was Toronto. So while the NL hesitated, McPhail sailed in and grabbed Toronto. Stole them, actually.

It took the McDougall group just two years to do what hadn't been possible for almost a century. Toronto was in.

What's a Little Snow?

Opening day was scheduled for April 7, 1977 in Toronto. It snowed. A lot. They played anyway. Beat Chicago 9-5 on two home runs by first baseman Doug Ault, who, like Rusty Staub in Montreal back in 1969, became Toronto's newest hero. Bill Singer throws the first pitch in anger. Jack Brohamer, second base, White Sox, creates a famous photo by cross-country skiing on a pair of catcher's pads, using bats for poles.

Anne Murray does the national anthems. 44,649 fans hang in for most of the game.

> **Know-it-alls**
>
> Q. What Blue Jays' third baseman left the game after a few years and became a star in the National Basketball Association?
>
> A. Danny Ainge.

Early Struggles

It was hardly a surprise that the team stunk for the first few years. But, unlike Montreal, the Blue Jays were unable to improve quickly. Under manager Roy Hartsfield and general manager Peter Bavasi (son of famous baseball man Buzzie), Toronto won 54 in 1977, 59 in 1978, and 53 in 1979. Hartsfield was let go and veteran baseball man Bobby Mattick took over for 1980 but after a 67 win mark couldn't get much else out of the club as attendance started to drop.

Mattick was let go after 1981 and replaced by Bobby Cox as manager.

Bavasi, who was a good organizer and promoter but not so hot as a player guy (he refused a trade in the first season that would have sent pitcher Bill Singer, whose arm was about done, to New York for an unknown lefthander named Ron Guidry, who went on to win 170 games), was replaced by the player personnel guy — Pat Gillick.

He would team with a smart money man named Paul Beeston, and the rest, as they say, was about to be history.

> **Know-it-alls**
>
> Q. What slugger hit .442 in the Jays' first month, April 1977?
>
> A. Otto Velez.

> **Quote, Unquote**
>
> "If this had been a prison break, there would have been 24 guys behind me."
>
> — Outfielder Rick Bosetti is happily traded by Toronto, 1981.

It should be noted, as Brunt wrote in 1996, that without Bavasi's hand on the tiller in the early years, "the Toronto Blue Jays would not ever have been what they are."

But his time had passed, and two new hands would guide the ship from then on.

Segap Wolley and a Guy with No Socks

Paul Beeston, a young accountant, was the first person hired by the new franchise in 1976, and he would go on to become team president. A class guy by any account, he was exceptionally bright when it came to handling the team budgets — especially in knowing when to open the bank account and sign free agents. He had the unusual habit of not wearing socks with his business suits, and a fondness for Cuban cigars.

He also had a true partner to handle the baseball side.

Pat Gillick had earned an enviable reputation as a scout in the Houston Astros and Yankee organizations as someone who could pick out a future talent no others could see. His encyclopedic knowledge of every player in pro ball brought Gillick the nickname Segap Wolley (Yellow Pages, backwards).

For most of their time with Toronto, the pair worked under Peter Hardy of Labatt, also a spectacularly decent man who, like Branch Rickey from another era, was known to all under him as Mr. Hardy.

When Gillick was handed full control of the on-field aspects of the team in the fall of 1981, the first thing he did was find a manager who could mould the Jays' talent into a contender. He found one that Ted Turner of the Atlanta Braves had just fired — Bobby Cox.

Bobby's Boys

Bobby Cox had some good young talent to work with when he came to Toronto in 1982, and he knew what to do with it — platoon (two guys sharing one spot).

With the Jays, Cox loved to platoon catchers Ernie Whitt and Buck Martinez, and was so steady in his switching of third basemen Garth Iorg and Rance Mulliniks they became known as Rance Mullinorg.

Know-it-alls

Q. Name the Blue Jay who burned his uniform in the clubhouse after a bad performance in the 1980s?

A. Damaso Garcia.

Youngsters such as shortstops Alfredo Griffin (a rookie of the year in 1979) and Tony Fernandez, Damaso Garcia at second, and an up-and-coming outfield that would settle around Jesse Barfield, Lloyd Moseby, and George Bell provided strong defence and good offence. And the pitching staff, led by Dave Stieb and including starters Jim Clancy, Luis Leal, and Doyle Alexander, was more than competitive.

Cox's team won 78 games in 1982, 89 in 1983, and 89 again in 1984, staying in the pennant race well into September each time.

Finally, in 1985, with attendance at the little ball park swelling to almost 2.5 million fans (they'd drawn

Chapter 25 ➤ Climbing the Tallest Mountain: The Toronto Blue Jays

1.7 million in the first year), Toronto won its first division title with 99 wins, helped greatly by a 17-10 season from Alexander (who came to the Jays in 1983 after the Yankees figured he was through as a pitcher), and the late season call up of Tom Henke to take over the closer's role from high-priced and oft-injured free agent Bill Caudill.

They wrapped it up on October 5, 1985, beating New York 5-1, and went on to face the Kansas City Royals in the American League championship series.

Which they promptly lost, four games to three, after leading 3-1. During that series, rumours flew that Cox was heading back to Atlanta. They turned out to be correct. Cox left, and third base coach Jimy Williams took over.

Sir David

Dave Stieb had been signed by the Jays as an outfielder out of Southern Illinois University, where he also pitched on occasion. After the Jays let him get hitting and fielding out of his system he moved to the mound full-time and proved to be an absolute thoroughbred, with a good fastball and curve to go with one of the nastiest sliders anyone had ever seen. He went to single-A ball in 1978 and was in the Majors by the halfway point of 1979, going 8-8 in 18 starts.

He was hotheaded, hard on his fielders when they made mistakes, and harder on himself when he goofed up. Though desperate to win a Cy Young award as best pitcher, Stieb never did. But there were seven all-star game appearances, 17 wins or better four times, and 176 victories overall including one when he came back in 1998 after five years out of the game.

What most people remember about him, however, was his flirtation with no-hitters. Five times he threw complete game one-hitters. In September 1988, in consecutive starts, Stieb took a no-hitter into the ninth against Cleveland only to have Julio Franco single with two outs, and had a no-hitter into the ninth against Baltimore when Tony Traber singled with two down.

Finally, the man whose biography was called "Tomorrow I'll Be Perfect" pulled it off. September 2, 1990, Stieb no-hit the Indians at Cleveland, winning 3-0.

> **Know-it-alls**
>
> Q. Name the catcher who broke his leg in a home plate collision but still had the presence of mind to finish a double play by tagging the next Seattle Mariner who came by?
>
> A. Buck Martinez.

> **Quote, Unquote**
>
> "I had Rick Burleson's bat. I had Buddy Bell's gloves. I had Tom Paciorek's helmet. All I needed was somebody's stroke."
>
> — Dave Stieb, pitcher, bats for himself in the 1981 all-star game.

Part 5 ➤ Baseball: Diamonds of the Great White North

Horseshoes, Hand Grenades, and Atom Bombs

They say close only counts in horseshoes, hand grenades, and atom bombs. The first two apply to the Blue Jays from 1986 to 1991 — second in 1987 by a whisker after losing a famous series to Detroit on the last weekend; first in 1989 under new manager Cito Gaston, losing the American League championship series to Oakland in five games; second and just two out in 1990; first and lost to Minnesota in the championship series in 1991, a year in which they drew over four million fans — almost unprecedented in baseball.

This was the middle of a stretch that saw Toronto win better than half its games for nine years.

But it was in the middle of this middle stretch that the atom bomb went off. An atom bomb named George Bell.

George and Jimy

George Bell was the Jays' most exciting player of the late 1980s era. An average outfielder at best, he was an artist at the plate, hitting 47 homers and driving in 134 RBI in 1987, the year he won the American League's prestigious Most Valuable Player award.

> **Listen Up!**
>
> On June 5, 1989, the Blue Jays left Exhibition Stadium and moved into the $560 million SkyDome, the world's first stadium with a fully retractable roof. The facility featured private boxes, bars, restaurants, a huge video scoreboard, and artificial turf. At the time it was considered state of the art and the wave of the future. Then, led by Camden Yards in Baltimore and Jacobs Field in Cleveland, the "state of the art" became baseball-only parks that harkened back to the old days of unique field measurements, real grass, and open skies. Just 10 years after it opened, SkyDome was considered by many to be obsolete as a baseball stadium.

He was also, like Stieb, a hothead, given to exploding at the media without notice, and coming up with interesting views on things. He once accused umpires of being racist and not liking Dominicans.

Over the winter, after 1987, someone in the Jays' brain trust decided it would be a great idea if Bell came out of the outfield and became only the designated hitter (as GM, Gillick has to take the responsibility here). They didn't really explain it well to the proud Bell, and left it to manager Williams to sort it out.

In spring training, Bell refused to go into a game when Williams ordered him to. Bell showed up his manager, who was doing what he was told to do, very publicly. Bell wound up as DH just seven times that year.

Williams, who many felt had been hung out to dry by the organization on this issue, became a bundle of nerves. He was eventually fired just 38 games into the 1989 season

Chapter 25 ➤ *Climbing the Tallest Mountain: The Toronto Blue Jays*

and replaced by hitting coach Cito Gaston. After a number of years in Atlanta as a third-base coach for Cox, Williams was given the Boston Red Sox managing job in the late 1990s and proved he was quite a capable boss.

Bell would play in Toronto through 1990 and finish his last three years splitting between the two Chicago teams.

Sittin' with Cito on Top of the World

It has been said that anyone could have managed the 1992 Blue Jays to the World Series title, they were so talented. Which is ridiculous, of course, since the roadside is littered with talented teams that couldn't win the big one.

> **Know-it-alls**
>
> Q. On September 14, 1987, the Jays hit a Major League record 10 homers in one game. Who hit them?
>
> A. Ernie Whitt, three; George Bell and Rance Mulliniks, two each; Lloyd Moseby, Fred McGriff, and Rob Ducey, one each.

The truth is that one Cito Gaston, formerly the batting coach, managed to keep the divergent personalities and mix of veterans and kids together, and bring them home a winner in 1992.

Pat Gillick had made a brilliant trade for second baseman Roberto Alomar and outfielder Joe Carter before the 1991 season, and for the following year he added veteran designated hitter Dave Winfield as a free agent and traded for star pitcher David Cone two-thirds of the way through the season. That added to an already deep team that was strong at all positions and had superb pitching, especially in relief, where Duane Ward

> **Listen Up!**
>
> Only one fielding play in World Series history is known as The Catch — Willie Mays in 1954 against Cleveland. Number two on the list may well be Toronto centre fielder Devon White's fourth inning, scamper to the centre field fence, back-handed, face smash against the wall item at SkyDome in game three of the 1992 Series against Atlanta off Dave Justice. He even had the presence of mind to fire the ball back to the infield where a botched umpire call denied the Jays what looked to be the first World Series triple play in 76 years.

Part 5 ➤ *Baseball: Diamonds of the Great White North*

> **Quote, Unquote**
>
> "I didn't do a whole lot, but I did it at the right time."
>
> — Dave Winfield comes up with the World Series winning double, 1992.

was the setup man for Tom Henke in a duo that practically guaranteed a win if Toronto led after the seventh inning.

After taking the East with 96 wins, Toronto beat Oakland in a dramatic six-game American League championship that included a huge comeback win in game four keyed by a home run from Roberto Alomar that turned around a 6-1 margin and gave the Jays a 7-6 win.

The World Series was full of drama. There was rookie Ed Sprague's winning pinch-hit homer in game two, the same contest in which a Marine Corps colour guard accidentally flew the Canadian flag upside down; one of the greatest catches of all time in game three; a brilliant outing (his last start as a Jay) by lefthander Jimmy Key in a game four win; and an extra-inning run-scoring double by Winfield to wrap up the series in game six. Catcher Pat Borders was the series MVP.

Toronto had its first-ever World Series victory, and Cito Gaston had become the first Black manager to take the big title.

> **Quote, Unquote**
>
> "Touch 'em all Joe, you'll never hit a bigger homer in your life."
>
> — Tom Cheek, Jays' radio announcer, in the seconds after Joe Carter's 1993 series winner.

Touch 'Em All Joe

Here's a tease: Baseball history was made at 11:39 p.m., October 23, 1993, SkyDome in Toronto. Game six, World Series. Philadelphia's Mitch "Wild Thing" Williams has two on and two out and Joe Carter standing between him and a huge save that will send the series to game seven. Williams has a two balls, two strikes count on the Toronto outfielder. He launches a slider…

Stop right there!

A little background, please.

Gillick did a little tinkering with the roster after the first World Series win the season before. Gone was Winfield, replaced by future hall of famer Paul Molitor. Back in town was shortstop Tony Fernandez (who would hit .306). In at the trading deadline was stolen base king Rickey Henderson. And signed in the off-season was pitcher Dave Stewart, the man with The Stare — the scariest look in all of baseball.

John Olerud flirted with .400 for a while before winning the American League batting title with a .363. Molitor was second at .332 and Alomar third at .326.

Chapter 25 ➤ *Climbing the Tallest Mountain: The Toronto Blue Jays*

So, everything goes right and the team cruises into first place with 95 wins, erasing the Chicago White Sox in six games to win the pennant.

On come the Phillies, upset winners over the Braves. Toronto wins three of the first five. Molitor will hit .500 and win the MVP award for the series.

Back to Williams' pitch. It's a slider too far in on Carter and too far down. The Toronto slugger pounds it over the left field wall for only the second World Series winning homer in history (Bill Mazeroski's in 1960 was first), and Toronto has back-to-back victories, the first team to repeat in 15 seasons.

Know-it-alls

Q. Who hit the first home run in the SkyDome?

A. Fred McGriff.

Languishing Through the Nineties

And then, the wheels fell off. A terrible 1994 season was made worse by the strike and the cancellation of the World Series. The fans took it to heart and failed to come back with as large numbers in 1995 (from over 4 million down to 2.8). The Canadian dollar took a nosedive, making it harder to compete. In that 1995 year, the team was horrible, winning just 56 times. Free agents began to leave — Roberto Alomar, the best second baseman the club ever had, took off for Baltimore.

Quote, Unquote

"We don't know who owns us, the industry's [screwed] up, and the team's in last place. It's a joy to be alive."

— Paul Beeston, 1995.

That was nothing. After 1994, Gillick had resigned, saying he was looking for other challenges. That turned out to mean Baltimore, as well.

In June of 1995, Labatt was purchased by Interbrew S.A., a Belgian beer giant, and fans and media worried they wouldn't care about the ball club nearly as much. They were right. The club went on the market, but when a suitable owner was not found, Interbrew decided to hang onto it.

Gord Ash was promoted from assistant general manager to the bosses' chair. At the end of 1997, Beeston also left the team to take over as president of Major League Baseball.

Gaston was fired near the end of 1997, and replaced for 1998 by Tim Johnson.

Crowds continued to fall, despite the presence of Hall of Fame shoo-in Roger Clemens, who won back-to-back Cy Young Awards as best pitcher right after Pat Hentgen did it in 1996.

Johnson won 88 games and finished third, but was fired in the spring of 1999 because he couldn't get out from under a lie he had told about serving in Vietnam during the 1960s. Clemens was traded to New York.

And 1999, under new manager Jim Fregosi, hit the halfway mark as an injury-plagued disappointment but pulled it together and made a run at a playoff spot.

Other Stars of the Era

- Bob Bailor was the first player chosen in the 1977 expansion draft by Toronto. He hit .310 in that first year as a shortstop. Played 11 seasons, 4 with the Jays, the rest with Baltimore, New York Mets, and the Dodgers. Became a long-time coach with Toronto's organization.
- John Mayberry was known as Big John. A 10-year veteran and two-time all-star when he came to Toronto in 1977, he played four and a half seasons at first base with the Jays and was a huge fan favourite.
- Fred McGriff debuted at first base with Toronto in 1986, spending five seasons before being traded before 1991 to San Diego in the deal that brought Joe Carter and Roberto Alomar to the Jays. Four-time all-star with the Padres and Atlanta.
- Kelly Gruber was a nine-year Jay at third base, making the all-star game twice. Member of the 1992 World Series team for which he hit a key homer against Atlanta. Once voted most popular athlete in Toronto.
- Left handed pitcher Jimmy Key was a key member of the team in the 1980s. Threw nine seasons with Toronto including the 1992 World Series. Signed as a free agent with New York Yankees. Played 15 seasons to 1998. Best year with Toronto was 1987, when he won 17 games.

The Least You Need to Know

- The Blue Jays began play in 1977.
- The first game was in a snowstorm.
- Pat Gillick and Paul Beeston built the team into one of the best in baseball.
- Toronto won its first division title in 1985.
- Dave Stieb and George Bell were the stars of the early years.
- The Jays won back-to-back World Series titles in 1992–1993.
- First Gillick, then Beeston, left the club in the 1990s.
- The last years of the century brought in difficult times.

Part 6
All the Sports You Can Eat

If you can throw it, carry it, slide on it, or go fast with it, Canadians will enjoy it. From curling to basketball, to any type of racing, be it in cars, snowmobiles, boats, or on horses, sports in this country have large and loyal followings.

And the heroes come in all shapes and sizes as well. From a four-legged star who did even better in retirement than on the track, to a beloved Quebecker who loved to go fast and push the envelope, Canadians have made names for themselves both across the land and across the globe.

In this section, and the appendices, we'll look at many of those sports and their legends.

Chapter 26

Curling: Hogging the Spotlight

In This Chapter

- ➤ The birth of the Brier
- ➤ The Richardsons
- ➤ The Wrench
- ➤ On to the world stage
- ➤ Women's curling
- ➤ Other stars

Curling is the source of constant amusement for one segment of Canada's sports-mad population, and the source of great pride and love for another. No sport takes as much ribbing from non-fans, both for its rules and for its legendary post-game fun at the curling rink. The fact remains, however, that curling is one of the country's favourite sports — of the 1.5 million people who curl around the world, 1.2 million of them are Canadians. In fact, there are twice as many curlers in Saskatchewan as in the entire United States. Curling also draws higher ratings on television each year than any sport other than hockey, and at times when Canadian teams haven't been playing in hockey playoffs, even higher. In this chapter, we'll take a look at curling's stars and the competitions, known as bonspiels, in which they compete.

Quote, Unquote

"It was the biggest moment of my life. I knew this was where I belonged."

— Matt Baldwin, three-time winner, on his first Brier, 1953.

Know-it-alls

Q. When did Macdonald Tobacco bow out of organizing and sponsoring the Brier?

A. 1979. Sponsorship was taken over by Labatt Breweries.

In the Hack

You may remember from Part 1 that curling was about the earliest recorded game played in Canada that was imported from elsewhere, with roots going back to the late eighteenth century. Scottish settlement established the game in western Ontario, and as many of those went further west to the prairies, the game went there as well.

These days, curling is the "national" sport of Saskatchewan and Manitoba, is hugely popular in Ontario and Alberta, and has somewhat less of a following (relatively speaking) in B.C., Quebec, and the Maritimes.

Across the Hog Line

It's called the Purple Heart. And it is symbolic of those rinks (four people) who have survived the toughest playdown in sports (four steps) to win their provincial championship and advance to the Brier — curling's national championship.

As writer Bob Weeks points out, it's somewhat surprising that with a game this popular it wasn't until after the First World War that the idea of a Canadian championship bonspiel came about. Part of the problem was straightening out a few of the rules differences from the west to the east (curling irons vs. curling stones, etc.), and especially, the differences in culture. Curling in the west, Weeks writes, was the game of farmers and small communities while in the east it was more of a sport for the elite.

A man named George Cameron set about bringing the boys from the west, whose championship was the famed Manitoba bonspiel, and those from the east together. It went slowly at first — tours back and forth, that sort of thing. But when the Macdonald Tobacco company got onboard in 1926, things picked up speed.

Actually, the name Brier came from a brand of tobacco, and the name has stuck ever since as the title of the men's nationals. The trophy itself is known as the Tankard.

The first national (which ran as an invitational) was played in 1927 at Toronto with the Murray Macneill rink from Halifax the winner. Brier championships stayed in Toronto until 1940, when the tournament moved to Winnipeg for the first time. Switching cities became the norm after the 1943–45 Briers were cancelled due to the war.

Women's national championships began in 1961 with the Diamond "D" Championships — a competition that has had various names including the Canadian Ladies championship, the Macdonald Lassie championships, the Canadian Ladies again, and finally the Scott Tournament of Hearts (named for the paper company).

Great curling, of course, has meant great curlers. And when you're talking great curler, you have to start with one rink above all.

> **Quote, Unquote**
>
> "I had tears in my eyes after the game. I was never so discouraged in my life."
>
> — Ernie Richardson to journalist Doug Maxwell about his first try at curling. He got over it.

Into the House of Richardson

Great story from Bob Weeks: Garnet (known as Sam) and Ernie Richardson of Stoughton, Saskatchewan, are in the stands watching the 1955 Brier with their parents when Sam turns and says "You know, Mom, we're going to get into this."

Okay, thinks mom. They've only been playing a couple of years. Right.

Sam was right on. Not only did the Richardsons (the boys, joined by cousins Arnold and Wes, and they weren't themselves brothers) get to the Brier, they flat out dominated it, winning four times over five years from 1959.

With Ernie as the skip, they also won four world championships, became national figures through sponsorships and promotions (Richardson brooms, Richardson boots, Richardson socks, etc.), and are now considered the greatest superstars the game has known.

> **Listen Up!**
>
> One of the most entertaining parts of watching curling for the uninitiated is listening to the skip yelling at his or her sweepers to work on the rock (clean), leave it alone (never), or sweep as hard as they can (hurry hard). Of all the skips, Ontario's Russ Howard, a two-time national and world champion, has the most recognized calls. His Hurrrrryyyyyy! Hurrrrryyyhaaaaaarrrrrd! have become synonymous with curling in many minds.

It was also the team's success that set off a huge row between eastern and western associations about amateurism, cash bonspiels, commercial sponsorship, and the like — aimed squarely at the Richardsons, says Weeks.

But the move to ban making money (not that curlers made a lot of money then, or now), was defeated and never reappeared.

The Richardsons finally lost at the Brier in 1964 and eventually disbanded as a team in 1968. But they left a legacy behind that would never be equaled.

> **Know-it-alls**
>
> Q. What Brier was known as the Bad-Ice Brier, for its lousy surface conditions?
>
> A. Edmonton, 1973.

Wrenched Right into the Button

If the Richardsons were the poster boys for curling in the 1950s and 1960s, Ed Werenich has been the same for men's curling in more recent years.

It's not that the Ontario firefighter, born in Benito, Manitoba, has won more Briers than anyone else in the era — he has two, same as Rick Folk, Ed Lukowich, Russ Howard (whose rink was the most consistent over these years), Kevin Martin, Pat Ryan, Jeff Stoughton, and Al Hackner — and certainly not that he's a superb athletic figure (Weeks says, "He looks no more like an athlete than someone's 100-year-old grandfather").

It's rather his paunchy build, fiery eyes, aggressive, tactically perfect play over eight Brier entries, and the fact he's as Canadian as Don Cherry, that has made The Wrench a source of fascination to fans, casual observers, and non-fans alike.

> **Know-it-alls**
>
> Q. Name the only husband and wife to both skip national championship rinks?
>
> A. Don Duguid (1970–71) and Betty Duguid (1967). Betty's, you notice, was first.

Teamed with Paul Savage, John Kawaja, and Neil Harrison, The Wrench won his first Brier in 1983. Afterwards, Werenich and Savage parted company for the second and final time, and Eddie was back in the winner's circle in 1990, with Kawaja, Ian Tetley, and Pat Perroud. And again, he won the worlds.

And Now a Word from Don Duguid

He's probably the most well-known figure on the Canadian curling scene, even if a lot of people would be hard pressed to identify the face.

He's Don Duguid, and in the late 1960s and early 1970s he was a dominant force at home and on the world stage, winning the Brier and the global crown in 1970 and 1971. At one point, Duguid's rink had 17 straight international victories.

When he retired, Duguid was recognized as the brightest curling mind on the planet, which made him perfect for television as the colour voice on Brier and world championship coverage. He's been at it ever since.

Shall We Join the Ladies?

From 1961 to 1982, when the women's championship became known as the Tournament of Hearts, rinks from the west absolutely ruled. Especially those of Saskatchewan's Joyce McKee, who won in '61 and came back in 1969 with a completely new rink, and Vera Pezer, from the land of wheat and winter, who took the title three straight years with her rink of Sheila Rowan, Joyce McKee, and Lenore Morrison, from 1971–73. Note that gave McKee five nationals as either skip or rink member.

As a matter of fact, over the first 21 years, eastern rinks won just twice, New Brunswick in 1963 and Quebec in 1975.

But while many western women had the advantage of having basically grown up in curling rinks, women from eastern Canada came to the game a little later. Eventually the balance was found, and from Nova Scotia's Colleen Jones in 1982 to Ms. Jones again in 1999, eastern teams have taken 8 of 18 — a little more even.

Nobody has won more Scott titles than Connie Laliberte of Manitoba, however. A winner with Chris More, Corinne Peters, and Janet Arnott in 1984, Laliberte won with Arnott, Cathy Gauthier, and Laurie Allen in 1992, and with Gauthier, Arnott, and Cathy Overton in 1996.

Laliberte won the world title only in 1984, however, which leads to another topic.

The women's worlds have been less of a sure thing for the women than the men. Canada has won the global crown 10 times in its 21-year history, led by Sandra Peterson's two victories with a rink consisting of Jan Betker, Joan McCusker, and Marcia Gudereit. Sandra Schmirler, by the way, won it in 1997 with the same threesome (which also won the first official Olympic gold in 1998 at Nagano).

As curling has gained popularity in Europe, teams like Sweden and Norway have become tough to beat.

Canada's men have won the worlds 25 times in 40 tries, including 6 times in the 1990s. If you don't win the men's global crown, you basically aren't allowed to come home.

> **Know-it-alls**
>
> Q. What two skips fought The Battle of the Sexes on ice, in 1986?
>
> A. Ed Werenich and Marilyn Darte. Werenich won.

Other Stars

- Howard "Pappy" Wood was an amazingly resilient man. An accomplished curler, Pappy won the Brier in 1925, 1930, and 1940

as a skip, and in 1932 as a third. He played in 65 straight Manitoba provincial championship bonspiels from 1908 to 1972, and made the Guinness Book of Records as a result.

- Heather Houston skipped her rink of Lorraine Lang, Diane Adams, and Tracy Kennedy to two straight national championships in 1988 and 1989. The Ontario foursome also won the worlds in 1989.
- Ken Watson was close to perfect in his Brier record. Representing Manitoba four times at the national final, Watson won three of them, in 1936, 1942, and 1949. In 1939, he created the world's largest high school bonspiel, in Manitoba.
- Ron Northcott was the best curler in the world in the late 1960s, taking his rink to Canadian and global championships three times — 1966, 1968, and 1969. He was known as The Owl.
- Matt Baldwin was the star of Canadian curling in the years immediately preceding the rise of the Richardsons. Winner of the Brier in 1954, 1957, and 1958, and of the Alberta championship five times. A huge crowd favourite for his emotional enthusiasm on the ice.
- Curling is so deep in this country that winning the junior nationals has never been a guarantee that you'd do well in the adult events. One skip who did pull off the double was Alison Goring of Ontario, junior winner in 1983, Scott tournament winner in 1990. Heather Godberson won the junior in 1996 and was a member of Cathy Borst's Scott winner in 1998.

The Least You Need to Know

- The Brier is the men's national championship and it began in 1927.
- The Richardsons from Saskatchewan are the most famous rink in history.
- Women's national championships began in 1961.
- Ed Werenich is the most recognizable figure from modern curling.
- Canada has dominated men's international curling.

Chapter 27

Basketball: Just a Humble Peach Basket

In This Chapter

- A Canadian invention
- The Edmonton Grads
- Toronto gets and loses the Huskies
- The birth of the Toronto Raptors
- The birth of the Vancouver Grizzlies
- Other stars

From the invention of the game by a Canadian in 1891 to the invention of our two National Basketball Association teams in the 1990s, basketball has always been a fringe sport in this country. No more. The game is growing by leaps and bounds (sorry), and is a favourite among school kids especially. In this chapter we'll look at the other game (after lacrosse) that we've given to the world.

Now Here's an Idea

The most famous Canadian among American school kids likely isn't John A. Macdonald (who?) or Jean Chrétien (what?). It's probably Dr. James Naismith.

> **Quote, Unquote**
>
> "You've been a great help to me."
>
> — The words James Naismith said would be the sweetest he could ever hear. Spoken by an ex-student.

Naismith was himself an excellent athlete who gave up a chance for life as a minister to teach physical education in the Young Men's Christian Association (YMCA) system. After graduating from McGill, the Almonte, Ontario native went on a two-year training course to Springfield, Massachusetts, in hopes of getting his YMCA Phys-Ed teaching certificate.

There, Naismith showed his creativity by inventing the first football helmet. He was then asked to come up with a game the men at the Y could play indoors in the winter. After thinking awhile, he remembered an old game called Duck on the Rock, and adapted it to a gymnasium and soccer ball by getting the Y's janitor to tack up a couple of peach baskets on the lower balcony rail (he originally had wanted wooden boxes).

Thus, basketball. Like the telephone, it was invented in America by a Canadian.

His YMCA class first played it on December 21, loved it, and a new sport was born, spreading throughout the U.S. and Canada, through the Y's and other sports clubs. One place it quickly appeared was in Edmonton.

Something for Future Secretaries to Do

Officially they were the Edmonton Commercial Graduates, but everyone knew them simply as the Grads.

They were put together by coach Percy Page, a teacher at the McDougall Commercial High School, beginning in 1914. After adding a few outside players for the 1915 season, the Grads went undefeated and won the Alberta championship. Page would stay as the team's bench boss for 25 seasons, during which they would win 502 games and lose just 20, put together a string of 147 games without a loss, and take the world championship 17 straight times.

Over four appearances at the Olympics, where women's basketball was a demonstration sport, the Grads went 27-0, outscoring their opposition almost 6-1.

Their best player was Noel MacDonald, who joined the team in 1933 and became its captain by 1936. Over her eight seasons, MacDonald averaged 14 points a game, scoring 1,874 points overall.

The Edmonton Grads, who travelled over 125,000 miles to play opponents, were disbanded at the beginning of the Second World War having given up the search for anyone who could challenge them.

In and Out in One Year

The first game in the history of the National Basketball Association (which began as the Basketball Association of America) was played on November 1, 1946.

In Toronto.

Yes, with a little money and some decent organization, the Toronto Huskies, who lost to the New York Knicks that night, could have remained a charter member of the league and not had to pay all those mega-millions for a franchise in the 1990s.

> **Quote, Unquote**
>
> "A rag-tag bunch earning about $65 a game and decked out in rumpled green jerseys."
>
> — John Strebig for the *Toronto Star*, writing in 1994 about the old Toronto Huskies.

The Huskies were put together by about a dozen owners who each threw in $10,000, bought some used uniforms from the Boston Celtics, rented Maple Leaf Gardens from Conn Smythe (who didn't think much of basketball, but liked the extra income), and tried to make a go of it.

They were less than mediocre (22–38, last place). People ignored them. After one money-losing season the Huskies folded up shop.

And that was it for the NBA in Canada for 50 years.

A Whole Lot of Almosts

Toronto almost got an NBA team four times from the 1970s to the 1990s:

- In 1975, when the league, happy with the way the Buffalo Braves had done playing some of its games at Maple Leaf Gardens in previous years, decided it would grant an expansion franchise to the city. Ruby Richman, a local lawyer who practically killed himself trying to bring the game he loved to the city, and Toronto Maple Leafs' owner Harold Ballard couldn't put the $6.5 million fee together to pull it off.

- In 1983, Ted Stepien, the owner of the NBA's worst franchise, the Cleveland Cavaliers, called a press conference to say it was 999 to one he'd move the club north and call them the Toronto Towers. Instead, under pressure from the NBA, he sold the team to American interests and it stayed put. Stepien then brought a minor league Continental Basketball Association team, the Tornadoes, to Varsity Arena. That lasted two and half seasons before the poorly run club packed up and moved to Florida.

- In 1986, the NBA announced it was looking for four expansion cities. A bunch of Toronto lawyers and entertainment industry types, along with legend Wilt Chamberlain, came up short. So did a similar Vancouver bid. The franchise cost of $42 million Canadian was too much.
- Toronto almost got an NBA team in 1992 when Larry Tannenbaum and his Palestra group came close to buying the San Antonio Spurs. Again, the league stepped in.

Meanwhile

Lest you think that basketball interest was tied to having an NBA franchise in Canada…

According to Basketball Canada, in 1980 there were 200,000 people registered as players across the land. Just 14 years later, before the birth of the Toronto Raptors and Vancouver Grizzlies, that number had jumped to 336,000, with 104,000 of them in Ontario alone.

As writers Brendan Connor and Nancy Russell point out, by 1994 there were 71 Canadians (43 men and 28 women) playing in American colleges, a bunch more playing pro in Europe.

And as professional experiments came and went (The World Basketball League, with a height limit of 6' 5", had teams in Calgary, Vancouver, and Saskatoon, and the National Basketball League, an all-Canadian experiment with six teams), basketball at the club, high school, and university level continued to thrive, as it does today.

The national university tournament in Halifax, Nova Scotia, is now one of the highlights of the college sports schedule in this country. And legends have been built. Especially at the University of Victoria, where the wife and husband team of Kathy and Ken Shields dominated college basketball for years.

Listen Up!

He was known simply as "Coach." Jack Donohue came to Canada from New York in the early 1970s to turn the national amateur men's program into a contender, which is exactly what he did. Previously known as the man who taught the great Lew Alcindor (Kareem Abdul-Jabbar) his high school basketball at Power Memorial, Donohue used his extensive skills and Irish charm to forge an identity for the game in his new country. After almost pulling off a medal with the 1976 Olympic team, he put together a definite contender for 1980 only to have the plug pulled by the Moscow boycott. Donohue, who settled permanently in Canada, stayed with the program until the late 1980s.

Chapter 27 ➤ Basketball: Just a Humble Peach Basket

The Big, Purple Dinosaur

No, not Barney.

How to make a long story short? Well, Larry Tannenbaum keeps Toronto at the forefront in the NBA's head office with a lot of hard work, but when the league announces in 1993 it will expand to Toronto, it throws bidding wide open to get the team. John Bitove Jr. then puts together a presentation that blows the NBA away and his group gets the franchise instead as he and his partners fork over $175 million (could have had it for under $50 million eight years earlier) to enter the lodge.

Former superstar Isaiah Thomas is hired as the team's general manager and he takes Damon Stoudamire as the first Toronto pick in the college draft. He's an instant star and wins rookie of the year. Brendan Malone is the first coach, lasting one season before getting replaced by Darrell Walker. The second year is great — 30 wins. Lots of optimism.

In the third season, all heck breaks loose. Bitove's partner Allan Slaight tries to force Bitove to buy his share of the team, but winds up holding the bag himself. Thomas and Slaight don't get along, the team stinks, Thomas tries to buy the team, can't, and leaves shortly after the season starts. Walker is fired in February, Stoudamire is traded to Portland, and the club wins just 16 times. The Raptors are the laughing stock of the NBA.

> **Quote, Unquote**
>
> "Mighty Mouse was little, but he was aggressive when he had to be."
>
> — Damon Stoudamire, Toronto Raptors, on his cartoon character nickname.

> **Know-it-alls**
>
> Q. Who scored the first point for the Toronto Raptors?
>
> A. Alvin Robertson, a three-pointer, November 3, 1995.

Glen Grunwald takes over as GM and brings stability to the team, which is bought by Maple Leaf Sports and Entertainment Inc. (owners of the Toronto Maple Leafs hockey team). The new facility — the Air Canada Centre — replaces the SkyDome (worst home arena in basketball) as the home court.

Grunwald hires former assistant Butch Carter as coach, trades for veterans Kevin Willis and Charles Oakley, and then drafts a superstar — Vince Carter — who becomes the second Raptor to win top rookie honours. The shortened 1998–99 season (labour troubles between players and owners) sees Toronto make a minor run at a playoff spot.

Optimism again takes the forefront.

Part 6 ➤ All the Sports You Can Eat

Know-it-alls

Q. What were the Vancouver Grizzlies originally to be known as?

A. The Vancouver Mounties.

Know-it-alls

Q. What happened in the Vancouver Grizzlies, first ever game?

A. Beat Portland on the road, 92–80.

Know-it-alls

Q. What NCAA school did Steve Nash attend?

A. Santa Clara.

A Far Less Grizzly Story

Vancouver's entry to the NBA is much simpler and cleaner. Realizing that Toronto was in line for a team, Arthur Griffiths, then owner of the Vancouver Canucks in the NHL, approaches the NBA to get in on what he sees as a good thing. That was 1993.

In February of 1994, Vancouver is recommended by the NBA expansion committee, and after a successful season ticket drive, the league grants a franchise in 1994. The team goes out and hires Stu Jackson as its general manager and tells the world they'll be known as the Grizzlies.

Brian Winters is the first head coach, and he gets the usual group of suspects to build with, plus Bryant Reeves of Oklahoma State, the team's first draft pick. Known as Big Country, he's a big centre.

For four seasons the team is lousy, eventually replacing Winters as coach with Brian Hill. Ownership changes when the Griffiths family sells everything (basketball and hockey teams and the arena) to John McCaw Jr. and Orca Bay Sports and Entertainment. The club does come up with a legitimate star of its own in Shareef Abdur-Rahim, who scores an average 18.7 points a game in his rookie 1996–97 season and is among the NBA's top ten scorers in his second year.

After wrapping him up to a long-term contract in 1999, the Grizzlies also have something to look forward to.

A Small Base on Which to Build

As the 1990s came to an end there were still but three Canadians playing in the NBA, and none in the Women's National Basketball Association (WNBA).

Longest serving was Montreal's Bill Wennington (12 seasons) who won four NBA championship rings with the Chicago Bulls.

Guard/forward Rick Fox was born in Toronto but grew up in the U.S. He played eight years with Boston and the Los Angeles Lakers.

Steve Nash, who grew up in B.C., was the second Canadian picked in the first round of the NBA's draft. An excellent point guard, after two seasons in Phoenix, he was traded to the Dallas Mavericks for 1998–99. Nash would lead Canada to a berth in the 2000 Olympic games.

Other Stars

- Leo Rautins was the first Canadian ever drafted first overall by an NBA team, going from Syracuse University to the Philadelphia 76ers (17th overall) in 1983. A member of the national club at just 16 years old, Rautins also played for the Atlanta Hawks in the NBA before starting a long career in the European pro leagues. Went on to a broadcasting career.

- Bev Smith came out of Salmon Arm, B.C., to become the best woman player Canada has produced. A guard/forward, Smith made the national team in 1978 at 16 years old, and played 18 seasons, helping earn a bronze medal in the 1979 world championships and a fourth at the 1984 Olympics. Retired after the 1996 Olympics and is now head coach of the national squad.

- Norman Baker was the best male basketball player of the century's first 50 years. As a Vancouver Hornet, he was a member of five national championship teams and once scored 1,862 points in a 70-game season. He was chosen to tour Europe and North Africa in 1950 with "The Stars of the World" and went on to play one season in the NBA with the Boston Celtics.

- Kelly Boucher of Calgary went to the University of Victoria before playing professional basketball in Israel. A member of the 1996 Olympic team, Boucher became the first Canadian to play in the Women's National Basketball Association, spending the 1997–98 season with the Charlotte Sting.

The Least You Need to Know

- Basketball was invented by a Canadian, Dr. James Naismith.
- The Edmonton Grads women's team was practically unbeatable around the world for almost 30 years.
- The first game in NBA history (then the BAA) was played in Toronto in 1947.
- Leo Rautins was the first Canadian picked in the first round of the NBA draft.
- Toronto and Vancouver received NBA expansion franchises in 1994.

Chapter 28

Racing: The Asphalt Jungle

In This Chapter

- First racing heroes
- Formula One
- Indy Car and CART
- The Racing Villeneuves
- Speedboating
- Other stars

Practically since the internal combustion engine was first invented Canadians have raced anyone who would go for it. But organized racing in Canada first got a real toehold in the 1960s when a number of tracks were built across the country. In saloon and sports cars, Indy-type cars, stock cars, Can-Ams, and Grand Prix automobiles, Canadians have had a presence. Some have risen to star status. And we've also had strong powerboats and even snowmobile racers. In this chapter, we'll look at racing in Canada.

All Eyes Looked to Bowmanville

Closed-course racetracks can be found everywhere across the nation, from small paved or dirt ovals to larger road layouts such as Shannonville in Ontario and Sanair in Quebec. But, it was when the world-class Mosport track opened in the 1960s, near Bowmanville, Ontario, that the international race community began coming regularly to Canada.

Formula One made its debut at Mosport with the inaugural Canadian Grand Prix in 1967, and the same year the Indy Car drivers raced north of the border as well (actually they came twice — the other race was at St. Jovite, Quebec).

Every kind of racing has been held at Mosport since — sports cars, Can-Ams (a distinctly North American series in the '60s and '70s), endurance, motorcycles, stock cars, go-karts, and more.

Over 30 years since it was built, and long after Grand Prix moved to Montreal and the city circuits of the Molson Indy Toronto and Molson Indy Vancouver had stolen the spotlight, Mosport was still attracting great races.

> **Know-it-alls**
>
> Q. Who won the first Canadian Grand Prix, in 1967?
>
> A. Jack Brabham. Denny Hulme was second, both driving Brabhams.

Ain't It Grand, Eh?

The creation of a Canadian Formula One stop gave home-grown drivers the opportunity to have a ride or two.

Peter Ryan, Al Pease, Eppie Wietzes, and George Eaton (he of the famous department store family) all tried their hand behind an F1 wheel, where they basically filled the role of the "leaker" – F1 lingo for back marker.

Canada's first serious run at F1 involvement came in the 1970s when Walter Wolff, an Austrian-born construction magnate from Montreal, entered a competitive team that included European drivers Jody Scheckter and former world champion James Hunt. Scheckter even won the Canadian Grand Prix in 1977. The effort died out by the end of the decade.

> **Know-it-alls**
>
> Q. What year did the Grand Prix move to Montreal?
>
> A. 1978.

But it took a quiet, driven young man from Berthierville, Quebec, who broke into F1 at the same time Wolff was running cars, to put Canada truly on the map of the world's automobile racing countries.

The Legend of Gilles

When Gilles Villeneuve was a car-crazy teenager, he confided to a friend that one day he planned to drive in Formula One. As writer Guy Robillard remarked, "In Berthierville, it was the equivalent of predicting he'd walk on the moon."

But walk on the racing world's version of the moon he did. Graduating from jalopies to stock cars to snowmobiles and anything else that would go fast, Villeneuve became a Formula Ford champion in Quebec in 1963 and eventually would dominate the Formula Atlantic series (in the 1976 series, he lost just one race).

Europe was watching. Villeneuve made his Formula One debut in a terrible McLaren car at the British Grand Prix in 1977 and drove so well in finishing 11th that even the glorious Ferrari team noticed. And, when Villeneuve shortly after lost his McLaren ride, Ferrari grabbed him.

Always pushing the outside of the envelope, Villeneuve won his first race in 1978 at the inaugural Canadian Grand Prix in Montreal (which made him an instant national legend) and in 1979 he was second in the driving standings behind his teammate Jody Scheckter. He would be near the top of the heap for three more seasons.

> **Quote, Unquote**
>
> "You had just attained the heights of glory and like a lightning bolt, destiny cruelly stole your life."
>
> — Fellow driver Clay Regazzoni pays tribute to Gilles Villeneuve on the latter's death.

On May 8, 1982 at Zolder, Belgium, Villeneuve was trying to charge by Jochen Mass on a straight during practice. Mixed signals put him on the wrong side for the upcoming corner, which he entered at too fast a speed. The resulting crash killed him.

In tribute, the Montreal race course on Ile Notre Dame was renamed Circuit Gilles Villeneuve.

Among those who had to bear broken hearts were his children, Melanie and Jacques. The boy would be heard from again.

Earul

"Howdy, Earul."

That was a familiar greeting away down south in Dixie for Earl Ross of Ailsa Craig, Ontario, who was the first (and still the only) Canadian to garner any success in American stock car racing.

With strong sponsorship from the Carling Black Label beer brand, Ross, an experienced local racer, joined the Grand National circuit in 1974 where he went racing with the big boys, including the legendary Richard Petty, Cale Yarborough, and Buddy Baker.

Working with team owner Junior Johnson (himself a major legend), Ross learned quickly that season and, in a year when only five different drivers would share wins over the 30 events, Ross grabbed one of them — September 29, 1974 at Martinsville, Virginia.

Ross won rookie of the year honours, but his sponsorship would quickly disappear and ol' Earl came home.

Back Home Again in Indiana

For open wheel racers in North America, heaven and hell has always been the Indianapolis Motor Speedway, home of the famous 500 mile race.

Canadians had tried their hands at it through the century, but the country began to make an impact in the early 1980s, when Ross Bentley of Port Coquitlam, B.C. made the 33-car field a couple of times. He was followed in short order by Ludwig Heimrath Jr. (whose father Ludwig was a lion on the sports car circuit racing for Porsche), driving for the Canadian backed Mackenzie Financial team, John Jones, Gilles' brother Jacques Villeneuve, Scott Goodyear, Paul Tracy, and Gilles' son Jacques and Greg Moore, the latter two in another Canuck sponsored team — Player's Racing.

The Brick Yard (the track's nickname) was tough on drivers, and the Canadians were no exception. Some had non-competitive cars, some had no luck, and others had mechanical difficulties.

Sunny days seemed to appear in 1994 when Goodyear lost the closest finish in Indy 500 history to Al Unser Jr.

The following year, Goodyear was leading a couple of laps from the end when he passed the pace car under caution (the pace car was going way too slow) and was penalized a lap. That handed the famous race to Gilles' son Jacques Villeneuve, the youngest winner ever at 23.

And again, Europe was watching.

The Invasion of the Continent

In the year of his 500 win and his Indy Car championship, Jacques Villeneuve was invited by Frank Williams to test a Williams Formula One car at Silverstone track in England. The test was a smashing success and that off-season, young Jacques followed his father's legend into the world of Grand Prix.

Williams was the strongest team at that time, and Jacques would be number two driver behind Damon Hill. The 1996 season was a dream. As Hill went on his way to taking the driver's championship, Villeneuve sat right behind, winning four times and heading into the final race at Japan with an outside chance of taking the crown himself.

Hill was let go by Williams that winter and Villeneuve took over as number one driver for 1997. After battling Ferrari's Michael Schumacher all season, and surviving an attempt by the German driver to purposely bunt him off the track in the last race, Jacques Villeneuve fulfilled his father's dream, and his own, by becoming world champion.

After an off-year with Williams in 1998, Villeneuve moved to the new British American Racing team, co-owned by his manager Craig Pollock, and struggled through the first half of 1999.

> **Quote, Unquote**
>
> "I would say he is much cleverer and brighter (about racing) than his father was."
>
> — Former driver John Watson on Jacques Villeneuve.

Let's Go Cart-Racing

IndyCar ran races at Sanair in 1984–86, but after deciding the track couldn't handle the high speed cars, abandoned it. Meanwhile, Molson Breweries jumped at the chance to host a race on a course around the famed Canadian National Exhibition starting with 1986 (Bobby Rahal won). The race was such a huge success, the company then sponsored the Molson Indy Vancouver, beginning in 1990 (Al Unser Jr. the winner).

> **Know-it-alls**
>
> Q. What driver has won the most Molson Indys in Toronto?
>
> A. Michael Andretti, five times.

Canadians continued to move up in IndyCar and in 1994 a high of five Canucks started the Molson Indy Toronto — Tracy, young Jacques Villeneuve, Goodyear, Bentley, and Claude Bourbonnais. Tracy (who won the Toronto race in 1993) was doing especially well at this time, driving for the famous Roger Penske racing team, but his penchant for wrecking the car began to grate on the owner, and he eventually let Tracy go to Team Kool Green.

Another excellent young Canadian racer, Greg Moore, came along in 1996, running for Player's.

The year that young Jacques won Indianapolis in 1995, relations between Tony George, owner of the Indy circuit, and the car owners soured, and a new circuit — Championship Auto Racing Teams (CART) was formed. Which meant no more running at Indy.

In 1999, three Canadians — Moore, Tracy, and Bourbonnais were still running regularly in CART, while Goodyear was in George's Indy Racing League.

In Harmsworth's Way

Speedboating has a strong history in the country going back to 1928 when Harold Wilson began developing the Little Miss Canada boats. He won the world championship in 1942 in the seven litre class, but missed the prestigious Harmsworth Trophy in 1948 in *Miss Canada IV* due to engine problems.

It was left to James Thompson to design and build the boat that would win the Harmsworth. *Miss Supertest III* set the world speed record for a propeller driven boat of 184.24 mph at Picton,

> **Listen Up!**
>
> It's only natural that the Canadian invention of the snowmobile would be turned into a high-powered racing machine. Snowmobile racing in Canada, under the auspices of the Canadian Snowcross Association, runs on ovals and has turned out some spectacular drivers, especially Gilles Villeneuve and his brother Jacques. The latter is a legendary figure in the sport, which is especially popular in Ontario and Quebec.

269

Part 6 ➤ *All the Sports You Can Eat*

> **Know-it-alls**
>
> Q. What is the name of the Canadian equivalent of the American NASCAR stock car series?
>
> A. CASCAR.

Ontario, in 1957, and then won the Harmsworth (ending 30 years of American victories) with Bob Hayward at the wheel in 1959, 1960, and 1961.

Then, tragedy struck. Racing on the Detroit River in the Silver Cup race on September 10, 1961, Hayward's test boat, *Miss Supertest II*, flipped, and he was killed. Thompson retired from speedboat racing as a result.

Miss Supertest III and the schooner *Bluenose* are the only non-living items ever inducted into Canada's Sports Hall of Fame.

Other Stars

➤ Kathryn Teasdale ran for years in Canadian stock and sports cars before earning a chance to try the Busch Grand National series (the next level down from U.S. stock car racing's big leagues) in 1998. She became the first Canadian woman to race in that series.

➤ Miguel and Yvon Duhamel were a force on the world motorcycle circuit in the 1990s, culminating with Miguel's world championship in superbike for 1998.

➤ Frank Holley became the first Canadian to win an NHRA drag racing crown by piloting the Chitown Hustler to the Funny Car championship in the 1980s.

➤ Alan Berg raced almost two seasons in Formula One in the early 1990s. The Calgary native struggled to qualify at times and couldn't continue because of sponsorship problems.

> **The Least You Need to Know**
>
> ➤ Canada got its own Grand Prix in 1967.
>
> ➤ The opening of Mosport in the 1960s gave racing in Canada a huge boost.
>
> ➤ Gilles Villeneuve became a Formula One legend before being killed in a race.
>
> ➤ Jacques Villeneuve (Gilles' son) was the first Canadian to win both the Indy 500 and the world driver's championship.
>
> ➤ The CART series (Indy-type cars) has two stops in Canada — Toronto and Vancouver.

Chapter 29

Horse Racing: A Star in the Barn and Other Stories

In This Chapter

➤ The birth of the Plate
➤ The ruling class
➤ Equine stars
➤ E. P. Taylor and Northern Dancer
➤ Big Red
➤ Standardbreds
➤ Other stars

From the time two men first raced their horses against each other in Canada, equine racing has been one of this country's most popular sports. At first, the Sport of Kings was roughly organized and centred in small communities, but by the middle of the nineteenth century, prominent men were slowly taking control, both cleaning up a sport that was susceptible to race fixing, and making serious inroads in developing the thoroughbred breed. At the same time, standardbred racing was growing in rural Canada with the same goals in mind. In this chapter, we'll look at the success of those attempts and the stars, both human and horse, that emerged as a result of them.

Quote, Unquote

"Horse Racing is ill-suited to Canadian life."

— Guelph clergyman Arthur Palmer, 1847.

Know-it-alls

Q. What races make up the Canadian Triple Crown?

A. The Queen's Plate, the Prince of Wales Stakes, and the Breeder's Stakes.

Know-it-alls

Q. Four of the most famous horses in history have ended their careers in Canada. Name them.

A. The Great Exterminator, Man O' War, Secretariat, and Cigar.

Two Plates Fit for Kings and Queens

The first King's Plate in Canada actually began in Quebec in 1836, and was competed for, off and on, right up to 1954. Ontario's version began in 1860, but it wasn't until 1881 when Colonel Casimir Gzowski and a number of other "respectable" citizens, interested in improving the thoroughbred breed, organized the Ontario Jockey Club that the race became the jewel of the racing calendar.

The OJC rented Woodbine Park in Toronto's east end in 1881 and pulled off a coup in 1883 by convincing the governor general and his wife to attend the then Queen's Plate, adding a royal air to proceedings that would be repeated many times over the following 112 years by visits from Britain's royal family.

Among the powerful owners in the early part of the century were the Seagrams, whose horses would win 20 Ontario Queen's and King's Plates between 1891 and 1935, and Colonel R. S. "Sam" McLaughlin, who won the King's Plate in 1934 with Horometer and did it back to back in 1946 and 1947 with Kingarvie and Moldy.

Horses for Courses

The first superstar among Canadian horses was Sir Barton, owned by J. K. L. Ross of Montreal and trained by Guy Bedwell, who won what was then the unofficial Triple Crown of the Kentucky Derby, Preakness Stakes, and Belmont Stakes, in 1919. The Triple Crown wasn't officially designated until 1939, but unofficially, Sir Barton, who ended his career with a loss to the famous Man O' War at Windsor's Kenilworth Park, was Canada's only Triple Crown winner.

The Pumper

Johnny Longden was known as the Pumper for his unusual riding style, but that didn't stop him from amassing over 5,000 victories as a jockey, starting in 1927 and finishing in 1966. Though considered one of the greatest jockeys of all time, his most famous victories came aboard Count Fleet, winner of the 1943 Triple Crown. Longden was renowned for his "feel" of an animal, which he put to excellent use.

You Can Call Him Mr. Taylor

Edward Plunkett Taylor, E. P. to his friends, was an engineer by education but made his millions in the brewery industry and his fame in horse racing.

Helped by trainer Bert Alexandra, Taylor started slowly in the 1930s but eventually built Windfields Farms into the powerhouse of the sport in Canada. Among E. P.'s tremendous horses were Windfields, Canadiana, Victoria Park, and, of course, Northern Dancer.

But his biggest influence may have been in "putting racing on an upper level and making it more profitable," says Louis Cauz.

Through involvement in the Ontario Jockey Club, Taylor was able to gather up most of the licences in Ontario, close down many unprofitable tracks, including three right in Toronto, and build the gem of race facilities in the country at the new Woodbine track northwest of Toronto in 1956. He also made the jockey club a public institution and went beyond the call of duty in ensuring open competition by offering half of his yearling stock for sale to all comers each year.

Taylor would eventually pass control of his empire to his son Charles. On the son's death in the 1990s, the operation was moved to the United States and cut back significantly.

Of all the things E. P. Taylor is remembered for, however, the one that transcends all others danced on four legs.

Quote, Unquote

"He looked like a frog on a log."

— An Australian commentator on jockey Johnny Longden's pumping style.

Know-it-alls

Q. What do comic and long-time horse racing commentator Michael Magee and legendary horseman E. P. Taylor have in common?

A. They are cousins. Industrialist Charles Magee was E. P.'s grandfather and Michael's great grandfather.

The Dancer

Northern Dancer, owned by E. P. Taylor, bred under the discerning eye of Joe Thomas and trained by Horatio Luro, is the most famous thoroughbred in Canadian history for two reasons:

First, in 1964, the product of sire Nearctic and dam Natalma (who herself was the daughter of Native Dancer, the Gray Ghost), darn near won the Triple Crown, taking the Kentucky Derby and Preakness before losing in the Belmont. He also won the Queen's Plate.

Second, and more importantly, when the horse was retired to stud he became the most proficient breeder in modern horse racing history. His son Nijinsky won the English Triple Crown in 1970. Another son, The Minstrel, was British horse of the year in 1977.

And as writer Trent Frayne points out, sons and daughters of the Dancer were extraordinarily expensive. In 1983, a son sold for $10.2 million, and in 1985 a grandson went for $13.1 million. And they kept winning. As did sons of sons. And great-grandsons, and so on.

All this from a stocky horse that was so undersized they had to build him a special trench in the breeding shed in which to stand the mare so he could mate with her.

> **Quote, Unquote**
>
> "A mean, rotten son of a buck."
>
> — Jim Coleman, writing on Northern Dancer's character around the barn.

Back in the Sulky Again

Cross a thoroughbred with a road horse and you have a standardbred (a breed first recognized in 1879). Stick a little cart, called either a sulky or a bike, behind it, put a driver on the cart and you have a fun horse to race that even the smallest of farmers could afford to run. The trotters and pacers were the sport of choice in small communities where races would be held at country fairgrounds and the like. But suddenly in the 1960s, the popularity of the standardbreds began to take off, and in some places even passed thoroughbreds in attendance. Canadian owners came to prominence, especially the Armstrong Brothers of Brampton (Ted, Elgin, and Charles), who developed an entire line that carried the name Armbro.

Harness stars included Helicopter, Strike Out, Armbro Omaha, Fan Hannover, Ralph Hannover, and Goalie Jeff. And Cam Fella, the greatest standardbred of them all.

Those horses in turn meant drivers such as Keith Waples, Michel Lachance, John Campbell, and Bill O'Donnell were suddenly famous among race fans, following in the hoof prints of such pioneers as Dan MacKinnon and Joe O'Brien.

One driver, however, rose above all.

Herve Filion was the first harness driver to win more than 400 races in a single season, totalling 407 in 1968. He eventually won 14,783 races and was a hero in both Canadian and American harness worlds.

Filion, however, disappeared from the scene in August 1995, after being arraigned on charges in New York for fixing a race at Yonkers Raceway. At this writing, the case had still not gone to trial.

Ronny and Big Red

"Riding Secretariat was like riding a Cadillac. But by his last two races, he had turned into a Rolls Royce."

Jockey Ron Turcotte once said that of Secretariat, considered by many the best thoroughbred runner ever. The two will always be linked. The picture of the man from New Brunswick guiding Big Red home in the 1973 Belmont Stakes for an incredible 31-length victory that wrapped up the first Triple Crown victory since Citation in 1948 will always remain in spectators' minds.

Secretariat was bred in Virginia and owned by Penny Tweedy. But it was to Canada, the home of Turcotte and the horse's famous trainer Lucien Lauren, that Tweedy looked when it came time for Big Red to run his final race prior to stud duty. Thus, in October 1973, the eyes of the sports world were turned on Woodbine Racetrack in Toronto and the Canadian International. Secretariat won easily (with Eddie Maple up because Turcotte had been suspended for bumping in New York) over a small field to the joy of the huge crowd on hand.

Turcotte, with 3,033 races and $29 million in purses behind him, took a terrible spill during a race in 1978 and was paralyzed. The accident happened at Belmont Park in New York, where he and Secretariat had ridden into history.

> **Listen Up!**
>
> Not only was Sandy Hawley one of the greatest jockeys of all time, he was, by all accounts, one of the nicest men in sports. A native of Oshawa, Hawley rode over 30,000 mounts in his career, winning almost 6,500 races, including four Queen's Plates. Hugely popular in Toronto and California, Hawley's best year was 1976 when he won the Woolf Award for meritorious service, and the Eclipse Award as North America's best jockey. Twice he was chosen Canada's athlete of the year. In the early 1990s, Hawley was diagnosed with skin cancer, and beat it. He retired July 1, 1998, finishing third in his final race at Woodbine.

Fitting Pud with a Halo

Racing in Canada had always been able to find room for the man-on-the-street owner. One of the most successful was Jim Fair, an Ontario dirt farmer known as the "Squire of Cainsville," who took the King's Plate in 1948 with Last Mark.

David "Pud" Foster was another of those. In 1983, he and trainer Dave Cross took a brilliant two-year-old named Sunny's Halo and turned him into the first Canadian Kentucky Derby winner since Northern Dancer. Set to skip the Belmont for the Queen's Plate, Sunny's Halo ran poorly at the Preakness and at Arlington Raceway in Chicago, and it was discovered he had injured an ankle. The Plate was out. But, out of respect for the Canadian race, Foster brought him to Woodbine anyway, parading Sunny's Halo to a standing ovation that summer.

One Last Kick at the Can?

Horse racing in Canada came to the millennium's end in trouble, simply caused by the proliferation of other places for gamblers to put their money. Especially hurtful was the growth in provincial lotteries, where, as Louis Cauz notes, $2 could be put down with

> **Know-it-alls**
>
> Q. What famous jockey spent a number of seasons manning the penalty box at Los Angeles Kings hockey games?
>
> A. Sandy Hawley.

the chance of winning a million, rather than just $5.30 for a victorious horse. Crowds at racing events began to take a fall, though special events still draw good houses, especially the Queen's Plate in Toronto.

One of the biggest paid crowds of the decade came in 1996, when Woodbine Racetrack was chosen to host the prestigious Breeder's Cup day, a multi-race spectacle that draws many of the best names in the racing world. It was the first time the Breeder's was held outside the United States, and on that occasion the day featured the final race of the great Cigar, which lost to Alphabet Soup in the Classic.

Other Stars

- George "The Iceman" Woolf won virtually every major stakes race in North America except the Kentucky Derby, including the Preakness in 1936, and rode a succession of famous horses including Seabiscuit and Whirlaway. Woolf died in 1946 in a spill at Santa Anita in California.

- Keith Waples and Mighty Dudley were the first driver and horse to break the two minute mile barrier, posting a 1:59.3 mark in a 1959 race. Waples had a long, successful career, topped in 1967 when he won 246 times in a single season, breaking the Canadian mark. Won the Little Brown Jug in 1972 with Strike Out.

- Avelino Gomez won 4,078 races in his career, including four Queen's Plates. Known as El Perfecto, the enthusiastic rider was enormously popular with the fans when he won, and often was booed when he lost. He died in a three-horse spill at Woodbine in 1980. Gomez is a member of both the Canadian and National Racing Halls of Fame.

- Bill O'Donnell — The Magic Man — was a superb driver known for his talent at coming from behind. O'Donnell had the first mile under 1:50 with Nihilator, and in 1985 was the first driver to make over $10 million in a year.

- Lt. Col. Dan MacKinnon is one of the legends in harness racing. He drove for 50 years, finishing in 1940. A holder of the world ice racing record with The Yank (horses wore special shoes), he was a key builder in the Maritimes, especially as owner of the Charlottetown Driving Park, from 1930.

Chapter 29 ➤ *Horse Racing: A Star in the Barn and Other Stories*

The Least You Need to Know

- ➤ Quebec and Ontario both had King's or Queen's Plates until 1954.
- ➤ Casimir Gzowski and Joseph Seagram were important early builders of the sport.
- ➤ Some of the finest jockeys in the world came out of Canada.
- ➤ Northern Dancer, a Canadian horse, is the greatest sire ever in modern thoroughbred history.
- ➤ Standardbred Racing became hugely popular in the 1960s.
- ➤ Provincial lotteries ate into horse racing's popularity in the 1990s.

Appendix 1

Special Events

There have been a handful of sporting moments in this country that don't necessarily fit a regular category. Here are five of them.

Don't Look Back (Someone *Is* Gaining on You)

There is a bronze statue at the corner of Renfrew and Hastings in Vancouver that commemorates one of the most dramatic moments in world sports history. It shows John Landy of Australia glancing over his left shoulder as Roger Bannister of England passes him on the right to win the 1954 British Empire and Commonwealth Games mile run at Empire Stadium.

That race has been known ever after as The Miracle Mile.

Bannister had been the first to break the famous four-minute mile barrier, and Landy had broken that record shortly afterwards with a 3:57.9. But in Vancouver, the two famous men would be running together.

Landy led going into the final lap with Bannister right behind. Realizing his only chance would be to try and take Landy off the final turn, the Englishman set himself up and went for it. At that moment, the Australian made the fatal error of glancing back over the wrong shoulder, and Bannister was past, winning in 3:58.8. Landy took silver in 3:59.9.

It was the first time two runners in the same race had beaten the four-minute barrier.

Canadian footnote: Third in that race was Canadian Rich Ferguson, a graduate of Leaside High School in Toronto, who went 4:04.6.

Appendices

The Lady of the Lake

Just 32 days after the Miracle Mile, a 16-year-old wisp of a girl from Toronto slipped in Lake Ontario at Youngstown, New York, for a 40-mile, zigzag swim that would make her a Canadian sports hero.

Her name was Marilyn Bell, and with her coach Gus Ryder, she had basically slipped into the attempt to cross the 32 miles to Toronto without being invited. Seems the Canadian National Exhibition, which sponsored the attempt for a first-ever crossing, had pinned its hopes on American Florence Chadwick, offering her $10,000 if she could pull it off.

Chadwick and three other challengers pulled out after 15 hours, leaving just Bell, who though slightly off-course and already exhausted, pulled herself together, ignored the eels that kept attaching themselves to her legs, and touched the breakwater at the CNE at 8:06 p.m. on September 9, 21 hours after the start.

By then word had spread, and over 250,000 people were there to greet Bell, who wound up with $50,000 in cash and gifts (including the 10 grand from the Ex). Bell would become the youngest to swim the English Channel, and after one more marathon she retired, eventually got married, and settled down to quietly raise four kids in New Jersey.

The Queen of the Channel

Cindy Nicholas came along 20 years later and broke Marilyn Bell's record for crossing Lake Ontario. But it was the English Channel that truly fascinated her. So much so that during her career, Nicholas swam the stretch between France and England a record 19 times, including both ways on five occasions. Her first crossing in 1975 broke the existing record. Her greatest triumph came on September 8, 1977 when she made the swim from the English side in a hair under nine hours, touched the French beach and stroked back again. The combined time was over 10 hours faster than it had ever been done.

Though later in life she would become a lawyer, Cindy Nicholas would always be known as the Queen of the Channel.

All I Need Is a Pair of Wheels

In 1985, Rick Hansen disappeared off the face of the earth. Or so it must have seemed.

The wheelchair athlete, who had lost use of his legs in a truck accident at 15, had already made a name for himself by setting the wheelchair marathon world mark and by competing in the first wheelchair event at an Olympic Games, in 1984.

Wanting something special and memorable to show the world that people with disabilities could do practically anything they set their minds to, Hansen dreamed up the Man in Motion world tour. And that's exactly what he did — he toured the world. Rolled 25,000 miles through six continents and 34 countries, arriving back in Vancouver over a year later, in October 1986.

The tour's theme music was David Foster's *St. Elmo's Fire,* sung by John Parr — "Wanna be a man in motion, all I need is a pair of wheels..." — which is what Hansen, who raised close to $10 million for spinal cord research, became known as: the Man in Motion.

143 Marathons of Hope

Out on the Trans-Canada Highway, about 20 kilometres east of Thunder Bay, Ontario, set back against the tree line, is a single white pole that marks the final step Terry Fox took on September 1, 1980, before abandoning his attempt to run across Canada.

The cancer that had claimed his right leg three years before had spread to the 21-year-old's lungs, and it had become too painful for the Port Coquitlam, B.C. resident to continue. 144 long days before, on April 12, 1980, Fox had dipped his foot into the Atlantic Ocean at St. John's, Newfoundland at the beginning of a journey he called the Marathon of Hope. His goal was to raise money for cancer research and increase awareness of the plight of cancer victims, and as he headed west national interest in the run had grown to epic proportions.

Taken back to hospital in New Westminster, B.C., Fox would pass away on June 28, 1981, already aware that something special, something incredible, was building across the land.

On his run, Fox had risen every day at 4:30 a.m. and run until early evening, averaging 26 miles each time. Except for one day off in Montreal, he reeled off 143 marathons on one good leg and his artificial right limb. Each stride involved a double hop on the left and a stride with the right so that, in effect, his left leg actually travelled the distance to the final goal in Vancouver.

The run itself raised $1.7 million and subsequent nationally televised telethon came up with another $10 million. Terry Fox had wanted to raise a dollar for every one of Canada's 24.1 million residents. On the day he died, the total was $24.17 million.

That same year, the first Terry Fox Run for Cancer Research events were held across the nation in September. By 1999, with the nineteenth version just ahead, those runs had raised almost $200 million across Canada and in 50 countries around the world.

Terry Fox's name, legend, and legacy will far outlive the brave young man.

Postscript: In 1986, Steve Fonyo, a B.C. resident who lost his left leg to cancer, set out to make the full run from St. John's to Victoria. He completed the task and raised $10 million for cancer research.

Appendix II

Other Things You Should Know

- Pat Fletcher was the last homebrew to win the Canadian Open Golf Championship, taking the prize in 1954.
- Al Balding was the first Canadian to find success on the U.S. PGA tour, winning the Mayfair Open in 1955 and three more tourneys in 1957.
- Stan Leonard finished second at consecutive Masters golf championships, in 1958 and 1959.
- George Knudson was the most successful Canadian men's pro golfer, winning a remarkable eight tournaments between 1961 and 1972. One of the highlights was a tie for second at the Masters in 1969. He went on to influence and teach many future pro and amateur stars.
- Moe Norman was so serious about golf he would practice driving and fairway irons endlessly, often to the detriment of both his overall game and putting. Won back-to-back Canadian amateurs in 1955 and 1956. After turning pro he struggled to find success. Considered one of the best strikers of a ball that ever lived.
- Marlene Stewart (later Streit) said in 1949 she would be the best amateur player in the world, and she achieved that, winning an incredible 34 straight times starting in 1955. She is the only woman to win all of the Canadian, British, Australian and U.S. ladies' amateur crowns.

Appendices

- Women golfers, led first by Sandra Post and in recent years by Dawn Co-Jones, Barbara Bunkowsky, Lorie Kane and Lisa Walters, are a powerhouse on the U.S. ladies' golf tour.

- Mike Weir's 1999 PGA campaign was the most successful since George Knudson. Included was a run at the PGA tournament, which would have made him the first Canadian to win a Major.

- Tommy Burns was the first Canadian to hold the world heavyweight boxing crown, winning the title in 1905 over Marvin Hart, despite being just 5' 7" tall (making him the shortest heavyweight champ in history).

- Yvon Durelle, the Fighting Fisherman, fought in one of boxing's best-ever bouts, losing the world light-heavyweight crown to American Archie Moore in 1958.

- George Chuvalo became the first man to go the distance with Muhammad Ali, at Maple Leaf Gardens in 1966. "He's the toughest (man) I ever fought," said Ali, a year later. Chuvalo never went down in 97 career heavyweight fights.

- Trevor Berbick won the World Boxing Council's version of the heavyweight crown in 1986 with a decision over Pinklon Thomas.

- Sam Langford, considered by *The Ring* magazine one of the best heavyweight fighters ever, couldn't get a shot at the world championship from 1908–1915 because champ Jack Johnson, thinking the public wouldn't watch two Blacks in the ring, refused to fight him.

- Carling Bassett (Seguso) is by far the best women's tennis player Canada has produced. A consistent performer, Bassett won three Women's Tennis Association tournaments in the 1980s, starting at Belgium in 1981, and on March 4, 1985, moved up to eighth on the world rankings — the first Canadian to make the women's top ten.

- Gerard Cote, Canada's greatest marathoner, won the famous Boston Marathon four times in the 1940s during a career in which he won 112 races, finishing second 56 times, and third on 26 occasions. Two years after retiring from competitive running, Cote set the world mark for eight miles on horseshoes.

- In 1921, on a windy day, the famous schooner *Bluenose* was launched in Lunenburg, Nova Scotia, and went on to become the fastest ship of her class on the eastern seaboard and a vessel of legend. Commanded by Angus Walters, *Bluenose* won a number of important saltbanker challenges over her racing career. *Bluenose* sank in January 1946, after breaking her back during a storm off Haiti. She was enshrined on the Canadian dime.

- Daniel Nestor was one of the top doubles tennis players in the world during the 1990s, winning 11 ATP titles up to the summer of 1999, mostly with partner Mark

Appendix II ▶ *Other Things You Should Know*

Knowles of the Bahamas. He also won a major singles victory by beating Sweden's Stefan Edberg in a Davis Cup world group first round match at Vancouver in 1992 by taking the final two sets of a five-set marathon.

▶ Jack Bionda is among the best box lacrosse players ever. While trying to make it in pro hockey (he played parts of four years in the NHL), Bionda led senior lacrosse teams in Victoria, Nanaimo, and Portland, Oregon to senior national crowns five times in 14 years and was a multi-time most valuable player.

▶ Dr. Jack Wright played in 11 Davis Cup tennis tournaments for Canada from 1923–1933, and was a three-time Canadian champion who rose to number three on the men's world rankings. He was voted the country's top player of the first half-century.

▶ Eric Coy could have been an Olympic gold medallist in discuss, but the Second World War intervened. He set a world record in 1938 that lasted 16 years, and was a heavy favourite for the 1940 Olympics, which were never held. He also held numerous world marks in snowshoeing.

▶ George Athans and George Jr. are the only father-son team in the Canadian Amateur Athletic Hall of Fame. George was an excellent alpine skier and organizer, while George Jr. became one of the globe's top water-skiers, entering his first world meet at the age of 13. He won two world titles, in 1971 and 1973.

▶ William "Torchy" Peden was one of the most famous bike racers in the world in the 1920s and 1930s, specializing in the six-day race in which two-man teams would ride around an indoor oval with the most laps completed over the six days winning. Peden did 148 six-day events, winning 38 times.

▶ Arnie Boldt was the first athlete with disabilities elected to Canada's Sports Hall of Fame. Boldt was just three when he lost his leg to an auger, eventually taking up disabled sports in 1973. At the International Olympiad in 1976, Boldt won two gold, in long jump (world record) and high jump.

▶ Tommy Ryan went down in history as the inventor of five-pin bowling. A Toronto alley owner, he came up with the idea in the first years of the century but neglected to patent the invention. Five-pin, rarely played in America, is the most popular form of bowling in this country.

▶ Sprinter Cyril Coaffee tied the world record for 100 yards in 1922 at 9.6 seconds, and held the national mark for 25 years.

▶ Karen Cromwell (Scarpa) won nine Canadian championships in barefoot water-skiing and finished third at the world championships in 1992. Men's competitor Don Baker came into 1999 ranked in the top five in jumping and slalom and was a two-time national champion.

Appendices

- Dorothy Lidstone in 1969 and Lucille Lessard in 1974 were the first two Canadians to win the world archery title.
- Barney Hartman is considered the greatest skeet shooter in history. He once shot 2,002 clays in a row without a miss.
- Jim Trifunov won a wrestling gold medal at the 1928 Olympics and was one of the best amateur fighters in Canadian history, winning 10 national titles and capping that with the British Empire bantamweight championship in 1930. He was three times an Olympian and once an Olympic coach.
- Canada's women's national soccer team made the 1995 World Cup in Sweden and were able to come up with just a tie in three games, a record that included a 7-0 loss to Norway. At the 1999 edition in the U.S., a stronger side finished with the same record, gaining just a disappointing tie with Japan and again suffering a terrible loss to defending World champions Norway.
- Canada's men's team made the World Cup final for the first time in 1986 at Mexico City, losing three games and failing to score a goal.
- Alison Sydor was three times the world mountain bike champion from 1994–1996, dominating the course and opponents with her aggressive style.
- Curtis Hibbert was a six-time national gymnastics title winner who took two medals at the World Championships — silver in the high bar in 1987 and bronze in the vault in 1992. He competed in two Olympics.
- Jonathon Power became the top-ranked squash player in the world in May 1999. He also lost a controversial Commonwealth Games final in 1998 during which he berated the official and was booed off the court.
- Ernestine Russell Weaver competed in two Olympic Games as a gymnast (1956 and 1960), won five Pan-American Games medals, and three times was Canada's top women's athlete.
- Gareth Rees is Canada's most honoured rugby player. Holder of 44 caps for representing his country the outside-half and centre is the all-time points leader for the national team and played in the 1992 and 1995 World Cup.
- Canada's men's rugby team went to France for the World Cup in 1992 and surprised many by beating Fiji and Romania before losing 19-13 to world power France in the preliminary round. The Canadians lost in the second round to the famous New Zealand All Blacks 29-13 in a well played game.
- Swimmer Leslie Cliff won a medal at the 1972 Olympics, but it was in other international competitions where she really shone, winning 27 gold, 19 silver, and 10 bronze medals in her career, including two gold at the 1974 Commonwealth Games.

Appendix II ➤ *Other Things You Should Know*

- By the time Lela Brooks reached 17 years old the speed skater had already earned six world records. Her 14-year career carried Brooks to 1935 when she decided to retire just before the Winter Olympics.

- Jerome Drayton won the marathon world championship at Fukuoka, Japan, in 1969, in just his first full season in the sport. He would go on to win the title twice more, ending his career with a win at the Boston Marathon in 1977.

- Jocelyn Lovell brought Canadian cycling back to international prominence during a 20-year career that included 40 national championships and three gold at the Commonwealth Games in 1978. Lovell, who designed his own bikes, had his career ended by a traffic accident.

- Irene Macdonald was Canada's most famous diver in the 1950s, winning a bronze at the 1956 Olympics to go with a silver and bronze in Commonwealth competition. She became a key diving official and well-known television voice after retiring.

Bibliography

Allen, Maury. *Baseball's 100: A Personal Ranking of the Best Players in Baseball History.* (Galahad Books, 1981)

Barclay, James A. *Golf in Canada: A History.* (McClelland & Stewart, 1992)

Batten, Jack. *Hoopla: Inside the Toronto Raptors' First Season.* (McClelland & Stewart, 1996)

Beddoes, Dick. *Greatest Hockey Stories.* (Macmillan Canada, 1990)

Beddoes, Dick, Jim Coleman, et al. *Winners: A Century of Canadian Sport.* (Grosvenor House/Canadian Press, 1985)

Bolton, Rod and Ann Douglas. *The Complete Idiot's Guide to Curling.* (Prentice Hall, 1998)

Boulton, Marsha. *Just a Minute: Glimpses of our Great Canadian Heritage.* (Little, Brown and Company, 1994)

Boulton, Marsha. *Just Another Minute: Glimpses of our Great Canadian Heritage.* (Little, Brown and Company, 1994)

Brown, Graham and Douglas Fairbairn. *Pioneer Settlement in Canada, 1763–1895.* (Prentice Hall, 1981)

Browne, Lois. *Girls of Summer: The Real Story of the All-American Girls Professional Baseball League.* (HarperCollins, 1992)

Brunt, Stephen. *Diamond Dreams: 20 Years of Blue Jays Baseball.* (Viking, 1996)

Cauz, Louis. *Baseball's Back in Town: A History of Baseball in Toronto.* (Controlled Media Corporation, 1977)

Cauz, Louis, ed. *The First Year.* (Controlled Media Corporation, 1978)

Cauz, Louis. *The Plate: A Royal Tradition.* (Deneau Publishers, 1984)

Bibliography

Cherry, Don, with Stan Fischler. *Grapes*. (Prentice Hall, 1982)

Chieger, Bob, ed. *Voices of Baseball: Quotations on the Summer Game.* (New American Library, 1983)

Connor, Brendan and Nancy Russell. *Slam Dunk: The Raptors and the NBA in Canada.* (Prentice Hall, 1995)

Cosentino, Frank. *Canadian Football: The Grey Cup Years.* (Musson Book Company Ltd., 1969)

Cosentino, Frank. *A Passing Game: A History of the CFL.* (Bain & Cox, 1995)

Cranston, Toller. *Zero Tollerance*. (McClelland & Stewart, 1997)

Creamer, Robert W. *Babe: The Legend Comes to Life.* (Simon & Schuster, 1976)

Currie, Gordon. *100 Years of Canadian Football.* (Pagurian Press, 1968)

Dheensaw, Cleve. *Olympics 100: Canada at the Summer Games.* (Orca Book Publishers, 1996)

Diamond, Dan, ed. *Hockey Hall of Fame: The Official Registry of the Game's Honour Roll.* (Doubleday Canada, 1996)

Dryden, Ken. *The Game.* (Totem, 1984)

Dryden, Steve, ed., and Mike Ulmer. *The Hockey News: The Top 100 NHL Hockey Players of All Time.* (Transcontinental-McClelland & Stewart, 1998)

Ducey, Brant E. *The Rajah of Renfrew: The Life and Times of John E. Ducey, Edmonton's Mr. Baseball.* (University of Alberta Press, 1998)

Frayne, Trent. *The Best of Times: Fifty Years of Canadian Sport.* (Key Porter Books, 1988)

Frechette, Sylvie, with Lilianne Lacroix. *Gold at Last.* (Stoddart, 1993)

Gordon, John. *The Grand Old Game: A Century of Golf in Canada.* (Warwick, 1995)

Greig, Murray. *Big Bucks & Blue Pucks.* (Macmillan Canada, 1997)

Guillet, Edwin C. *Early Life in Upper Canada.* (University of Toronto Press, 1963)

Gzowski, Peter. *An Unbroken Line.* (McClelland & Stewart, 1983)

Gzowski, Peter. *The Game of our Lives.* (PaperJacks, 1983)

Humber, William, and John St. James, eds. *All I Thought About Was Baseball: Writings on a Canadian Pastime.* (University of Toronto Press, 1996)

Humber, William. *Diamonds of the North: A Concise History of Baseball in Canada.* (Oxford University Press, 1995)

Hunt, Jim. *Bobby Hull.* (Ryerson, 1966)

Hunter, Douglas. *Champions: the Illustrated History of Hockey's Greatest Dynasties.* (Penguin Studio, 1997)

Kendall, Brian. *Great Moments in Canadian Baseball.* (Lester Publishing, 1995)

Kendall, Brian. *100 Great Moments in Hockey.* (Viking, 1994)

Kendall, Brian. *Shutout: The Legend of Terry Sawchuk.* (Penguin, 1996)

Laing, Jane, ed. *Chronicle of the Olympics.* (Dorling Kindersley Inc, 1996)

Lavender, David. *Winner Take All: The Trans-Canada Canoe Trail.* (McGraw-Hill, 1977)

Leonetti, Mike, and Harold Barkley. *The Game We Knew: Hockey in the Sixties.* (Raincoast Books, 1998)

Bibliography

Macfarlane, John. *Twenty-Seven Days in September.* (Hockey Canada, 1973)

McDonald, David and Lauren Drewery. *For the Record: Canada's Greatest Women Athletes.* (Mesa Associates, 1981)

McFarlane, Brian. *It Happened in Hockey.* (Stoddart, 1991)

McFarlane, Brian. *More It Happened in Hockey.* (Stoddart, 1993)

McFarlane, Brian. *One Hundred Years of Hockey.* (Deneau Publishers, 1989)

McFarlane, Brian. *Proud Past, Bright Future: One Hundred Years of Canadian Women's Hockey.* (Stoddart, 1994)

McFarlane, Brian. *Stanley Cup Fever.* (Pagurian Press, 1978)

McFarlane, Brian. *Still More It Happened in Hockey.* (Stoddart, 1994)

McKinley, Michael. *Etched in Ice: A Tribute to Hockey's Defining Moments.* (Greystone, 1998)

McKissack Jr., Fredrick. *Black Hoops: The History of African Americans in Basketball.* (Scholastic, 1999)

Metcalfe, Alan. *Canada Learns to Play: The Emergence of Organized Sport, 1807–1914.* (McClelland & Stewart, 1987)

Michel, Doug, with Bob Mellor. *Left Wing and a Prayer: Birth Pains of a World Hockey Franchise.* (Excalibur, Undated)

Milton, Steve. *Skate Talk: Figure Skating in the Words of the Stars.* (Key Porter Books, 1997)

Morrison, Scott. *Toronto Blue Jays: 1992 World Champions.* (Sun Publishing, 1992)

Morrow, Don, Mary Keyes, et al. *A Concise History of Sport in Canada.* (Oxford University Press, 1989)

Neish, Jim, and Mark Dottori. *Canadian Football League Facts, Figures & Records, 1998 Edition.* (CFL/General Publishing, 1998)

O'Brien, Andy. *Fire-Wagon Hockey: The Story of the Montreal Canadiens.* (Ryerson, 1970)

O'Connor, Tim. *The Feeling of Greatness: The Moe Norman Story.* (Master's Press, 1995)

Orser, Brian, with Steve Milton. *Orser: A Skater's Life.* (Key Porter Books, 1988)

Podborski, Steve, with Gerald Donaldson. *Podborski!* (McClelland & Stewart, 1987)

Podnieks, Andrew. *Canada's Olympic Hockey Teams: The Complete History.* (Doubleday Canada, 1997)

Rampersad, Arnold. *Jackie Robinson: A Biography.* (Alfred A. Knopf, 1997)

Roxborough, Henry. *Canada at the Olympics.* (Ryerson, 1963)

Roxborough, Henry. *One Hundred-Not Out: The Story of Nineteenth-Century Canadian Sport.* (Ryerson, 1966)

Searle, Caroline, and Bryn Vaile, eds. *The IOC Official Olympic Companion 1996.* (Brassey's Sports, 1996)

St. George Stubbs, Lewis. *Shoestring Glory: Semi-Pro Ball on the Prairies, 1886–1994.* (Turnstone Press, 1996)

Stojko, Elvis. *Heart and Soul: Elvis Stojko In His Own Words.* (Rocketeer Publishing, 1997)

Teitel, Jay. *The Argo Bounce.* (Lester and Orpen Dennys, 1983)

Tewksbury, Mark. *Visions of Excellence: The Art of Achieving Your Dreams.* (Viking, 1993)

Thiele, Stephen. *Heroes of the Game: A History of the Grey Cup.* (Moulin Publishing, 1997)

Bibliography

Thorn, Jim, Pete Palmer, et al. *Total Baseball: The Official Encyclopedia of Major League Baseball, Sixth Edition.* (Total Sports, 1999)

Turner, Dan. *Heroes, Bums and Ordinary Men: Profiles in Canadian Baseball.* (Doubleday Canada, 1988)

Villeneuve, Jacques, with Gerald Donaldson. *Villeneuve: Winning in Style.* (HarperCollins, 1996)

Vipond, Jim. *Gordie Howe, Number 9.* (Ryerson, 1968)

Waldman, Carl. *Encyclopedia of Native American Tribes.* (Facts on File, 1988)

Wallechinsky, David. *The Complete Book of the Olympics, 1992 Edition.* (Little, Brown and Company, 1991)

Wallechinsky, David. *The Complete Book of the Winter Olympics, 1994 Edition.* (Little, Brown and Company, 1994)

Weeks, Bob. *The Brier: The History of Canada's Most Celebrated Curling Championship.* (Macmillan Canada, 1995)

Whitney, Alex. *Sports & Games the Indians Gave Us.* (David McKay Company, 1977)

Williams, Tiger, with James Lawton. *Tiger: A Hockey Story.* (Seal, 1985)

Wise, S. F. and Douglas Fisher. *Canada's Sporting Heroes: Their Lives & Times.* (General Publishing, 1974)

Young, David. *The Golden Age of Canadian Figure Skating.* (Summerhill Press, 1984)

Other Sources

Butt, Debbie, ed. *Vancouver Grizzlies Media Guide, 1998–1999.*

Canada's Sports Hall of Fame thumbnail sketches of members.

Diamond, Dan, ed. *Toronto Blue Jays Official Guide, 1999.* (Diamond and Associates, 1999)

Kaplan, Rick, ed. *Toronto Raptors Official Guide, 1997–1998.*

(No editor listed). *MolsonIndy 1998 Media Guide.*

(No editor listed). *Montreal Expos Official Guide, 1998.*

The Boy in Blue: Ned Hanlan and the Passion for Rowing. From the files of Canada's Sports Hall of Fame.

Web Sites

www.montrealexpos.com
(History of the Expos)

www.canadianboxing.com
(Boxing history, with links to other sites including Boxing on the Web)

www.ontariojockeyclub.com
(Ontario Jockey Club with links to other horse racing)

Index

A

All American Girl's Professional Baseball
   League   214, 219
Allan Cup   38
Alou, Felipe   235–236
Argo Bounce   174
Argonaut Rowing Club   18
Asahis   203, 207
Ash, Gord   247
Ault, Doug   241
Auto Racing   265–270

B

Babb-Sprague, Kristin   130–131
Bailey, Ace   43, 48–49, 52
Bailey, Donovan   125, 132–134
Baker, Bonnie   215
Bain, David   29–30
Bannister, Dr. Roger   279
Barilko, Bill   58

Baseball   201–248
   early   13, 15, 18–21, 31
   prairie   205, 207–208
   women in   211 214–215
Basketball   13, 257–263
Basset (Seguso), Carling   286
Bauer, Father David   139–140
Baumann, Alex   120–122
Bavasi, Peter   241
B.C. Lions   178, 187, 195, 198–199
Beachville (Ontario)   18
Bedard, Myriam   149, 153, 158
Beers, Dr. Geroge   6
Bees   10, 13
Beeston, Paul   239, 242, 247–248
Beliveau, Jean   57–58, 67
Bell, George   244–245, 248
Bell, Marilyn   280
Bertoia, Reno   211, 217–218
Biathlon   149, 153–155, 158
Black Monday   233, 238

Index

Blacks
    in Baseball   203, 206, 210
    in Football   181, 183
    in Hockey   85–86, 93
Blainey, Justine   91
Bluenose   286
Bobsled   7, 156–157
Bone, Jamie   184
Boucher, Gaetan   149, 154–155, 158
Boutilier, Martin (Brother Matthias)   207–208, 210
Bowman, Scotty   58, 63, 71, 79
Boxing   11, 13, 29, 129, 284
Brier, The   252–253, 256
Brochu, Claude   234
Bronfman, Charles   230, 234
Brown, George   25
Browning, Kurt   145–146, 158
Butler, Rich   226
Butler, Rob   226

C

Calgary Cannons   222
Calgary Flames   67, 79–80, 84, 88
Clagary Stampeders   165, 172–173, 178, 187–190, 192, 195
Canadian Baseball Association   19
Canadian Football League   18, 159, 176, 178–179, 181–199
Canadian Grand Prix   266–270
Canadian Press   195
Canadian Rugby Union   163, 167–168, 172
Canadian Youth Team (Baseball, 1991)   226, 228
Canoeing (early)   11
Carnegie, Herb   86
Carter, Joe   245–246
Carter, Vince   261
Catherwood, Ethel   102
CFL Expansion   193–194
Checkers   11
Cherry, Don   71, 81, 84, 254

Choctaw   4
Chuvalo, George   286
Clancy, Francis Michael (King)   45–49
Clarke, Bobby   241–243
Clarke, Nig   207–208
Cleveland, Reggie   224–225
Conacher, Lionel   45, 161, 166, 170
Cooke, Jack Kent   212
Cox, Bobby   241–243
Cranston, Toller   137, 144
Creighton, James   17, 21
Cricket   12, 16
Cromwell (Scarpa) Karen   285
Crothers, Bill   112
Cullan, Father Ronald   217–218
Cummings, Gail   91
Curling   10–13, 15, 251–256
Cyr, Louis   23, 27–28, 30

D

Davis, Victor   120–121
Dawson City (hockey team)   36–37
deCoubertin, Baron   21
Deerfoot   8
Desmarteau, Etienne   98–99
Dibo   8
Dixon, George   28–29
Donohue, Jack   260
Drapeau, Jean   116–117, 230
Drayton, Jerome   289
Dubin Inquiry   125, 127
Ducey, John   212
Duggan, George   29
Duguid, Don   254–255
Duhamel, Miguel and Yvon   270

E

Eagleson, R. Alan   64–69, 81–82, 84
Eastern Canadian Hockey Association   37
Edmonton Eskimos   166, 172–175, 178, 187–190, 199

Index

Edmonton Grads   257–258, 263
Edmonton Legislators   206
Edmonton Oilers   66, 76–77, 88
Edmonton Trappers   222
Edwards, Dr. Phil   104
Espositio, Phil   64, 68, 72
Etchevarry, Sam   171, 174, 178, 198

F

Field Hockey   13, 16
Figure Skating   29, 142–147
Flutie, Doug   191, 196, 199
Football   159–199
    early   12, 15, 17–19
Fowler, Dick   211, 213–214, 219
Fox, Terry   281
Francis, Charlie   126–127
Frechette, Sylive   125, 128, 130–131, 134
Fuhr, Grant   85, 88

G

Garapick, Nancy   117–188, 123, 133
Gaston, City   244–246
Geoffrion, Bernie (Boom Boom)   61
Genereaux, George   109
Gibson, George (Moonie)   205
Gillick, Pat   239, 242, 245–246, 248
Globe & Mail (as *Toronto Globe*)   25, 166
Godfrey, Paul   240
Golf   98–99, 104, 283
Grant, Bud   171, 176
Gray, George   28
Greene, Nancy   149, 152, 158
Gretzky, Wayne   55, 70, 75–77, 82, 142, 192
Grey Cup   159–160, 163–168, 171–173, 175, 178–198
    winners   169, 179, 190, 199
Guelph Maple Leafs (baseball)   20

H

Halifax Rules (hockey)   17
Hamilton Tiger Cats (Tigers)   44, 173, 175–176, 178, 185, 187, 189–190, 194–195, 198
Hanlan, Ned   23, 25–27, 30
Hansen, Rick   280–281
Harmsworth Trophy   269–270
Harvard University   17–19, 21
Hawley, Sandy   275
Heddle, Kathleen   134
Heggtveit, Anne   149, 151, 158
Henderson, Paul   63–64, 67, 73
Hewitt, Foster   50
Hewitt, W.A.   16, 50
Hiller, John   221, 224
Hockey   31–93
    early   15–17
Hodgson, George   99–100, 104
Hoffman, Abby   61–62, 88, 122
Horse Racing   271–277
    early   12–13
Howard, Russ   253
Howe, Gordie   6, 56–57, 67
Hungerford, George   112
Hurley   13, 16
Huron   1, 4

I

Imlach, George (Punch)   60–61
Innuit   7
International League (baseball)   20
Iroquois   1, 4
Ismail, Raghib (Rocket)   192–193, 199
Irwin, Arthur (Foxy)   204, 205

J

Jackson, Donald   143
Jackson, Roger   112–133
Jackson, Russ   171, 177
James, Angela   89
Jarry Park   230, 240
Jenkins, Ferguson Jr.   206, 221, 223–224, 226, 228
Jerome, Harry   111–112, 114

Index

Johnson, Ben 95, 125–128, 132, 134
Jones, Colleen 255
Jones, Mack 231, 238
Joy, Greg 119

K

Kerr, Bobby 97–98
Kidd, Bruce 112
King's College 16
King's Plate (Ontario) 271–272, 275, 277
Kingston 16, 17
Knudson, George 285
Kreiner, Kathy 152

L

Lacrosse 3–8
Lafleur, Guy 71–72, 79
Laliberte, Connie 255
Lalonde, Newsy 38, 41
Lancaster, Ron 171, 189, 196
Landy, John 281
Laumann, Silken 131–132, 134
Lee, Bill (Spaceman) 232–233
Lee-Gartner, Kerrin 153
LeMay Doan, Catriona 155
Lemieux, Larry 129
Lemieux, Mario 75, 78, 84
Lethbridge Mounties 222
Lewis, Lennox 129
Limpert, Marianne 133
Lindros, Eric 83–84, 141–142
Little, Olive Bend 215
London Tecumsehs 19–20
Longden, Johnnie 272–273
Lord Stanley of Preston 33–34
Lovell, Jocelyn 289

M

MacDougall, Hartland 29
Magnussen, Karen 144

Mahovlich, Frank 60–61
Malone, Joe 41
Manley, Elizabeth 145
Maple Leaf Gardens 48, 50, 52
Marchildon, Phil 211, 213, 219
Martinex, Dennis 234–235
Mauch, Gene 231–232
McBean, Marnie 134
McDougall, Don 240
McGee, Frank (One Eyed) 36–38
McGill University 17–19, 21, 165
McGuire, Dawn 89
Medicine Hat Blue Jays 222
Memorial Cup 55
MicMac Sticks 16
Mi'kmaq 1, 16
Miller, Shannon 92–93
Miracle Mile 279
Miss Supertest III 269–270
Molson Indy Toronto 269
Molson Indy Vancouver 269
Moodie, Susanna 9–10, 12
Moon, Warren 183, 185–186
Montreal AAA (football) 168, 172
Montreal AAA (hockey) 34
Montreal Alouettes 172, 174–175, 184, 186–191, 193–194, 196, 198–199
Montreal Canadiens 37, 40–42, 45–47, 50, 53–55, 57–58, 62–63, 70–73, 79, 82, 84
Montreal Expos 221–223, 228, 229–238
Montreal Gazette 35
Montreal Hockey Club 34
Montreal Maroons 51
Montreal Olympic Games 115–117, 123
Montreal Royals 209, 212, 219, 222
Montreal Star 36
Montreal Victorias 34–35
Montreal Wanderers 37–38, 40, 45
Morenz, Howie 43, 45–47, 52
Mosport 265–266, 270
Mulroney, Brian 21, 127

Index

N

Naismith, Dr. James   257–258, 263
National Hockey Association   40
National Hockey League   40–84
    birth of   33, 40
Native Peoples   1, 4–8, 12
Nelson, Rocky   218
New Brunswick-Maine Baseball League   205
Nicholas, Cindy   280
Nootka People   5
Northern Dancer   271, 273–274, 277

O

O'Brien, J.A.   37, 40
Olympic Games
    early   15, 21
    summer   95–135
    winter   92, 137–159
Olympic Hockey   92–93, 137–142, 147
Olympic Stadium (Montreal)   117, 232
Olympics (Canadian Gold Medals)   102, 123, 135, 147
O'Neill, Tip   203–204, 206, 210
O'Ree, Willie   86–87, 93
Orr, Bobby   63–67, 73
Orser, Brian   144–145
Orton, George   97–98, 104
Ottawa Rough Riders   168, 169, 177, 182, 185, 187, 189–191, 193–195, 199
Ottawa Senators   40, 45, 195
Ottenbrite, Anne   122

P

Pacific Coast Hockey Association   33, 38
Paris Crew   24–25, 30
Parker, Jackie   171, 174–175
Patrick, Frank   38–39, 45
Patrick, Leslie   38–39, 45
Paul, Robert   143, 145, 147
Pictou Standard   20
Peden, William (Torchy)   287
Podborski, Steve   150
Puck (invention)   17
Puhl, Terry   225, 228
Purple Heart   252

Q

Quebec Bulldogs   40, 44
Quebec Nordiques   65–67, 73, 76, 80
Queen's Plate (Ontario)   271–273, 175, 177

R

Rat Portage   35–36
Rautins, Leo   263
Raymond, Claude   231
Read, Frank   109–111, 114, 132
Rebagliati, Ross   151
Rheaume, Manon   90
Richard, Maurice   6, 54–56, 78
Richard Riot   55–56
Richardsons, The   251, 253–254, 256
Richmond Hill Dynes   222
Rider, Fran   89
Robertson, Bruce   116
Robinson, Jackie   211, 216–217, 219
Rogers, Steve   233
Ross, Earl   267
Rounders   12
Rosen, Goody   211–213
Rosenfeld, Bobbie   49, 102
Rowing   15, 24–27 109–114, 120, 121, 123, 131–134
Rubenstein, Lorne   29–30
Rugby   17, 288
Ruth, George Herman (Babe)   203, 207–208, 210

S

Sailing   20, 129
Sarnia Imperials   168

297

Index

Saskatchewan (Regina) Roughriders   166–169, 173, 187, 189–190
Sawchuk, Terry   58–59
Scott, Barbara Ann   137, 142–143, 147
Secretariat   271–272, 274–275
Sir Barton   272
Shinny   6, 16
Shore, Eddie   48–49
Skalbania, Nelson   186
Skiing   149–155
SkyDome   244
Smith, Graham   118–119
Smith, Larry   93, 194
Smythe, Conn   43, 45, 47–50, 52
Snowmobile Racing   269
Snyder, Gerry   230
Soccer   13, 18, 288
Sonshine, Harry   174
Southam, Gordon   39
Speedboating   265, 299
Speed Skating   154–156, 158
Speed Skating (short track)   156, 158
Stanley Cup   33, 59
    awarding of   34, 40
    first winning   of 34
Staub, Rusty   231, 238, 241
Standardbred Racing   271, 274, 277
Stewart (Streit), Marlene   285
Stieb, Dave   242, 243–244, 248
Stojko, Elvis   146
Stoudamire, Damon   261
Strike, Hilda   103
Sunny's Halo   275
Sutherland, James   16
Sutter Family   78
Sydor, Alison   288

T

Tanner, Elaine   107, 113–114
Taylor, Cyclone   37–38, 41
Taylor, E.P.   271, 273
Taylor, Dr. Ron   221–223
Team Canada 1972   65, 67, 72
Team Canada 1998 (women's)   89
Tennis   286–287
Tewksbury, Mark   120
Thomas, Isaiah   257
Thomson, Earl   100
Toboggan   7, 11
Toronto Arenas   40
Toronto Argonauts   166, 169, 171–172, 174, 177, 182, 185, 188–192, 196, 198
Toronto Blue Jays   221–222, 228–229, 234, 239–248
Toronto Huskies   257, 259
Toronto Maple Leafs (baseball)   204–205, 208–209, 212
Toronto Maple Leafs   45, 51, 53–54, 56, 60–62, 67–71
Toronto Olympic Bid   129
Toronto Raptors   257, 260–261, 263
Toronto Star   108
Toronto Sun   169
Toronto Telegram   140, 169
Triple Crown (Canada)   272
Triple Crown (U.S.)   272
Turcotte, Ron   274–275

U

University of British Columbia   198
University of Regina   197
University of Saskatchewan   197
University of Toronto   164–166, 170
University of Victoria   260
University of Western Ontario   20, 184, 198

V

Vancouver Canadians   222
Vancouver Canucks   64, 73, 88
Vancouver Grizzlies   157, 160, 262–263
Vancouver Sun   101
Vanier Cup   184, 197

Vezina, Georges   41
Victoria Rink   18
Villeneuve, Gilles   265–267, 270
Villeneuve, Jacques (Uncle Jacques)   268–269
Villeneuve, Jacques   227, 265, 268–270
Vimy Ridge   39
Voyageurs   7, 8

W

Wagner, Barbara   143, 147
Waldo, Carolyn   128
Walker, Larry   221, 225–228, 234, 236
Ward, Pete   224, 227
Weir, Mike   286
Wennington, Bill   262
Werenich, Ed   251, 254–256
White, Deacon   210
Williams, Dick   231, 233
Williams, Jimy   243–245
Williams, Percy   101, 104
Windsor, Nova Scotia   16
Winnipeg Blue Bombers   168–169, 175–178, 189, 198–199
Winnipeg Jets   66–67, 80
Winnipeg Victorias   34–35
Women
    in Native culture   5
    in Sports   23, 34, 49, 61, 85, 88–93, 102–103, 107–108, 113, 117–118, 128–134, 141–143, 144–147, 151–158, 211, 214–215, 251, 253, 255–256, 262
Woodstock Young Canadians (baseball)   19
World Hockey Association   63, 65–67, 73, 76
Wrestling
    Native   5, 8
    early settlers   11, 13
Wright, Joseph   25
Wright, Joseph, Jr.   25

Y

Youppi   237

Z

Zorra (Ontario)   18

About the Author

Malcolm Kelly was born in England and raised in Toronto. As an athlete he ran sprints in track, played baseball, football, and water polo, and eventually went into coaching and managing at the AAA minor baseball level, helping to found the North Toronto Baseball Association. After graduating from the University of Toronto in 1981, he first worked professionally for *Thomson Newspapers* in Midland, Ontario, then spent two years in professional basketball as a public relations man. For 12 years he held many different jobs at the *Town Crier*, Canada's largest community monthly newspaper chain before spending a season covering the Toronto Blue Jays for *Canadian Press* and two years doing the Toronto Raptors for *CP* and the *National Post*. He has also covered the Toronto Maple Leafs and many individual events such as auto racing, tennis, and basketball for the *Ottawa Citizen*. Currently, he works for the Toronto section of the *National Post*. Mr. Kelly lives in Toronto with his wife Barbara, son Patrick, and their dachshund Auggie.

Photo Credits

Early Canadian curling: National Archives of Canada; Ned Hanlan: Canadian Sports hall of fame; Howie Morenz at Madison Square Garden: O-Pee-Chee Collection/Hockey Hall of Fame; Jean Belliveau and Maurice Richard, training camp, 1953: Prentice Hall Archives; Wayne Gretzky: Canapress/*Edmonton Journal*/Ken Orr; Bobby Kerr & Percy Williams: Canadian Sports Hall of Fame; Gaetan Boucher: Canadian Press; Donovan Bailey winning in Atlanta: Canadian Olympic Association/Claus Andersen; Lionel Conacher: Canadian Football Hall of Fame; Mud Bowl: Canadian Sports Hall of Fame; Ferguson Jenkins: Canapress/AP Photo; Joe Carter hitting World Series winning home run, 1993: Canapress/Shaun Best; James Naismith: University of Kansas archives; Edmonton Grads women's basketball team, 1924: National Archives of Canada; Northern Dancer winning Kentucky Derby, 1964 with E.P. Taylor: Canapress/AP Photo; Marilyn Bell: Canadian Sports Hall of Fame; Paul Henderson's 1972 Canada-Russia winning goal: *The Toronto Star*/F. Lennon.